SAVE THE
LAST DANCE
FOR ME

❖ REFERENCE SERIES ❖

1 ALL TOGETHER NOW
The First Complete Beatles
Discography, 1961-1975
by Harry Castleman & Walter J. Podrazik

2 THE BEATLES AGAIN
[Sequel to *All Together Now*]
by Harry Castleman & Walter J. Podrazik

3 A DAY IN THE LIFE
The Beatles Day-By-Day, 1960-1970
by Tom Schultheiss

4 THINGS WE SAID TODAY
The Complete Lyrics and a Concordance
to The Beatles Songs, 1962-1970
by Colin Campbell & Allan Murphy

5 YOU CAN'T DO THAT
Beatles Bootlegs
& Novelty Records, 1963-1980
by Charles Reinhart

6 SURF'S UP!
The Beach Boys On Record, 1961-1981
by Brad Elliott

7 COLLECTING THE BEATLES
An Introduction & Price Guide to Fab Four
Collectibles, Records & Memorabilia
by Barbara Fenick

8 JAILHOUSE ROCK
The Bootleg Records of
Elvis Presley, 1970-1983
by Lee Cotten & Howard DeWitt

9 THE LITERARY LENNON:
A COMEDY OF LETTERS
The First Study of All the Major and Minor
Writings of John Lennon
by Dr. James Sauceda

10 THE END OF THE BEATLES?
[Sequel to *The Beatles Again* and
All Together Now]
by Harry Castleman & Walter J. Podrazik

11 HERE, THERE & EVERYWHERE
The First International Beatles
Bibliography, 1962-1982
by Carol D. Terry

12 CHUCK BERRY--ROCK 'N' ROLL MUSIC
Second Edition, Revised
by Howard A. DeWitt

13 ALL SHOOK UP
Elvis Day-By-Day, 1954-1977
by Lee Cotten

14 WHO'S NEW WAVE IN MUSIC
An Illustrated Encyclopedia, 1976-1982
by David Bianco

15 THE ILLUSTRATED DISCOGRAPHY
OF SURF MUSIC, 1961-1965
Second Edition, Revised
by John Blair

16 COLLECTING THE BEATLES, VOLUME 2
An Introduction & Price Guide to Fab Four
Collectibles, Records & Memorabilia
by Barbara Fenick

17 HEART OF STONE
The Definitive Rolling Stones
Discography, 1962-1983
by Felix Aeppli

18 BEATLEFAN
The Authoritative Publication of Record
For Fans of the Beatles, Volumes 1 & 2
Reprint Edition, With Additions

19 YESTERDAY'S PAPERS
The Rolling Stones In Print, 1963-1984
by Jessica MacPhail

20 EVERY LITTLE THING
The Definitive Guide To Beatles
Recording Variations, Rare Mixes &
Other Musical Oddities, 1958-1986
by William McCoy & Mitchell McGeary

21 STRANGE DAYS
The Music Of John, Paul, George & Ringo
Twenty Years On
by Walter J. Podrazik

22 SEQUINS & SHADES
The Michael Jackson Reference Guide
by Carol D. Terry

23 WILD & INNOCENT
The Recordings of
Bruce Springsteen, 1973-1985
by Brad Elliott

24 TIME IS ON MY SIDE
The Rolling Stones
Day-By-Day, 1962-1986
by Alan Stewart & Cathy Sanford

25 HEATWAVE
The Motown Fact Book
by David Bianco

26 BEATLEFAN
The Authoritative Publication of Record
For Fans of the Beatles, Volumes 3 & 4
Reprint Edition, With Additions

27 RECONSIDER BABY
The Definitive Elvis
Sessionography, 1954-1977
by Ernst Jorgensen, Erik Rasmussen &
Johnny Mikkelsen

28 THE MONKEES:
A MANUFACTURED IMAGE
The Ultimate Reference Guide to
Monkee Memories & Memorabilia
by Ed Reilly, Maggie McManus &
Bill Chadwick

29 RETURN TO SENDER
The First Complete Discography Of Elvis
Tribute & Novelty Records, 1956-1986
by Howard Banney

30 THE CHILDREN OF NUGGETS
The Definitive Guide To
"Psychedelic Sixties" Punk Rock
On Compilation Albums
by David Walters

31 SHAKE, RATTLE & ROLL
The Golden Age Of American Rock 'N' Roll,
Volume 1: 1952-1955
by Lee Cotten

Available only through Popular Culture, Ink., P.O. Box 1839, Ann Arbor, Michigan 48106
Phone: 1-800-678-8828

32 THE ILLUSTRATED DISCOGRAPHY
OF HOT ROD MUSIC, 1961-1965
by John Blair & Stephen McParland

33 POSITIVELY BOB DYLAN
A Thirty-Year Discography, Concert &
Recording Session Guide, 1960-1991
by Michael Krogsgaard

34 OFF THE RECORD
Motown By Master Number, 1959-1989
Volume 1: Singles
by Reginald J. Bartlette

35 LISTENING TO THE BEATLES
An Audiophile's Guide to the
Sound of the Fab Four, Volume 1: Singles
by David Schwartz

36 ELVIS--THE SUN YEARS
The Story Of Elvis Presley In The Fifties
by Howard A. DeWitt

37 HEADBANGERS
The Worldwide MegaBook Of
Heavy Metal Bands
by Mark Hale

38 THAT'S ALL
Bobby Darin On Record,
Stage & Screen
by Jeff Bleiel

♦ REMEMBRANCES SERIES ♦

1 AS I WRITE THIS LETTER
An American Generation
Remembers The Beatles
Edited by Marc A. Catone

2 THE LONGEST COCKTAIL PARTY
An Insider's Diary of The Beatles,
Their Million-Dollar Apple Empire
and Its Wild Rise and Fall
Reprint Edition, With Additions
by Richard DiLello

3 AS TIME GOES BY
Living In The Sixties
Reprint Edition, With Additions
by Derek Taylor

4 A CELLARFUL OF NOISE
Reprint Edition, With Additions
by Brian Epstein

5 THE BEATLES AT THE BEEB
The Story Of Their Radio Career, 1962-1965
Reprint Edition, With Additions
by Kevin Howlett

6 THE BEATLES READER
A Selection Of Contemporary Views, News,
& Reviews Of The Beatles In Their Heyday
Edited by Charles P. Neises

7 THE BEATLES DOWN UNDER
The 1964 Australia & New Zealand Tour
Reprint Edition, With Additions
by Glenn A. Baker

8 LONG LONELY HIGHWAY
A 1950's Elvis Scrapbook
Reprint Edition, With Additions
by Ger Rijff

9 IKE'S BOYS
The Story Of The Everly Brothers
by Phyllis Karpp

10 ELVIS--FROM MEMPHIS TO HOLLYWOOD
Memories From My Twelve Years
With Elvis Presley
by Alan Fortas

11 SAVE THE LAST DANCE FOR ME
The Musical Legacy Of The Drifters,
1953-1993
by Tony Allan with Faye Treadwell

12 TURN ME ON, DEAD MAN
The Complete Story of the
Paul McCartney Death Hoax
by Andru J. Reeve

♦ TRIVIA SERIES ♦

1 NOTHING IS BEATLEPROOF
Advanced Beatles Trivia
For Fab Four Fanciers
by Mike Hockinson

Available only through Popular Culture, Ink., P.O. Box 1839, Ann Arbor, Michigan 48106
Phone: 1-800-678-8828

FORTY YEARS AFTER: THE DRIFTERS VISIT THE WHITE HOUSE, JUNE 5, 1993.
(L. to r.): Roland Turner, Joe Cofie, Roy Hemmings, President Bill Clinton,
Tina Treadwell, Johnny Moore, First Lady Hilary Clinton, and Faye Treadwell.

SAVE THE LAST DANCE FOR ME

The Musical Legacy
of The Drifters,
1953-1993

by
Tony Allan
with
Faye Treadwell

Popular Culture, Ink.
1993

Book design and layout by Tom Schultheiss.
Text edited by Candace Morton.
Cover design by Diane Bareis.
Computer programming by Alex Przebienda.

ISBN 1-56075-028-6
LC 92-81113

Published by Popular Culture, Ink.
P.O. Box 1839, Ann Arbor, MI 48106 USA

PCI Collector Editions
are published especially for discerning collectors and libraries.
Each Collector Edition title is released in limited quantities
identified by edition, printing number, and number of copies.
Unlike trade editions, they are not generally available in bookstores.

(This is a Limited First Edition copy: only 1000 printed.)

Printed in the United States of America

"The best rock-and-roll books in the world!"

Contents

FOREWORD, by Charles "Dr. Rock" White ix

CHAPTER 1: Turn Your Radio On 1
CHAPTER 2: Sanctifying the Devil's Music 13
CHAPTER 3: The Original Drifters 21
CHAPTER 4: Spreading the Gospel 31
CHAPTER 5: Drifting Away: The Tragedy of
           Clyde McPhatter... 39
CHAPTER 6: Rockin' and Driftin' 53
CHAPTER 7: Crowning the Drifters 71
CHAPTER 8: Save the Last Dance for Me 79
CHAPTER 9: Drifting Down Broadway 89
CHAPTER 10: The Times They Are A'Changing.................. 105
CHAPTER 11: Live on Stage—The Drifters? 123
CHAPTER 12: Bringing Back the Good Times 135

Appendices

APPENDIX 1: Name Variations.. 157
APPENDIX 2: The Drifters: A Group Family Tree,
            1953-1993 159
APPENDIX 3: Discography 167
APPENDIX 4: The Drifters' Hit Singles: American &
            British Charts.. 195
APPENDIX 5: Non-related "Drifters" Recordings 201

IN MEMORIAM: Doc Pomus and Mort Shuman 203

INDEX 205

THE WHITE HOUSE
WASHINGTON

May 21, 1993

Ms. Faye Treadwell
c/o Howell Begle
901 Fifteenth Street NW, Suite 700
Washington, DC   20005

Dear Ms. Treadwell:

On behalf of President and Mrs. Clinton, I would like to invite The Drifters to perform at the White House on Saturday, June 5, 1993. Their performance will be part of the 25th reunion celebration for President Clinton's Georgetown University Class of 1968.

The President and Mrs. Clinton would be honored if The Drifters would present their concert at a dinner that will be held outdoors on the South Lawn of the White House.

Please send their personal appearance rider to me for discussion. You may contact me directly at....

With Best Wishes,

Ann Stock
Social Secretary

TEXT OF THE LETTER INVITING THE DRIFTERS TO THE WHITE HOUSE
(Not a facsimile. White House phone and fax numbers removed.)

Foreword

The Drifters' name instantly creates a feeling of exhilaration and expectation, in my mind at least, which goes back to the first time I heard "Save the Last Dance for Me" as a teenager in love. That song had a refreshing directness, an earthy sensuality, and, it seems to me, a miraculous balance of sophistication and simple finesse; it never lost touch with a coaxing desire to dance and romance. It would become clear only later that this fusion of South American baion rhythms, superb string accompaniment, and beautiful vocals (topped by the soaring lead of Ben E. King) heralded a major breakthrough in popular music. "Save the Last Dance for Me" still sounds as fresh today as it did then. But the legacy of "Save the Last Dance for Me" is only part of Drifters' story, for so high have been their standards that this is only one of many of their songs that have become an essential part of twentieth century popular music. "Come on over to My Place," "There Goes My Baby," "Under the Boardwalk," "On Broadway," "When My Little Girl Is Smiling," "Money Honey," "White Christmas," "Down on the Beach Tonight," and "Kissing in the Back Row of the Movies" are all familiar greats.

In *Save The Last Dance For Me*, Tony Allan and Faye Treadwell guide us through the Drifters' story, a story as colorful and fascinating as the music itself, a story which tells of the giants of rhythm and blues (Clyde McPhatter, Ben E. King, and Johnny Moore), a story which gives insights into the myriad mini-stories and sub-plots of the transformations that have taken place within the group.

So come along on the exciting journey of the Drifters, who are still, nearly forty years after their original formation, giving endless joy to millions and millions of people.

Charles "Dr. Rock" White,
author of *The Life and Times of Little Richard,*
broadcaster and conservationist

THE DRIFTERS WITH AUTHOR TONY ALLAN (1990)
(L. to r.): Peter Lamarr, Johnny Moore, Tony Allan, John Thurston, Joe Cofie.

Acknowledgements

This part of any book is necessary, even though it often tends to become cliched (which perhaps explains why it often goes unread). However, lots of people deserve a mention for all their help and encouragement, so here goes: Firstly, we would like to dedicate this book to Sarah Johnson (Faye's mother), and to the memory of George Treadwell; Faye Treadwell, for starting the ball rolling; Phillis, for all her support and enthusiasm; Jim Davidson, for all the hours spent typing; Alison Hilbourne and all at "Well Now Dig This" for pointing me in the right direction; Johnny Moore, whose anecdotes were invaluable; Jerry Wexler, for the hospitality which was much appreciated; Les Quinn, for coming up with invaluable information; Michael J. Sweeney; Marvin Goldberg; Joe and May; Margaret and the girls at Baxter, Clark and Paul for their help with the initial stages; Kid Campbell and the staff at A & R Booksearch; Atlantic Records; Tanya, Lynsey and Debbie, for all their help; Chas. "Dr. Rock" White; Roger Greenaway; Léann and Ross, and Tina Treadwell; Galen Gart of Big Nickel Publications, for allowing us to reproduce some early Drifters advertisements from his outstanding rhythm and blues series of books, *First Pressings: The History of Rhythm and Blues*; and a special mention for Phil Luderman, the Drifters' longtime road manager—I know he's not mentioned in the text, but his warmth and friendliness are appreciated by all who encounter him. Finally, a big thank you to Tom Schultheiss of Popular Culture, Ink., and, of course, to Drifters' fans everywhere.

Tony Allan

Chapter 1

Turn Your Radio On

At the end of the 1940s, mainstream American popular music—long under the dictate of the large music publishing houses—had degenerated into a tasteless hodge-podge of styles. Simply put, publishers who had reigned supreme since the early days of sheet music tended to favor show songs. This style had been challenged only during the Big Band era of the 1930s, when most of the name bands played original compositions, temporarily making the publishing houses somewhat superfluous as demand decreased for their made-to-measure ditties.

During the early forties, many of the former band vocalists had begun to gain popularity in their own right. Yet, singers like Frank Sinatra were still forced to turn to the publishing houses for new material, only to be supplied either with the standard show songs or with tunes that sounded very much like them. The only relief from these songs, if indeed they can be called that, was to be found in the novelty genre, which produced smash hits like Eileen Barton's "If I'd Known You Were Coming, I'd Have Baked a Cake," or even worse, singing cowboy Gene Autry's "Frosty the Snowman." Thus, by the end of the decade, Tin Pan Alley once again ruled the roost; the swing era had been merely a temporary aberration.

The entire popular music genre had stagnated. To escape from the blandness, some white teenagers, at whom this music was supposedly aimed, began to turn the dials on their radios in an attempt to escape from the noise that "assailed" their ears. What they stumbled upon in the process was the sound of black America—rhythm and blues, or to use the term the white establishment of the time did, "race music." The term "rhythm and blues" was shortly to be coined by a young

Billboard contributor and future Atlantic Records producer named Jerry Wexler, who picked the name in an attempt to kill off the derogatory "race" term. Wexler would later say that he should have called it "rhythm and gospel," but rhythm and blues it soon became.

Black acts were not totally unknown to white America. During the thirties and forties, both the Inkspots and the Mills Brothers had enjoyed huge success, although these vocal groups never upset the apple cart because their combination of sweet harmonies and pleasant melodies were not at odds with the music white America had become accustomed to hearing. They seemed, however, a long way away from the sounds that wafted clandestinely into the solid homes of white Americans via the radios of their teenage sons and daughters.

Across the airwaves came a music far removed from the cozy tunes of Doris Day and Mantovani. Names like Roy Brown, the Orioles, and Muddy Waters entered the parlance of those "in the know." Unlike the prevailing white music, black music had not stagnated but constantly evolved, from spirituals to gospel, from jazz and blues to the newly termed rhythm and blues. Three styles now dominated black radio: the urban blues sound of those such as John Lee Hooker and Muddy Waters (in essence, an electrified update from the old country blues of the 1920s and 1930s—to the old themes of money, women, and bad luck, electric guitars and crashing drums had been added to hammer home the message); the "jump" style as purveyed by Roy Brown, Bullmoose Jackson, and Wynonie Harris (this often drew upon "risky" blues lyrics—double entendres—and featured shouting vocalists over honking saxes and a driving beat); and, finally, the vocal group sound, long a tradition in black culture, which was now emerging as the most popular of all the styles present in black music.

Most rhythm and blues recordings were to be found mainly on small independent labels, which made them difficult to obtain. The record industry was dominated by a handful of major labels, whose executives ignored the new black acts because they considered them to have limited appeal. Some of these labels, such as RCA-Victor with its "Bluebird" series, had

2

long operated in the Negro market, but the recordings were considered to be aimed merely at the black audience and featured mostly older bluesmen such as Sonny Boy Williamson, Big Joe Williams, and Big Bill Broonzy, all of whom owed much to the older rural traditions (Williamson, however, prior to his tragic death in 1948, had recorded in a harder style).

Almost invariably, then, the majors (RCA-Victor, Columbia, Decca, MGM, Capitol, and Mercury) relied upon the safe, antiseptic music of the day, and because they all had extremely efficient distribution systems—essential given the vastness of America—that gave them access to regional retailers nationwide, their records were readily available to potential buyers. Although they may have believed they were satisfying a demand with such fare, their attempts to please everyone ultimately pleased only a few. Their disregard for anything removed from the norm extended from the blues to country swing and boogie, so that even though people such as Hank Penny and Pee Wee King were popular with white audiences, they were overlooked in favor of crooners like Perry Como and Al Martino.

To fill the gap created by this blinkered attitude, particularly in the emergent rhythm and blues market, a host of independent labels sprang up following World War II. In Chicago, Leonard and Phil Chess set up the Aristocrat label (the forerunner of Chess Records); in New York, Herb Abramson and Ahmet Ertegun founded Atlantic Records; in Memphis, Sam Phillips started his Memphis Recording Service, a venture which would evolve into the legendary Sun label. On the West Coast, there were several labels based in Los Angeles: Art Rupe's Specialty, the Bihari Brother's Modern/RPM, and Lew Chudd's Imperial (which gave the world Fats Domino). Though almost exclusively operated by whites, these small labels were still at a disadvantage insofar as they did not have the distribution networks of the major labels and had to rely on an unorganized network of independent regional distributors. To get their records into the marketplace, the owners of small labels often had to take to the road themselves, where more often than not they had to plead with the distributors to take their

SAVE THE LAST DANCE FOR ME

records.

Gradually, releases on independent labels began to chalk up massive sales. Roy Brown's original "Good Rockin' Tonight" on Deluxe proved to be one of 1947's biggest singles (although it appeared only on black charts), and John Lee Hooker's "Boogie Chillen" sold, so it is said, a million for Modern in 1948 (although this fact was probably never officially acknowledged).

Despite these huge successes in the "jump" and "urban" blues styles, the underlying trend in black music was the vocal group sound, which had a long tradition in black culture, back to the slave days and probably beyond to Africa. The style had found some degree of white acceptance throughout the thirties and forties when watered down versions were popularized by groups like the Four Tunes, the Four Knights, the Inkspots, and Mills Brothers, all of whom enjoyed mass popularity. Although—in terms of hit records—the Mills Brothers could claim to be *the* black vocal group (seventy hits between 1931 and 1968), in terms of influence the Inkspots were the *boss* group.

Formed as the Percolating Puppies in the early thirties, the Inkspots originally consisted of Bill Kenny (lead tenor), Charles Fuqua (second tenor and guitarist), Deek Watson (baritone and guitarist), and Orvil "Hoppy" Jones (bass). Their repertoire initially consisted of jive and jump numbers, although their first attempts fell on deaf ears. Even a name change (to the Inkspots) failed to light many fires. They were seemingly going nowhere fast, until a sudden change of style catapulted them to stardom.

In 1939 their ballad styling of "If I Didn't Care" scored across the board, topping hit listings in both the white and "race" markets. It effectively defined what would thereafter be their style. The Inkspots' sweet sounds were apparently tailor-made for the sombre mood of an audience seeking relief from the harsh reality of war. The melancholic and nostalgic quality of Bill Kenny's voice, complemented by the talking bass of Hoppy Jones, endeared them to the nation. Though they were black, their recordings did not betray that fact, and their "off-white" sound saw them score nearly fifty chart hits between

4

1939 and 1951. More importantly, however, they greatly influenced much that followed. Although many of their recordings sound quaint and mannered today (a Hip-Hop or Public Enemy fan would no doubt be amazed), elements of the group's influence linger on, particularly Bill Kenny's tenor stylings, traces of which can be found in the ballads of the young Elvis Presley, and Hoppy Jones's bass, which may arguably have been the most influential ingredient of all.

It would be difficult for even their most ardent admirer to classify the Inkspots as a rhythm and blues group, even though their recordings have turned up on rhythm and blues compilations. But the first group upon whom the term has been bestowed was heavily influenced by them—the Ravens.

Formed in New York in 1945, the Ravens initially consisted of Warren Suttles (baritone), Ollie Jones (tenor), Leonard Puzey (second lead), and Jimmy Ricks (bass). They at first mimicked the smooth harmonic stylings of both the Inkspots and the Mills Brothers, but soon hit upon their own sound. It was quite by accident: at a live concert, bassman Ricks came in too early, and such was the audience's reaction that the group decided to feature him on lead. In 1947, they reputedly sold a million copies of their revival of "Ol' Man River" (a show tune, once again, originally sung by Paul Robeson in "Show Boat"), issued on National Records. Despite constant changes in personnel, they remained on the rhythm and blues charts until 1954; major success in the white market eluded them, however. Ollie Jones went on to join the Blenders and later the Cues (of "Burn That Candle" fame); Jimmy Ricks pursued a solo career, but was never averse to falling back on the old group name when he toured, which he continued to do well into the sixties.

Although the Ravens have been dubbed "the granddaddy of rhythm and blues groups," in all honesty this is probably an overstatement, for their style was too rooted in the past to really be considered innovative. The accolade no doubt belongs to a group from Baltimore called the Orioles.

Initially known as the Vibranaires, a name under which they achieved some local success in the mid forties, the group consisted of Sonny Til (born Earlington Tilghman) on lead, George Nelson on second lead, Alexander Sharp on tenor, and Johnny Reed on bass. The combo was rounded out by Tommy Gaither on guitar. The members had all been childhood friends and regarded music as secondary to their day jobs—Til drove a truck for Western Electric, for example—and it was only in 1948 that they seriously considered a professional career in music.

A Baltimore songwriter, Dorothy Chessler, heard them and asked them to make a demo of one of her songs ("It's Too Soon to Know"). Changing their name to the Orioles, she then became their booking agent and manager, and took them to New York. Chessler arranged a spot for them on Arthur Godfrey's "Talent Scouts." Although they failed to win, they attracted the attention of Jerry Blaine, who was then head of Natural Records, which recorded them on "It's Too Soon to Know"/"Barbara Lee." When the record appeared in 1948 it was obvious that this was a departure from the usual black vocal group sound—the Orioles had a sweet and relaxed sound, which backed up Til's seemingly cool and detached lead with wordless patterns as opposed to the standard repetition of the words of the lead vocalist. They scored an immediate hit, and between 1948 and 1952 had a succession of rhythm and blues chartbusters with a series of sweet and sentimental ballads. More importantly, the Orioles were the catalyst for black vocal groups as they moved away from the earlier styles.

By 1950, vocal group records were beginning to outsell other rhythm and blues styles, and the growing audience led to the formation of more and more groups that began to dominate the release schedules. This period saw the formation of many classic groups, among which the Five Keys and the Larks were standouts. The latter featured one of the great unsung heroes of black vocal groups—Gene Mumford (he was to front the 1957 Dominoes on their worldwide smash revival of Hoagy Carmichael's "Stardust," although it hardly did him justice). Billy Ward's Dominoes started out in 1951 and were one of the outstanding rhythm and blues vocal groups attracting the new white teenage audience to black radio programs. Coincidentally, this

6

audience had grown large enough to come to the attention of white record store owners, who increasingly found themselves asked by white teens for black rhythm and blues hits.

One such owner was Leo Mintz, who ran a store in Cleveland. Mintz was so taken aback by the trend that he called a disk jockey friend of his, Alan Freed, and invited him to come by the store and witness the phenomenon for himself. Freed accepted and, after spending some time at Mintz's shop, decided that the time had come to change the pattern of white music broadcasting.

Alan Freed seemed an unlikely character to spark a musical revolution, for he was almost thirty (he had been born December 15, 1932) at the time and hosted a classical music program—hardly the basis for teenage rebellion. He had fronted a jazz band called the "Sultans of Swing" in his youth (a fact no doubt noted by Mark Knopfler), and following a spell in the army had earned a masters degree in engineering at Ohio State University. Despite a hearing problem which had cropped up in the army, he moved into radio work in the forties, ending up at WKEL in Cleveland in 1950. He may have been hosting a classical music show, but he was a fan of rhythm and blues saxmen Red Prysock and Big Al Sears as well as the sophisticated blues of Ivory Joe Hunter. This fondness for rhythm and blues (combined with what he had seen at Mintz's record store) more than likely influenced his decision to alter the format of his show, although a more drastic change would be hard to imagine.

Nevertheless, Freed began to host his "Moondog's Rock and Roll Party" in June 1951 on WJW, where, with a whiskey bottle never far from his reach, he broadcast rhythm and blues to white America. Though he apparently adopted the term "rock and roll" to disguise the music's negro background, Freed may not be accused of racism, for here was a white man playing that "nigger music" to white youths—it was all right for blacks to play it because no one heard it anyway (or so it was thought). The new name would hardly have placated racists either, for "rock and roll" was a black euphemism for sexual intercourse. The term had been used by black musicians in the late forties to describe dance music (which is probably where Freed picked it up), and the expression had long been used in blues (in 1936 the great Robert Johnson said he'd be rockin' to his end, and in 1950 L'il Son Jackson recorded a song called "Rock 'n' Roll." Possibly the earliest record to combine the terms, however, was Frankie Jaxon's "My Baby Rock's Me (With a Steady Roll)," cut in 1929 with Tampa Red's Hokum Jug Band, although Jaxon was definitely not singing about dancing. Doubtless, blues buffs will come up with any number of even earlier examples of the combination.

Freed's fame quickly spread, for not only did he play all the latest (hot) rhythm and blues records but the seeming chaos of the show (with the disk jockey banging on telephone books in time with the music and joining in the vocals) captured the spirit of the new music perfectly. Freed was particularly fond of the vocal groups, and records by the Larks, the Orioles, and others were never far from the turntable. His success was such that by 1952 he was confident enough to stage his first "live" rock and roll show in Cleveland. The occasion was marred, however, when thirty thousand turned up for seats in an auditorium with a capacity of ten thousand and the authorities, no doubt panicked, cancelled the show. What followed was the first riot in the name of rock and roll.

In 1953, the Orioles' recording of Darrel Glen's "Crying in the Chapel" became one of the first records by a black vocal group to break into the white pop charts, and Alan Freed's influence was more than demonstrated when thirty thousand records were reportedly sold in the Cleveland area alone the day after he played it. Despite this, Freed remained one of the few white disk jockeys to play the record.

Freed moved to New York's WINS in 1954, where he continued to break down racial barriers both with his choice of records and his manic jive style. Though loathed by the establishment, he fronted national television shows and appeared in the early rock and roll films "Rock around the Clock," "Don't Knock the Rock," "Mr. Rock and Roll," and "Go Johnny Go." Most of the major names of the time (Little Richard, the Teenagers, Chuck Willis, Johnny Burnette, Chuck Berry, the Five

8

Keys, and the Drifters, the subject of this book) appeared on his radio shows, usually singing their latest waxings live (a series of bootleg albums documenting these performances surfaced a few years ago and are worth looking for). Gradually, though, the establishment began to fight back, and Freed was their prime target. When he refused to sign an affidavit denying he had ever taken payola (the illegal practice of accepting gifts or cash in exchange for playing certain records), he was fired by WABC, his then current station. The practice of payola was widespread, but Freed's scalp was wanted, and he was driven from the airwaves. His career never recovered. He pled guilty to a charge of commercial bribery in 1962, was given a suspended sentence, and was fined three hundred dollars. He died of uremia on January 20, 1965, before he could be further hounded with tax evasion charges.

It may be too much to say that Alan Freed was entirely responsible for rock and roll, but his contribution was immense, and his constant refusal to play watered-down white covers of rhythm and blues hits is something that should commend him to us all. Some, such as Hunter Hancock, may dispute his claim to being the first white rhythm and blues disk jockey, but to most his name is synonymous with early rock and roll.

In the meantime, the popularity of rhythm and blues had not gone unnoticed. In 1951, a hillbilly vocalist named Bill Haley recorded a cover version of Jackie Brenston's driving "Rocket 88" (it featured Ike Turner's band and was produced by Sam Phillips). Though watered down and rather anemic compared to the original, it was a significant departure for Haley, whose previous output had included horrendous cowboy songs. In some quarters Haley's "Rocket 88" is said to have been the first rock and roll record. This is questionable, but it is probably a better record than Haley's attempt at Jimmy Preston's "Rock the Joint," which transformed a rockin' boogie into a square dance.

Much more authentic were the efforts of Johnny Otis, who though white surrounded himself with black musicians and produced top-drawer rhythm and blues music. Otis had to wait until 1957 for real commercial success, but Bill Haley scored a national hit in 1953 with his "Crazy Man Crazy" on Essex, which set off his meteoric rise to fame. True to form, disk jockeys ignored Haley's original and played Ralph Marterie's cover on the major Mercury label (this time, though, their patronage proved useless—Marterie's record flopped).

Now taking note of what was happening on the independent labels, the majors began to issue a slew of inferior covers of rhythm and blues hits (Haley's was an exception, but it was an independent record). Some examples: "Kokomo" (originally out by Gene and Eunice, covered by Tony Bennett [?] on Columbia and Perry Como on RCA/Victor, both too horrible for words); "Such a Night" (the Drifters first on Atlantic, covered by Johnny Ray on Columbia and Dinah Washington—at least she was black—on Mercury); "Earth Angel" (originally by the Penguins on Dootone, and covered by the squeaky clean Crewcuts on Mercury; ironically, the Penguins were later signed by Mercury in a deal which also took the Platters to the label). Without exception, these covers are terrible (sorry, Dinah). Though note for note copies of the original, they lack the spark that made the originals great.

Nothing could halt the growth of the beast known as rock and roll. More and more white artists discovered the rhythm in the blues, most significantly in Memphis in 1954 when a young truck driver cut a version of an old Arthur Crudup blues tune called "That's All Right, Mama." The singer was Elvis Presley, and he unleashed a tide of young white vocalists who performed a variation of rhythm and blues called rockabilly that combined country roots with the new-found drive of black music. Presley himself went on to dominate the music scene for two decades, although whether he ever again matched the recordings he made in 1954 and 1955 is debatable. They captured the mood of the times, a time when it was really worth turning on the radio.

One strand of black music—gospel—appeared to be unaffected by the changes taking place in the field of secular music (its exponents regarded the blues as the property of the Devil anyway). A product of the gospel-singing tradition, however, was soon to make a contribution to the Devil's music that in its own way would be as earth-shattering as the upheaval created by Alan Freed's championing of rhythm and blues music.

CHAPTER 2
Sanctifying the Devil's Music

Religion has always played a key role in the life of black Americans. Even before their African forefathers were transported forcibly to the new world, religion was a dominant part of their culture.

On arrival in America they found many of their religious ceremonies outlawed, for their new white masters feared they could be used as a means of fostering rebellion, and the slaves were instead encouraged to embrace Christianity. At camp meetings in the early 1800s, however, blacks nevertheless developed "sorrow songs" such as "Steal Away," "Swing Low Sweet Chariot," and "Go Down Moses" that seemed to reflect their feelings about enslavement.

Following their emancipation, the spirituals, as they were now called, took on a more aggressive, joyous feel, and songs such as "In That Great Gettin' Up Morning" and "Git on Board, Little Children" came to be known as "jubilee spirituals."

At the end of the Civil War, attempts were made to improve the quality of religious songs in black churches, but this resulted in white influence replacing much of the rhythmic drive and passion of black singing. The Fisk Jubilee Singers, who sang black melodies in a cultured manner modelled on white hymnal styles, rose to prominence as a result of this influence.

The influence of the Fisk Singers was so strong that black religious song, which was often composed by whites, became bland in the extreme, with little relevance to the people for whom it was intended.

In the late nineteenth century, gospel hymns that restored much of the lost rhythm of the earlier hymns emerged,

13

SAVE THE LAST DANCE FOR ME

but even they relied heavily on the white hymnal tradition. This style of gospel song became the most widely used in Baptist churches during the opening quarter of the twentieth century, although the compositions of Charles Tindley, which addressed the needs of the poor and oppressed, became popular in the Pentecostal Holiness and Sanctified churches. (Tindley's gospel songs included "Stand by Me," "Leave It Here," and "We'll Understand It Better By and By.")

By 1930, however, black gospel music was not held in very high esteem, particularly among the younger generation who regarded its conservatism as "Uncle Tom" in nature. But under the influence of several men and women, among whom were William Herbert Brewster, Roberta Martin, and particularly Thomas A. Dorsey, gospel music was to revive and take on a whole new significance.

Thomas A. Dorsey was born on July 1, 1899, in Carroll County, Georgia, the son of a Baptist minister and a church organist. He learned to play the guitar and piano, composing his first gospel song, "If I Don't Get There," at an early age.

On moving to Atlanta he came under the influence of local blues musicians and began singing the blues as "Barrelhouse Tommy." He moved to Chicago during World War I, where he studied composing and arranging, working at the same time as an agent for Paramount Records. One of his songs, "Riverside Blues," was recorded by King Oliver in 1923. After a stint with Les Hite's Whispering Serenaders in 1923, he formed the Wildcats Jazz Band, which often featured Gertrude "Ma" Rainey on vocals. He recorded with her as "Georgia Tom" before forming a duo with Tampa Red; their ribald blues "Tight Like That" was a big hit in 1928. He continued in this vein from 1928 to 1932, either with Tampa Red alone or with the addition of Bob Robinson (the trio was known as the Hokum Boys), specializing in humorous double-entendre blues songs.

His gospel song "Someday, Somewhere" was published in 1921, and in the early thirties he turned exclusively to that idiom. He organized the first gospel choir at the Ebenezer Baptist Church in Chicago in 1931, and in 1932 opened the Thomas A. Dorsey Gospel Songs Publishing Company, the first firm to promote black gospel music; the same year, along with gospel singer Sally Martin, he founded the National Convention of Gospel Choirs and Choruses,

His early gospel songs had been very much in the style of Charles Tindley, based on hymns and spirituals but lacking the rhythm he was to start using in his post-blues gospel songs. After a couple of failed attempts at recording gospel music, he began to sell his songs on the street, accompanying himself on piano outside churches, often joined by other singers. Before long, Negro church services, especially those involving sanctified Baptists, took on an entirely new dimension, the congregation leaping and hollering, driven along by a foot-stomping pianist who, more often than not, was Thomas Andrew Dorsey himself.

Dorsey discovered Mahalia Jackson and Clara Ward, but more importantly he created modern gospel music by bringing back the fire and passion natural to black vocalists which had all but been erased by the Fisk Jubilee Singers and their successors. At the same time, he unknowingly laid the foundations for future developments in the world of secular music.

Gospel music grew in popularity during the forties and early fifties, creating its own stars such as the Soul Stirrers, Swan Silvertones, and Sister Rosetta Tharpe, along the way. It even had its own radio stations and disk jockeys, one of the best of whom was Joe Lubic, who staged gospel shows in the style of the rhythm and blues packages.

There had been relatively few links between the gospel and blues singers even though they often traveled roughly the same road. But, as with all such unwritten laws, there were exceptions to the rule. Blind Willie Johnson had sung religious songs over a blues background in the 1920s, and the golden girl of the gospel scene, Sister Rosetta Tharpe, was heavily influenced by the blues. In general the styles did not mix, for the gospel singer was bound for glory while the blues singer was forever damned—the fire, emotion, and passion of gospel singing had no place in the secular field. At least it didn't until the appearance of Clyde Lensey McPhatter.

Born in Durham, North Carolina, on November 15, 1932

THE MOUNT LEBANON SINGERS (1949)
Rear (l. to r.): William Anderson, David Baldwin, Clyde McPhatter;
Front (l. to r.): Wilmer Baldwin, James Johnson, Charlie White.
(Photo from the collection of Marv Goldberg)

THE DOMINOES (1951)
Rear (l. to r.): Joe Lamont, Billy Ward, Bill Brown;
Front (l. to r.): Clyde McPhatter, Charlie White.
(Photo from the collection of Marv Goldberg)

(some biographies give the date as 1931 or 1933), Clyde McPhatter was the fourth child born to George and Beulah (also known as Eva) McPhatter. His father and mother were, like Thomas Dorsey's, a Baptist minister and a church organist, and he was singing in the church choir alongside his brothers Leroy, James, and George and sisters Bertha, Esther, and Gladys at an early age. By the age of ten his soprano was leading the choir, and his father hoped Clyde would follow him into the church. The young McPhatter dreamed instead of football stardom, although he did have connections with a local gospel group, the Four Internes. Coincidentally, Eugene Mumford had been a member of the group, the same Gene Mumford who would go on to sing with the Dominoes in the mid-fifties.

Clyde's dream dissolved abruptly after George McPhatter moved his family from Durham to Teaneck, New Jersey, when Clyde was about fourteen years old. He attended Cooper Junior High and Chelsea Vocational School, and came into contact with a gospel-singing group known as the Mount Lebanon Singers, who took their name from the Mount Lebanon Church on 132nd Street in Harlem.

Clyde was invited to join the group, which was made up of brothers David and William "Lover" Baldwin (brothers of novelist James Baldwin), Charlie White, William "Chick" Anderson, and James "Wrinkle" Johnson.

After Clyde joined, the group became well enough known to tour the eastern states, continuing to do so even after Clyde graduated and took a job as a clerk with a music publishing firm. By this time McPhatter was known as one of *the* vocalists on the gospel circuit. (During this period he also appeared on the bill of Harlem's famed Apollo Theater's "Amateur Night," a performance which he later claimed had made him a winner, though that fact has subsequently been disputed.)

Clyde might have continued in this fashion for a longer period had not fate taken a hand in the form of Billy Ward. Ward was a product of the renowned Julliard School of Music, and had won an award at the age of fourteen for his composition "Dejection." Following a spell in the army, Ward began his own voice training school on Broadway in the early fifties.

Though he principally coached gospel singers, Ward also had a job as arranger and coach for a rhythm and blues group called the Ques, and was toying with the idea of forming his own vocal group. When he told Joe Lamont (a member of the Ques) of his plans, Lamont suggested he contact Clyde McPhatter, whom he knew from his own gospel singing days. (The Ques had appeared on an amateur talent show in late 1950, where they had performed Leadbelly's "Good Night Irene." Ward took a dub of the song to King Records, but Syd Nathan was unimpressed—he was apparently looking for another Orioles.)

Billy Ward got in touch with Clyde, who then called at Ward's studio for an audition, bringing Charlie White along with him. (Bill Pinckney has said that he was the one who originally took Clyde to Billy Ward. Pinckney seems to have known Ward before Clyde did, and Bill has been quoted as saying: "Clyde and I were only discussing with Billy Ward, then somehow or other, the next thing I know, Clyde and Charlie White were with him.") Billy Ward apparently wanted a lead vocalist similar in style to the Inkspot's Bill Kenny, and although the young McPhatter admired Kenny's sweet tenor, his own singing style was much more earthy and bluesy. On hearing Clyde sing, however, Ward changed his plans and hired him immediately.

Persuading his new vocalist to resign from his office job, Ward formed the original Billy Ward and the Dominoes. Clyde was on lead tenor, Charlie White on second tenor, Joe Lamont on baritone, and Bill Brown on bass (Brown came from a New York gospel group, the Five Internationals, with whom Joe Lamont had also sung). Ward, though only the pianist and arranger, took the main billing.

Billy Ward returned to Nathan with a demo of "Do Something for Me," and Nathan signed the Dominoes to his Federal subsidiary. They were an immediate success in the rhythm and blues field, scoring a number six hit with "Do Something for Me" as a first release. Their follow-up release, "60 Minute Man," became one of the biggest rhythm and blues hits of 1951 and was the song that established the Dominoes in the music world.

18

Ralph Bass, the group's producer, noticed the gospel inflections in Clyde McPhatter's vocals and brought some of this quality to the fore in his productions of "The Bells" and "Have Mercy Baby." Clyde attacked the doom-laden "Bells" and the hard-driving "Mercy" with the emotion of a sanctified Southern Baptist, something entirely new in the world of rhythm and blues where lead vocalists tended to adopt the cool, detached stance of Sonny Til. Most of the records were not overtly influenced by gospel music, but those that showed traces of the style hinted at what could be.

The group spent most of 1951 and 1952 actively on the road, but Clyde began to grow dissatisfied with the setup. Ward had them on a fixed salary, which meant that they were always short of cash, and Clyde, moreover, was growing increasingly bitter about the billing of the combo inasmuch as many of the rhythm and blues public believed Billy Ward to be the lead vocalist. Group members were also expected to behave in an almost military manner; Ward imposed fines for such things as scruffy appearance, dirty shoes, and tardiness.

Matters came to a head in Providence, Rhode Island, where Clyde finally decided to leave the group. Ward later said he had fired his vocalist, but McPhatter was equally adamant that he had left voluntarily. Waiting in the wings to replace him was a young singer from Detroit who had been traveling with the Dominoes and studying Clyde. His name was Jackie Wilson—but that's another story.

Back in New York, Clyde contacted David Baldwin, saying he intended to form a group of his own; what happened on May 6, 1953, speeded up the process considerably.

On that night, Ahmet Ertegun, long one of Clyde's fans, went to see the Dominoes at Birdland in New York. Discovering that the group had a new lead singer, Ertegun asked what had become of Clyde McPhatter. Ward answered that he had been fired. That might have been that, except that Ertegun was not only a fan, he was the president of Atlantic Records.

The following day, Ertegun tracked McPhatter down to a rooming house in Harlem and offered him an Atlantic contract. He also agreed that Clyde should form a group to showcase his vocals.

Ahmet Ertegun and his partner Jerry Wexler (the *Billboard* writer who had coined the phrase "rhythm and blues"), who had only recently joined the company, thought they could revolutionize rhythm and blues by allowing McPhatter to perform in a style derived completely from gospel with as few concessions as possible to secular music. They envisioned a rhythm and blues vocal group that would sing with the emotion and power found in gospel music, a concept that at that time was alien.

By allowing Clyde McPhatter free reign to exploit his gospel influence, and by recording Ray Charles in a gospel style that was completely different from his earlier Nat "King" Cole vocals, Atlantic laid the foundations for the music that would become known as "soul" a decade later.

Many other artists were none too overjoyed by this merging of gospel and rhythm and blues—bluesman Big Bill Broonzy reportedly said that Charles was "crying sanctified and should be in church"—but the roots of much that followed were laid down in 1953 when Clyde McPhatter and the soon-to-be Drifters really did sanctify the Devil's music.

CHAPTER 3

The Original Drifters

What's in a name? Mention the Drifters to anyone who has been a music fan over the last thirty-five years and chances are that most will be able to name some of the classic songs associated with the group. Many will no doubt be able to debate the merits of the various line-ups and even who, exactly, was in the original formation.

Very few, if any, will be able to recall "I'm the Caring Kind" or "Wine Headed Woman," but these were the first songs ever released under the Drifters' name in 1950 (Coral 65037). The group involved, however, had no connection with the subjects of this book, and who they were has long been lost in the mists of time. The recording company, Coral, was a subsidiary of the Decca organization, which was renowned more for middle-of-the-road artists. How a black vocal group managed a release on this label is quite a mystery—Decca may have been trying to cash in on their success with the Inkspots. In any event, Coral went so far as to issue a second record by the group, " I Had to Find Out for Myself"/"And I Shook" (Coral 65040). Neither record sold well. A third unrelated record, "I Don't Want to See You Cry Anymore"/"The Dog, the Cat and Me" (London 16011) also appeared in 1950, this one by Ernie Andrews and The Drifters. (Should any Drifters' freaks feel the need to know more about these recordings, be aware that they are very fortyish in style and sound very dated today.)

You can't, it seems, keep a good name down. In 1951, Excelsior Records issued "Mobile"/"Honey Chile" by the Drifters, who may or may not have been the same group recorded by Coral the year before. This record managed to obtain a review in *Billboard* (July 7, 1951), but though not too bad in a bluesy sort of way, it was not highly rated. Again, very much a product

21

of its time, the record sank without a trace.

Confused? Well, there's more to follow. The Los Angeles-based Class label issued a Drifters' recording of "Three Lies" (Class 500) around 1953, and the following year Crown 108 featured "The World Is Changing" by the Drifters. These recordings are very obscure and difficult to find. Rama Records of New York seems to have gone one better, listing Rama 22 as "Besame Mucho"/"Summertime" by the Drifters but apparently forgetting to release it.

All these recordings, which may or may not have been made by totally different groups, have one thing in common: they have nothing whatsoever to do with the Drifters who came into existence in May 1953. (For more on non-related "Drifters" recordings, see Chapter 11.)

Armed with the Atlantic contract, Clyde McPhatter gathered together some of his old Mount Lebanon colleagues, namely David Baldwin, William "Chick" Anderson, and James "Wrinkle" Johnson. (Charlie White had left the Dominoes for the Clovers, and William Baldwin did not participate in the reunion.) An acquaintance from the neighborhood, fourteen-year-old "Little David" Baughan, was brought in as the fifth member. Thus, the quintet that gathered in May 1953 consisted of Clyde McPhatter (lead tenor), David Baughan (tenor), William Anderson (tenor), David Baldwin (bass), and James Johnson (bass).

Before moving on, we should say that some confusion surrounds McPhatter's departure from the Dominoes. David Baldwin has said he received a telegram from Clyde (who was in California) saying that he was leaving the Dominoes and returning to New York to form his own vocal group. Baldwin alleges that he—Baldwin—then gathered together William Anderson, James Johnson, and David Baughan to form the first Drifters with Clyde. This, however, differs from Ertegun's account and Ertegun has stuck with his story through the years; Wexler, moreover, has corroborated Ertugen's account.

How the Drifters came to be called the Drifters has also been the source of some confusion. The explanation usually given is that the name was obtained when each member threw a written suggestion into a hat and David Baldwin's emerged.

22

Baldwin said he hit upon the name while looking at a book on birds belonging to his father (Baldwin said this in an interview with Marv Goldberg, but Goldberg thinks Baldwin threw it out as an afterthought because no one seems to have heard of a bird called or even nicknamed a Drifter; still, it was the age of bird groups, a trend started by the Ravens.) Other explanations have been put forward—one credits Clyde McPhatter's mother, and Goldberg thinks McPhatter may have been toying with the idea, or that it came from George Treadwell. The most common alternative explanation has been that they became the Drifters because all the members had "drifted" from other groups, a suggestion put forward in an Atlantic press release. Baldwin's story has remained the one most quoted, but no one really knows for sure. Articles published at the time say that the Drifters did not appear until August 1953, hence the group, as some believe, may have had no name when they gathered for their first recording session (the Atlantic files, however, do list the group as Clyde McPhatter and the Drifters).

However formed, however named, the group began rehearsing immediately, and on June 29, 1953, Clyde McPhatter and the Drifters entered the studios of Atlantic for the first time and recorded four numbers—E. Hinds's "Gone," Clyde McPhatter's "Lucille," Ertegun and Wexler's "Let the Boogie Woogie Roll," and Ertegun's "What'cha Gonna Do."

The results proved unsatisfactory. The gospel/rhythm and blues fusion Ertegun and Wexler had hoped for failed to materialize. What they heard was a tenor-dominated sound that failed to highlight Clyde's lead vocal. They were also less than impressed with the group's name, which to them conjured up a country and western band. Though McPhatter was agreeable to replacing the personnel, he was adamant the name be retained (his refusal to change the name lending some credence to the theory that it was Clyde's mother who named the group). Of the recordings made that day, only "Lucille" was to see the light of day—it was released as a b-side the next year. The version of "Gone" cut at this date was believed at one time to have been lost in a fire at Atlantic Records' office. However, some years ago Jerry Wexler gave a copy of it to Drifters and vocal group researcher Marv Goldberg, who has subsequently aired it on oldies radio shows. He has done so with Jerry Wexler's blessing, although Wexler insisted that the disk jockey talk over sections of the recording, presumably to prevent bootleggers from duplicating it and issuing pirated copies. The general consensus among those who have been fortunate enough to hear this version is that it is superior to the subsequent re-recording.

The original recordings of "Let the Boogie Woogie Roll" and "What'cha Gonna Do" remain unheard.

There are perhaps two reasons why this initial line-up failed to work out. The first is the fact that their voices may have been too light and too similar to be effective; the second, that Anderson, Johnson, and Baldwin had not sung together since the Mount Lebanon Singers had disbanded in 1951 (when Clyde and Charlie White left to join the Dominoes) and had never sung with David Baughan.

Clyde McPhatter, now back to square one, set about recruiting another set of vocalists. He called upon two friends who were both gospel singers and offered them the chance to join the group. Gerhart and Andrew Thrasher promptly accepted. Originally from Wetumpka, Alabama, the Thrasher brothers were veterans of the gospel circuit. They had sung with the Silvertone Singers and, along with their sister Bernice, had been part of the Thrasher Wonders when the musicologist Moses Asch recorded them around 1947. Asch made several trips to the South during the forties to record Negro talent and had chanced upon the Thrasher Wonders. The recording ("Moses Smote the Waters") was issued on a collection of Asch's field recordings and is the first to feature any future members of the Drifters.

Bill Pinckney (born August 15, 1925, in Sumpter, North Carolina) was the next person McPhatter called. Pinckney's singing career began in 1946 in Dalzell, North Carolina, where he formed his first gospel group with David and Herbert Glover, Matthew Gallashald, and James and Wesley Mack. Called the Singing Cousins, they performed regularly in Southern churches before breaking up in 1949, the year Bill moved to New York.

24

In New York, Bill played sandlot baseball with the New York Blue Sox in New York City's Central Park, Pennsylvania, and New Jersey. He also worked at Sutton Motors, a Ford dealership. In 1951, he formed the Jerusalem Stars with James Green, Jimmy Griffen, Bill Massey, and Brook Benton (the same Brook Benton who in the late fifties and early sixties scored a succession of smash hits; his stay with the Stars was not long, however). Following the Stars, Bill got together with Jimmy Powell, James Bryant, and Gerhart Thrasher, naming this particular combination the Southern Knights. Despite the fact that his experience was strictly gospel-based, Pinckney gladly accepted McPhatter's invitation. An accomplished vocalist with a range that took in tenor, baritone, and bass, he initially joined the group as a tenor.

The jigsaw puzzle was completed with the acquisition of yet another one of Clyde's friends, bass Willie Ferbee (the group met him at a dinner; he was not a gospel singer—he had worked as a laborer). Thus, the second edition of Clyde McPhatter and the Drifters was just about ready to roll. Just about. Since many similar groups carried a guitarist with them, the Drifters decided to add one. (The Drifters' first guitarist was Arthur Hamm, followed by Chauncy Westbrook. Walter Adams played on "Money Honey," and upon his death was replaced by Jimmy Oliver.)

The next recording session was scheduled for August 9. Atlantic, unlike the majority of the independents, meticulously prepared for their sessions; they left nothing to chance, rehearsing the material and the musicians well in advance. In this, their arranger Jesse Stone played a major role. When Atlantic's initial jazz releases failed to make any impact, Stone, a jazz and blues musician in the twenties, began to write material himself (he found writing in the rhythm and blues style and its child, rock and roll, very easy). He also played piano, acted as bandleader, and had even written parts for the back-up vocalists.

Born on November 16, 1911, in Atchison, Kansas, Stone had a long history in jazz and blues music. His parents, Fred and Julia, had both been musicians, and he had been perform-

THE DRIFTERS FEATURING CLYDE McPHATTER (1953)
(L. to r.): Bill Pinckney, Willie Ferbee, Clyde McPhatter,
Andrew Thrasher, and Gerhart Thrasher.
(Photo courtesy Michael Ochs Archives/Venice, CA)

ing since he was four years old, principally through the encouragement of his mother.

During the 1920s he worked with the legendary Big Joe Turner in Kansas City, where he also formed a band known as Jesse Stone and The Blues Serenaders, who recorded "Starvation Blues" on Okeh Records in 1926.

Throughout the twenties and thirties, he worked as a pianist/arranger for various bands, including Duke Ellington's in 1936.

He recorded "Snakey Feeling" for Variety in 1937, but had to wait until 1942 for his first real commercial success, when Benny Goodman scored with Stone's composition, "Idaho."

Eventually landing in New York in the mid-forties, he worked for a while at Harlem's famed Apollo Theater before joining the newly established Atlantic Records in 1947.

Atlantic executives, and particularly Jerry Wexler, detested the amateur attempts of many independents who constantly issued substandard productions. Wexler recalls how at one session Hy Weiss, a street hustler who ran Old Town Records and who was infamous for his production-line method of recording vocal groups, overheard a musician discussing the key to a certain song and immediately switched on the control room microphone to tell the offending musician that there were no keys in his studio, play and get the fuck out. Not that all Old Town Records were bad. The story merely illustrates an attitude that seems to have been prevalent among many of the independents who cared little for the music or the artists.

Thus, before the August recording date, Atlantic had selected the material and assembled the veritable cream of rhythm and blues session men (Sam "The Man" Taylor on tenor sax, drummers Connie Kay or Panama Francis, David Rae and Heywood Henry on baritone sax, and Mickey Baker on guitar).

The first number recorded was "The Way I Feel," a slow ballad written by a former Big Band vocalist called Johnny Parker and originally recorded in 1951 by the Four Knights.

The dreamy atmosphere of this number was shattered by the next. Jesse Stone had provided the Drifters with a song called "Money Honey," and it was this song that finally brought

27

Ertegun's and Wexler's vision into reality. Stone had dreamed up a bagpipe opening for the number in which the backing vocalists sang "Aah-Dom, Aah-Dom"; the vocalists chants, driven on by the drums, were followed at once by the sound of Clyde's voice, which grew more intense during the song and highlighted his gospel tendencies. McPhatter's voice (not, as Wexler pointed out, a forced falsetto but a naturally pure tenor) soared above what was an infectious and irresistible song, and the result can only be described as perfection.

The other tracks cut that day were remakes of the June session's "Gone," "What'cha Gonna Do," and "Let the Boogie Woogie Roll." "Gone" was subsequently used as a b-side, but inexplicably the great "Let the Boogie Woogie Roll" remained unheard until May 1960 when it appeared credited to Clyde McPhatter only. The version of "What'cha Gonna Do" was thought unsuitable for release.

"Money Honey" backed with "The Way I Feel" was issued on Atlantic 1006 in September 1953. After a rather slow start, it shot to number one in the rhythm and blues charts (November 1). It failed, though, to cross over onto the white national Hot 100, despite the fact that black groups were becoming increasingly popular in the wake of the success of the Orioles and the promotions of Alan Freed.

The failure of "Money Honey" to hit the national charts is not hard to understand. Things were changing, but the dominance of the major labels proved hard to overcome. The year, after all, was 1953, the year Patti Page topped the hit lists with the appalling "How Much Is That Doggie in the Window"—a feat that prompted one music lover to remark that no one listened to the radio during the charming Miss Page's reign at the top of the charts for fear of having their ears assailed by that horrendous ditty.

"Money Honey" topped the rhythm and blues charts over the Christmas period. (At the same time, Eddie Fisher's revolutionary [!] "Oh My Papa" serenaded the mass white audience from the number one spot on the *Billboard* Hot 100.) "Money Honey" would later see covers by Elvis Presley, Little Richard, Johnny and the Hurricanes, and even (horror of horrors) Pat Boone; but none ever surpassed the original, which has stood the test of time and sounds as fresh today as it did then.

Just before Atlantic released "Money Honey," they solved a niggling problem with Clyde McPhatter's contract. Federal Records apparently still held claim to Clyde from his time with Billy Ward's Dominoes. The matter was resolved when Atlantic engineer Tom Dowd accompanied Clyde to a lawyer's office on 42nd Street. When they emerged, Clyde was free to turn the world of rhythm and blues upside down.

CHAPTER 4

Spreading the Gospel

Just as "Money Honey" was topping the rhythm and blues charts, producers Ahmet Ertegun and Jerry Wexler recalled the Drifters to the studios on November 12, 1953. Although Wexler would later say they knew nothing about making records (Wexler, in fact, admitted "We didn't know we were producers [or] what was a producer. Nobody knew what a producer did."), the productions Wexler and Ertegun made with Clyde McPhatter and the Drifters belie the statement, for they always managed to coax excellence from the group.

At this session the Drifters recorded "Don't Dog Me," which had been written by Ertegun and Wexler; "Warm Your Heart," composed by the same duo with the assistance of Tom Dowd; "Such a Night," which had been submitted by Lincoln Chase, a graduate of New York's Academy of Music and a Decca recording artist; and "Bip Bam," a number which leaned towards the emerging rock and roll style and which Jesse Stone had written under the pseudonym Charles Calhoun (a name he was to use for his composition "Shake, Rattle and Roll," one of the first classic rock and roll songs).

Wexler and Ertegun not only recorded but submitted ideas during the sessions, a fact underscored by what happened during the production of "Such a Night." As the group ran through the song with Jesse Stone, Jerry Wexler kept hearing a bass riff in his head. Taking this bass line of "Boomp-A-Doomp-A-Doomp-A-Boomp," which he had heard first on Eddie Heywood's "Begin the Beguine" in 1944 (it had also been used by Francis Craig on "Near You" in 1947), Wexler grafted it onto the Chase composition and gave the number a completely different feel.

Even though "Money Honey" was still atop the rhythm

and blues charts, Atlantic released "Such a Night" in January 1954, backing it with "Lucille," which the first Drifters group had recorded in January 1954. Surprisingly, "Lucille" picked up strong sales in its own right, entering the Most Played Jukebox Chart on March 6. "Such a Night" crashed onto the rhythm and blues charts shortly after and climbed to number five, with "Lucille" close behind at number seven. "Such a Night" was covered by Dinah Washington, but the hit for the white market was recorded by Johnny Ray of Columbia and took the "Nabob of Sob" into the U.K. Top 10.

The failure of the original to score with the mass white market is not hard to understand, for the song was overtly sexual and the listener was left in little doubt as to why the night was so special. The year was 1954, after all. The cover versions watered down the sexual overtones of the original, and none are comparable to Clyde McPhatter's rendition—a voice soaring up and down the scale with true gospel fervor.

The other cuts from the session fared less well. "Warm Your Heart" was an uninspired and routine ballad saved only by the Drifters' performance, and "Don't Dog Me" was released only as a Clyde McPhatter b-side in February 1960. "Bip Bam" did appear as a single but proved one of the group's least successful.

Since the August session, some changes had taken place in the Drifters' lineup. Willie Ferbee (the bass man) had become ill shortly before the group was to go on tour and had been unable to carry on. His place had been taken by Bill Pinckney, who was equally at home with tenor and bass. Walter Adams, who had been the guitarist on the "Money Honey" recording date, had unfortunately died, and Jimmy Oliver had been brought in. Although Oliver never recorded with the Drifters, he did become an integral part of the group, for he contributed songs and was responsible for their musical arrangements on the road. More importantly, though, the group had acquired a new manager—George Treadwell, a thirty-four-year-old native of New York who had made a name for himself in the forties as a jazz trumpeter at Monroe's Up Town. Treadwell had become involved with the group through the accountant

32

Lew Lebish, and his appointment was one of the most significant moves the Drifters were to make, although they probably were unaware of it at the time.

The group hit the road almost immediately after cutting "Money Honey" and proved as sensational in concert as they had been on record. Many rhythm and blues fans of the time considered them to have the most exciting act of any group, or solo act for that matter. Clyde McPhatter sang, did the splits, and back-flipped on one side of the stage, while the others tap-danced and performed acrobatics on the other. Their act was often accompanied by flashing theater lights, which created a rather strong effect, hitherto unseen. Gerhart Thrasher in particular let his exuberance overcome him and often lifted the microphone and swung it above his head before hurling it to the ground with a crash. (His behavior supposedly prompted Apollo Theater owner Frank Schiffman to install stationary microphones to prevent Thrasher from completely destroying what was left of his stock.) This visual display was backed up with nearly perfect vocals, and with Clyde McPhatter's soaring and intense leads guaranteed to create mayhem among the audience, the Drifters brought the frenzy of a sanctified Southern Baptist's prayer meeting onto the rhythm and blues stage—a new experience for many of their fans.

The group criss-crossed the country in 1954 with the various rhythm and blues caravans. The experiences, though, were not always pleasant. For example, while enroute from New York to Atlanta, the car they were driving broke down, forcing them to stop over in Fredericksburg, Virginia. They received the repair bill and found they did not have enough money to proceed. They wired for more and to pass the time decided to look around town. As they cruised the streets, they were shocked to find themselves stopped by the police, who demanded that they follow them to a local loan company. The firm, it seems, had been robbed by some black men whose description appeared to fit that of the Drifters.

The woman in the office could recall only that one of the robbers had been wearing a red suit. None of the Drifters was dressed in a red suit, but the police nonetheless decided that the suit had been replaced in a quick change act. They then asked the Drifters, who were now under the gaze of six-gun-toting officers, to open the trunk of the car. Bill Pinckney had the keys and as he reached down to give them to the police he heard the audible click of a gun and thought he was about to be shot. The search of the car turned up nothing, but it was still several hours before the group was allowed to go on their way. They left Fredericksburg wiser in the ways of Southern cops, and the incident brought home the fact that integration in America was still far from a reality. Black acts still had to find (if they could) black boarding houses and restaurants when on the road, and the attitude of the Fredericksburg police force graphically illustrated that the majority of whites were suspicious.

Despite their performance schedule, Jerry Wexler managed to fit in a couple of recording sessions, one on February 4 and one on March 14.

The February session had been set up to record what was thought to be a routine Christmas single, but the results were nothing short of sensational. The old standards "White Christmas" and "The Bells of Saint Mary's" were the chosen, but each of them re-

ceived radically different readings. "The Bells of Saint Mary's" was given a slow, atmospheric rendering reminiscent of the old spirituals. "White Christmas" featured a shared lead between the bass of Bill Pinckney and the tenor of Clyde McPhatter that echoed the Ravens version of 1948, but the complex arrangement took the number much further that it had been before. (The arranger in the session, Howard Biggs, had in fact been involved in the Ravens version, and he supplied the "Jingle Bells, Jingle Bells" finale on the Drifters version.) When Elvis Presley recorded a Christmas album in 1957, he duplicated the arrangement used that February night, and the British group the Darts had a U.K. hit with a similar version in 1980.

The session was a particularly productive one, for, apart from the seasonal single, it produced "Honey Love," which had been written by McPhatter and Wexler, as well as another attempt at Ahmet Ertegun's "What'cha Gonna Do," which in reality owed a great deal to the gospel group Radio 4's recording of the same name (where the Drifters sang "When the joints on fire," its religious predecessor asked "What 'cha gonna do when the world's on fire").

The lyrics of "Honey Love" were very much in the tradition of risky blues, but the light mambo rhythm was in marked contrast to the heavy blues background that had been used before. As was the case with "Such a Night," there was little doubt about what Clyde meant when he said he wanted it in the middle of the night, and many of the more conservative radio stations banned the song when it was released.

The third version of "What'cha Gonna Do" was perhaps the best track Clyde McPhatter and the Drifters ever recorded, for it was more or less a straight gospel performance with secular words. Hank Ballard would later take the melody and rename it "The Twist," setting off a worldwide dance craze in 1958. (Jerry Wexler met Ballard a few years later in a New York delicatessen and light-heartedly asked him about the source. Ballard admitted that he had lifted the song from the Drifters and that he and Syd Nathan, the owner of King Records, were expecting a lawsuit, which never materialized.) Released in May 1954, "Honey Love" (as if to prove that

35

a media ban meant little) shot to the top of the rhythm and blues charts, remaining there for twenty weeks. Although it was considered unfit for the more refined white audiences, the song was later covered by white acts, including Johnny Otis and The Four Seasons.

After the February session, the March 14 recording session was an anticlimax; nothing that would equal the classics produced the previous month was recorded. However, the Drifters reading of Jimmy Hodges country and western standard "Someday You'll Want Me to Want You" was noteworthy, neatly obliterating the songs country roots with a splendid rhythm and blues treatment, complete with a Bill Pinckney "talking bass" middle section echoing that of Hoppy Jones of the Inkspots.

Two of the other songs cut, Ertegun and Wexler's "Try Try Baby" and "There You Go," failed to see the light of day until 1959 when they were released as Clyde McPhatter solos. The fourth song, "If I Didn't Love You Like I Do," which had been supplied by rhythm and blues writer Julius Dixon, remained unissued until 1960 when it suffered the same fate. (The tracks did not appear as Drifters recordings until 1971 when they were issued as part of the anthology album *Greatest Recordings—The Early Years* on Atlantic SD33-375.)

At the beginning of May 1954, Clyde McPhatter received some unwelcome news—his draft notice, obviously a major blow to the continued success of the Drifters. (We should note that Clyde, while a member of the Dominoes, had been under the impression that Billy Ward had somehow kept him from being called up and believed, rightly or wrongly, that once the Drifters hit big, Ward had informed the draft board of his eligibility. The story may be far-fetched—but *anything* is fair in love and war.)

Atlantic nonetheless issued "White Christmas"/"Bells of Saint Mary's" in time to catch the Christmas market. They were rewarded not only with a rhythm and blues smash but with the first Drifters' record to make it to the *Billboard* Hot 100. It climbed only to number eighty, but the fact that it crossed over onto the pop charts raised the hope of a major breakthrough (it was to reappear in the hit lists in 1960 and again in 1962).

Although 1954 finished on a relatively high note, the imminent departure of the Drifters' lead singer put the future of the group in doubt for McPhatter was what set them apart from the host of rhythm and blues groups striving for similar success.

CHAPTER 5

Drifting Away:
The Tragedy of Clyde McPhatter

Clyde McPhatter's draft notice did not noticeably affect the Drifters immediately, for he was initially stationed with the special services unit (the entertainment branch of the army) at Fort Dix, New Jersey, and this allowed him to appear with them at least on their major concert dates. He also managed to take part in a recording session on October 24, 1954.

In Drifters terms, though, that recording session was not very productive. Atlantic cut four tracks, but decided to release nothing immediately. Ertegun and Wexler held back the recordings. Two of the numbers, "Everyone's Laughing" and "Hot Ziggety" did subsequently appear as Clyde McPhatter singles in 1955 (Atlantic 1070), with no mention of the Drifters. "Three Thirty Three" remained in the vaults until 1971 when it appeared on an anthology album. "Sugar Coated Kisses," the fourth song, has the dubious distinction of being the only track recorded by Clyde McPhatter and the Drifters unissued in any form. ("Gone," "Let the Boogie Woogie Roll," and "What'cha Gonna Do" from the June 1953 were all re-recorded and issued.)

Before leaving our discussion of this session, we should note that from time to time over the years some critics have questioned whether the vocal group on "Everyone's Laughing"/ "Hot Ziggety" was in fact the Drifters. The Atlantic sessions files and Jerry Wexler himself confirm that it *was* the Drifters behind McPhatter.

Although he was still appearing occasionally with the Drifters, by the time the song "Bip Bam" stalled in the rhythm and blues charts in November 1954, Clyde McPhatter was more or less out of the group. He made his final appearance with the Drifters in January 1955 when Alan Freed staged his first New

WINS

America's #1 Music station presents
America's #1 "Rock'n Roll" Disc Jockey

ALAN  FREED

"ROCK'N ROLL PARTY"

MONDAY THRU SATURDAY · 7:00 - 9:00 P.M.
MONDAY THRU THURSDAY · 11:00 P.M. - 1:00 A.M.
FRIDAY AND SATURDAY · 11:00 P.M. - 2:00 A.M.

Over 15,000 paid admissions for the first "Rock'n Roll" party
at St. Nicholas Arena, New York on January 14th and 15th.
Greatest advance sale in the history of American dance promotions. Thousands turned away.

Our thanks to the great array of performing artists:

BUDDY JOHNSON ORCHESTRA · JOE TURNER · THE CLOVERS

FATS DOMINO · THE MOONGLOWS · THE HARPTONES · THE DRIFTERS

ELLA JOHNSON · DANNY OVERBEA · DAKOTA STATON

RED PRYSOCK and NOLAN LEWIS

"ROCK 'N ROLL PARTY" **WINS**

available nationally to stations:
call, wire or write to
BOB LEDER, WINS, New York
...... 50,000 WATTS · 24 HOURS A DAY

|||||1010||||

York rock and roll show at the St. Nicholas arena, an event that attracted an audience that was seventy percent white to see what was in fact a black rhythm and blues show. (Following his departure from the Drifters, McPhatter did, occasionally, sing with the group. When he happened to be on the same package tour, for example, he would re-join them for a rendition of "Lucille," although this practice ceased as time progressed.) Clyde, dressed in army regalia, bade farewell to the setup which had proven so successful for him. He did not, of course, know it then, but he would never again reach the artistic heights he had in the company of Gerhart and Andrew Thrasher and Bill Pinckney. Indeed, aside from recorded material like "The Bells of St. Mary's," "White Christmas," and "Someday," their stage act included famed performances like the McPhatter/Pinckney duet on "Easter Parade," which was unfortunately never recorded.

McPhatter had made know his intention of pursuing a solo career even before he received his draft notice, and although his spell in the army naturally delayed his plans, he remained determined. Atlantic attempted to keep him in the public eye by issuing two singles in 1955, "Everyone's Laughing"/"Hot Ziggety" (Atlantic 1070), recorded, as we have said, with the Drifters in October 1954; and "I Gotta Have You"/ "Love Has Joined Us Together" (Atlantic 1077), recorded with Ruth Brown in 1955. Neither set the world on fire.

By the time he was discharged from the army in 1956, his career had undergone some important changes. He was now managed by Irving Feld (the rest of the Drifters remained with George Treadwell), who in addition to running the Superdisc label was the promoter behind the huge rock and roll shows that were beginning to force their way onto the American scene. Feld's Biggest Rock and Roll Show of 1956 was typical of the type he arranged. Bill Haley, the Platters, Teen Queens, the Colts, the Flamingos, Big Joe Turner, LaVern Baker, the Teenagers, Bo Diddley, and the Drifters all shared the stage with Clyde McPhatter. (When such shows started to lose their popularity in the late fifties, Feld, no doubt putting his experience to good use, moved into the circus world; he eventually bought Bartram's and Ringwold's and became the king of the circus.)

Atlantic, who at first had not been pleased, to put it mildly, with Clyde's decision to go solo (they felt that vocal groups ruled the roost), decided to change the sound of his recordings, a decision that was also to change the direction of his career.

Although his recordings with the Drifters had been undeniably magnificent, their success had been limited to the rhythm and blues charts. The recording session of August 25, 1955, held while Clyde was still in the army, pointed him in the new direction. The tracks recorded that day, "I'm Not Worthy of You"/"Seven Days," had much more of a pop sound and marked the end of his exclusively rhythm and blues period. "Seven Days," though rhythm and blues based, had a sound commercial enough to break into the national charts where, despite competition from white cover versions by the abominable Crew-Cuts, Sammy Lawson, and Dorothy Collins, it reached number forty-four early in 1956, just before Clyde left the army. (A third song, "My Definition of the Blues," was not issued.)

The next release, "Treasure of Love" (Atlantic 1092), fared even better, climbing to number sixteen in the summer of 1956. The fact that Clyde was able to promote the song twice a night on the Irving Feld package show no doubt helped.

It seemed he was now a true rock and roll star, but the illusion shattered when the follow-up, "Thirty Days," disappeared from view. Atlantic on this occasion had gone over the top in their attempt to "poppify" Clyde, and the song was little more than a trite pop tune which hardly did justice to his talents.

Wexler and Ertegun allowed Clyde more leeway when they cut "Without Love" and "Rock and Cry" on October 10, 1956, giving his natural talent rein once more. But as Wexler himself admits, the arrangements of the Ray Ellis vocal group detract from the recordings and date otherwise excellent performances by McPhatter.

When released in early 1957, "Without Love" became a

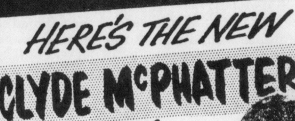

HERE'S THE NEW
CLYDE M^cPHATTER
HIT!

SEVEN DAYS

I'm Not Worthy of You

ATLANTIC #1081

HERE'S THE NEW
CARDINALS
HIT!

LOVELY GIRL

Here Goes My Heart to You

...NG CORP.

YORK 19. N. Y.

CLYDE MCPHATTER
AS A SOLO PERFORMER
Top: Atlantic Records display ad;
◄ Left: McPhatter circa 1957.

solid hit and peaked at number nineteen on the national charts. McPhatter continued to find success the following two years, particularly with "Long Lonely Nights" (Atlantic 1149), "Come What May" (Atlantic 1185), "A Lover's Question" (Atlantic 1190—this one sold over a million copies on its way to number six in the charts and was his biggest hit—and "Lovey Dovey" (Atlantic 2018). McPhatter, however, felt stifled artistically; the constant tour shows, he felt, were doing nothing for his growth as an artist. As Jerry Wexler said, Clyde saw himself as a black Perry Como, with the audience to match (Como was at this time one of the most successful artists in America and had had a succession of hit records—which even included the so-called rock and roll "Juke Box Baby"—along with a nationally-syndicated television show).

At any rate, when his Atlantic contract came up for renewal early in 1959, Clyde McPhatter did the seemingly unthinkable and left the label that had given him his greatest triumphs. He moved to MGM. The reason he left is not known, exactly. Some have said that Irving Feld thought that Atlantic was a small-time operation unable to properly promote an artist of McPhatter's standing; others, that Atlantic was reluctant to pay him a fifty-thousand-dollar re-signing fee. Jerry Wexler thinks the former was the case and says that personally he was deeply saddened by McPhatter's departure.

His decision to sign with MGM was to prove a mistake, for the label was completely unequipped to record and promote an artist like Clyde McPhatter. The company had been founded in the early fifties and had had some initial success releasing show material (usually supplied by MGM pictures), but the rock and roll explosion had caught them unawares. By the late fifties they had adjusted, but their two biggest stars in the field, Conway Twitty and Connie Francis, were a long way removed from Little Richard, Jerry Lee Lewis, and Elvis Presley.

Clyde was put into the hands of their new arranger, Ray Ellis, with whom he had worked at Atlantic during 1956 and early 1957. Without the restraining influence of Wexler and Ertegun, Ellis fashioned a completely white pop sound behind McPhatter during sessions recorded in 1959 in New York City.

Clyde attempted to assert himself and almost succeeded on "Let's Start All Over Again," "I Need You So," and "The Glory of Love," but in most cases the backing tracks swamped him.

MGM issued "I Told Myself a Lie"/"The Masquerade Is Over" (MGM 12780) as the first single; but, after a brief chart run in which it climbed to number seventy, it dropped from sight.

"Where Did I Make My Mistake" (MGM 12816), the next release, had echoes of "Treasure of Love," but even this throwback to his 1956 hit failed to fire the public's imagination. The flipside, "Twice As Nice," did manage to pick up some radio plays, which enabled it to reach number ninety-one on the *Billboard* charts, but it was hardly the major success both Clyde and MGM had hoped for.

No doubt to recoup some of the forty thousand dollars (a lot of money at the time) they had advanced McPhatter, MGM put out the seemingly prophetic "Let's Try Again" (MGM 12843). They must have thought they had hit the jackpot this time, for the record reached a dizzy number forty-eight in the charts. But the follow-up, "When the Real Thing Comes Along"/"Think Me a Kiss" (MGM 12877) stalled at number sixty-six, and despite two more releases—"This Is Not Goodbye"/"One Right After Another" (MGM 12949) and "The Glory of Love"/"Take a Step" (MGM 12988)—Clyde McPhatter's time on the MGM label was soon over.

This parting of the ways was welcomed by his fans, for almost nothing of note had come from the association. The recordings he made at MGM merely echoed the general softening of rock and roll then prevalent, in which the performers were drowned out by "girly" choruses and melodramatic strings, and nothing but blandness was created.

While he was still with MGM, Clyde embarked on his first tour of the U.K. He was part of a package show that included Bobby Darin (who had started out rockin' on U.S. Decca in 1956 before moving to Atlantic, where he was now being promoted as a younger, hipper Sinatra), the king of twang—guitarist Duane Eddy, and the then British chart sensation Emile Ford. Although he was not well known in Britain, where he had only charted briefly in 1956 with "Treasure of Love," Clyde was well received and his performances belied his lackluster MGM recordings. Nonetheless, he was so concerned about his recent lack of chart success that he was on the verge of packing it in, as he would later tell British rock and roll fanatic "Waxie Maxie" Needham when that one-man preservation society interviewed him in the mid-sixties.

(Needham was a fifties music freak who attained a degree of notoriety in the U.K. in the sixties when, using the logo "The Quest for Merrill Moore," he bombarded the music press with letters regarding that early fifties pioneer. So successful were his efforts that he persuaded the owner of a small British label, Jeff Kruger of Ember Records, that thousands were demanding Moore's material, prompting Kruger to lease tracks from the copyright holders, Capitol Records, who were oblivious to Max's pleas to issue Moore's recordings. It is a shame that Needham could not have shown the same devotion to Clyde McPhatter, who was virtually as unknown in the British Isles as Needham's piano-playing hero.)

With his career seemingly on a downward spiral, and now no longer on MGM's roster, McPhatter seemed fated for the show business wilderness. Clyde was saved from oblivion by the appearance of Clyde Otis, who had composed "A Lover's Question" with Brook Benton (the same Brook Benton from Bill Pinckney's old gospel group), and which had been a huge hit for McPhatter in 1958. Otis had come to New York almost penniless from Prentiss, Mississippi, in the mid fifties and had fought his way up the ladder to become, by 1960, the head of Mercury's New York office and one of the most successful black men in the recording industry. He had long been an admirer, and when Clyde left MGM he jumped at the chance to sign him to Mercury. Otis, who had been instrumental in taking both Brook Benton and Dinah Washington onto the pop charts, was confident he could do justice to Clyde's talent and rescue his career.

Clyde signed with Mercury on June 13, 1960, and recorded his first tracks on June 17. Belford Hendricks was the arranger and Otis the producer. The artistic renaissance hoped for failed to materilize, however. McPhatter apparently wanted to be deluged with strings, no doubt to emulate Brook Benton's success with "It's Just a Matter of Time." Otis tried to dissuade him, but Clyde insisted. The results were overly lush. Black artists seemed to crave a mass white following (and who could blame them), but in striving to do so they often lost their natural feel, and this was certainly the case with McPhatter when he made these initial Mercury recordings.

To cover themselves should this Las Vegas style fail to hit (which it did), Mercury cut the up-tempo "Ta Ta"/"I Ain't Givin' Up Nothing" (Mercury 71660). "Ta Ta" had been written by Clyde and the Drifters' old guitarist Jimmy Oliver, and was close in style to much of McPhatter's best work. It was what his audience wanted and it returned him to the charts, where the tune peaked at number twenty-three in late 1960.

Clyde Otis left Mercury in 1961, placing McPhatter's recording career in the hands of Shelby Singleton, who had set up his base of operation in the country and western capital, Nashville. Over the next year, Singleton recorded Clyde using a variety of material—rhythm and blues, remakes of his Drifters and Dominoes hits, and straight blues—but only "I Never Knew" (Mercury 71841) saw any real chart action.

Late in 1961, a song written by sixteen-year-old Billy Swan called "Lover Please" attracted Singleton's attention. The song had originally been recorded by the hillbilly group of which Swan was a member (Milt Mirley and the High Steppers), and later recorded by Denis Turner for Louis Records. Turner's record had been cut by Elvis Presley's former bass player Bill Black, but when Black refused to sell the master, Singleton decided to have McPhatter cover it. McPhatter did not like the song but agreed to cut it in February 1962, with an arrangement by Stan Applebaun, who was then one of the Drifters' arrangers. Applebaun's instrumental break featured an elaborate string arrangement, but Singleton replaced this with a rousing King Curtis sax break accompanied by the hand-clapping of the string players.

Rush-released, "Lover Please" (Mercury 71941) climbed to number seven on the charts, eclipsing all the other versions.

47

It was McPhatter's first appearance in the Top 10 since the release of "A Lover's Question" in 1958. To capitalize on this success, Mercury quickly followed up with "Little Bitty Pretty One" (Mercury 71987), which Bobby Day and the Satellites had recorded in 1957. The record reached number twenty-five but was to be McPhatter's last major hit.

He remained with Mercury until 1965, during which time he cut eight albums which were all released—a fact that seems incredible, given his lack of consistent success with single releases. Clyde gave many notable performances on these albums, especially on "Spanish Harlem," "Up on the Roof," and "On Broadway," which were all released on *Songs from the Big City* (Mercury MG20902). He was still a masterful vocalist when given worthy material.

In 1965, Clyde married for the second time; her name was Lena Rackley. Until the early sixties, he had been married to a woman who had remained very much in the background and was known only as Nora (it was said that she had known Clyde since high school; a member of the latter-day Moonglows, Billy McPhatter, is supposedly Clyde's son and it may be true that Nora is his mother).

By 1965, Clyde was beginning to show the signs of a problem with alcohol, caused partly by his natural shyness and partly by the slump in his fortunes. He was ill at ease with people he thought his social betters, unable to see that his vocal talent was the envy of those he aspired to be. Shelby Singleton had hoped that the *Songs from the Big City* album would resurrect Clyde's career, but the album, even though most of it is excellent, failed to do so.

Clyde moved to Amy Records in 1966. They issued five singles, but by the middle of 1967 he was once more in the wilderness. His marriage to Lena was on the rocks, thanks mostly to his now almost constant drinking; but Lena and Clyde had adopted a child (Patrick) and Lena no longer wished to go on the road, and this may have been part of problem, too.

With nowhere to go, he decided for some reason to move to Great Britain to try and start his career rolling again. He had only been there once before, on the March 1960 tour, but he

48

probably knew that several other "older" American acts (Gene Vincent and Little Richard, for instance) had enjoyed considerable success in both Britain and Europe.

Thus, early in 1968, after an unsuccessful attempt to enter the country in January when he had no work permit, Clyde arrived in Britain. Universal Dancing had offered him a contract, and he attracted the interest of U.K. record companies, at least at first.

He signed with Deram, a branch of Decca which tended to record the more progressive side of rock and roll. On June 8, 1968, he recorded "Only a Fool," "Symphony," and "Thank You Love." The first was issued as a single (Deram 202) but went nowhere in the charts even though it was excellent. Deram recorded him again in October, but once again nothing came of it.

Clyde at least managed to retain some of his old magic on live dates for he rekindled from time to time some of the spirit of his fifties shows. Most of his performances, though, were lost on club audiences who were there only to dance to the latest chart hits. His stage show was peppered with back-flips and gospel whoops, but these became more and more erratic as his dependence on alcohol grew.

Still, hope springs eternal. In July 1969, B&C Records, which was willing to take a chance on anyone, recorded "Denver"/"Tell Me" (B&C 106). They had planned to record an album but, when the single flopped, it failed to materialize.

To make matters worse, Clyde was arrested for loitering with intent. The case was dropped, but disclosures made at the time revealed that Clyde was in a poor way financially—he was apparently earning only fifteen pounds a night on some dates.

The British experiment a failure, Clyde returned to the States in 1970. He began to pick up dates on the back of the rock and roll revival which was gaining momentum for fifties and sixties acts. He phoned Jerry Wexler and asked to come back to Atlantic, but Wexler was preoccupied with the career of Aretha Franklin and could not help. He sent McPhatter some much-needed money, though.

Clyde McPhatter's return had been noted by Clyde Otis,

however, who decided to see if American Decca was interested in him. They were, and two sessions were arranged in Philadelphia (June 24-25, 1971), which at the time was the soul capital of the music world. The results of the sessions were uneven, for Clyde was drinking heavily (from a hip flask). Traces of his old style remained, though. Unfortunately, the subsequent album, *Welcome Home* (Decca DL75231), and its two singles, "Book of Memories" (Decca 32719) and "The Mixed up Cup" (Decca 32753), fell on deaf ears.

His drinking, moreover, made the promoters of the "oldies" shows suspicious of him; his performances were becoming more and more haphazard. On April 29, 1972, while Clyde was appearing with rock and roll madman Screamin' Jay Hawkins at the Camelot Inn in Brooklyn, Marcia Vance, a fan of Clyde's, approached Hawkins and asked him to introduce her. Hawkins readily obliged. But as the introductions were being made, Clyde McPhatter said possibly the saddest words an artist ever has, "I have no fans." He was courteous and polite to his remaining fan, but as Vance watched Clyde—surrounded by the members of his family—she was saddened to see such a once-great artist reduced to the level of a drunk.

Clyde had hoped to tour Africa, but the farthest he got was Houston, Texas, and here his contract for several performances was cancelled after he allegedly kissed his male pianist and indecently exposed himself.

The Houston incident occurred at the end of May. On June 12, Clyde was back in Manhattan, ready once more to kill his problems with drink. He had apparently taken up with a woman known only as Bertha, who accompanied him on his drinking bouts. On that night, Bertha and Clyde eventually went to bed, drunk, in her apartment. The next morning Clyde did not wake up. He had died during the night of a heart attack, brought on, no doubt, by years of alcohol abuse. Perhaps the greatest tragedy was that he had never acknowledged he had a problem and so denied himself any chance of a cure.

McPhatter was taken from the Nesbitt funeral parlor (175 Englewood Avenue in Englewood, New Jersey) on June 19, 1972, and after a service conducted by the Reverend Williams was laid to rest at eleven in the morning in George Washington Memorial Park (Paramus, New Jersey).

Although this is the end of the story of Clyde McPhatter, he deserves a few more words, for his contribution to popular music was beyond measure.

Clyde McPhatter was a major factor in the development of soul music, which grew out of the rhythm and blues of the fifties and became the dominant black music of the sixties. He may not have been the first black gospel singer to sing the Devil's music, but he was arguably the first to bring the emotional power of gospel to the world of blues. Before him, it had been considered improper to sing with sincerity to anything or anyone but the Lord; Clyde grafted his intense gospel tenor onto a rhythm and blues format that at that time was marked by the cool, detached stylings of such lead vocalists as the Orioles' Sonny Til.

He spawned a host of imitators. Among them are Nolan Strong (brother of "Money" hit-maker Barrett Strong) of the Diablos, whose version of "Someday" (Fortune Records) sounds like a Drifters' clone; Dee Clark; Jackie Wilson, who replaced Clyde in the Dominoes; Bobby Sheen, who as "Bob B. Soxx" did a perfect McPhatter imitation on "The Bells of St. Mary's" (produced by Phil Spector); and Smokey Robinson. Those who followed him in the Drifters (David Baughan, Johnny Moore, Bobby Hendricks, and even Johnny Lee Williams) all owed much to his style.

Others who may not have been obviously influenced by him have nonetheless acknowledged their debt. Otis Redding, a vocalist who reaped the popularity of the glory years of sixties soul, paid his debt when he cut "A Lover's Question." (Prior to his rise to fame, Otis Redding fronted a pirate Drifters group which toured the Southern states. Aside from his Little Richard impressions, Redding supposedly aped Clyde McPhatter to perfection, a talent he employed in his group's act.) Little Richard, never one to admit he has been influenced by anyone, openly said he had emulated Clyde's vocal style in his early days; Richard also cut the only version of "Without Love" (1965) that even approaches Clyde's and also had a stab at

"Money Honey" (both for Vee Jay). The "Annie" series of Hank Ballard and the Midnighters bears more than passing resemblance to the McPhatter-lead Drifters. Elvis Presley was on record as saying he wished he could sing like Clyde McPhatter; he also made a credible attempt at "Money Honey."

McPhatter kept his own influences under wraps, but they probably included Dan Grisson from the Jimmie Lunceford Band, and Pha Terrell, who sang with Andy Kirk. Both sang high tenor, a style beloved of black audiences because it is so close to gospel.

Although the recordings he made with the Drifters never broke through onto the white charts, with the exception of the seasonal success of "White Christmas," they were heard by the growing white teenage audience who listened secretly to the rhythm and blues stations—a fact acknowledged by the appearance of white covers by such artists as Pat Boone and Johnny Ray that never matched the real thing. That Clyde never took his rightful place among the major soul artists of the sixties remains one of the great mysteries of life. So many of the stars of that era (Wilson Pickett, Sam Cooke, Otis Redding, to name but a few) followed his lead and mixed gospel and blues. For some reason, Clyde missed out. That he was worth more than merely performing his old hits in revival shows is beyond doubt, but for some reason he seldom reached the greatness so obviously within him. His greatest recorded legacy is surely the work he did with the Drifters, for here his vocals managed to transcend all the known rules of popular music.

Listen to the Dominoes with Clyde on lead, the glorious Drifters' tracks, the joyous sound of "A Lover's Question" or "Lover Please." All shine like beacons in a music industry of so many lesser lights. Clyde McPhatter may be gone, but his soul is still with us. He will never be forgotten and this sad world is a better place for the short time he lived in it.

CHAPTER 6

Rockin' and Driftin'

Meanwhile, back in the Drifters' camp, efforts were being made to replace Clyde McPhatter. The logical step was to ask David Baughan, whose voice bore an uncanny resemblance to Clyde's, to rejoin the group—he had been a member in May 1953.

When the first lineup of the Drifters disbanded in the summer of 1953, Baughan joined the Checkers, who were with Federal Records, a subsidiary of King. The Checkers had been influenced by the Dominoes (even their name reflects this), and bass singer Bill Brown had been with the original Billy Ward lineup. They had several excellent records out. "The White Cliffs of Dover," in which Baughan's tenor was indistinguishable from McPhatter's, was the best.

When he received the call to rejoin the Drifters, Baughan readily agreed and took McPhatter's place as lead vocalist on the dates McPhatter could not make because of his army duties. Baughan was a member of the group when they recorded in New York on April 21, 1955. The session was not very successful, and Wexler and Ertegun found none of the tracks worthy of release. Baughan lead the group on "Honey Bee," written by blues singer Dossie Terry; Bill Pinckney did the honors on "Steamboat" and "No Sweet Lovin,'" from bandleader Buddy Lucas. The fourth song recorded was the ballad "Drifting Away from You," which featured Gerhart Thrasher.

Featuring Baughan's high tenor leads to good effect, "Honey Bee" was actually quite a good record. Along with "No Sweet Lovin'," it appeared as a b-side in 1961; the other two tracks remained in the can.

The Drifters were on the road throughout 1954 and 1955, often taking part in the package shows put together by

THE DRIFTERS (EARLY 1955)
(L. to r.): Gerhart Thrasher, Bill Pinckney, Andrew Thrasher,
Jimmy Oliver and David Baughan.
(Photo from the collection of Marv Goldberg)

the Gale Agency. In one such show, they shared the stage with Roy Hamilton, the Counts, the Spaniels, LaVern Baker, Big Maybelle, and Faye Adams, supported by the bands of Rusty Bryant and Eskine Hawkins. Billed as the "Biggest Rhythm and Blues Show," the tour set off in August 1954 and lived up to its name.

David Baughan was not proving a good choice for lead vocalist, for he was difficult to get on with and though still in his mid-teens had a drinking problem. His behavior deteriorated to such an extent that the Drifters considered bringing in another vocalist.

When in 1954 the Drifters had been in Cleveland on tour, the lead singer of the Hornets (they had started life as the Cleveland Quartet; the other members were James "Sonny" Long, Ben Iverson, and Gus Miller), Johnny Moore, had asked if he could join the group. Moore, born in Selma, Alabama, in 1934, had recorded several tracks with the Hornets for Chess Records, of which the best were "Big City Bounce" and "Rockin' and Ridin'," but the recordings were obscure. Inasmuch as the Drifters had just recruited Baughan, Moore's offer had been refused. But in November of 1954, Baughan's problem was still a concern and when on Thanksgiving day the Drifters chanced to meet Moore at the movies, Bill Pinckney asked him to audition. The only place to do so was the men's room. Leaving Baughan asleep in the seats, the Drifters adjourned. Moore sang "Money Honey" and "The Way I Feel," and following some discussion, Pinckney invited him to join.

Moore went home and informed his mother that he thought he had a chance to join the Drifters, even though he really did not believe it himself. The next morning, just as he was about to leave home for work in a local factory, Bill Pinckney phoned to say the group was waiting for him. Still thinking he was dreaming, Moore met up with Pinckney and the rest of the Drifters and appeared for the first time with the group in Atlanta, Georgia, on a bill that included Dinah Washington and the Checkers. As a result of what was happening, however, David Baughan's behavior began to change for the better, so much so that in March 1955 the Drifters let Moore go. He returned home, where he reorganized the Hornets. (Moore was recalled again in August by Percy Livingstone, who was the group's road manager until 1956—Bill Pinckney fulfilled this role before and after Livingstone's arrival and departure.)

The problems the Drifters were having with their lead vocalist were not apparent to the record-buying public, for Atlantic continued to issue Drifters' recordings that featured Clyde McPhatter. Following the Christmas smash hit "White Christmas," they released "What'cha Gonna Do" backed by the August 1953 recording of "Gone." The record reached the eighth position on the rhythm and blues charts on June 4, 1955, and kept the group in the public eye.

The Drifters, still touring with David Baughan, played a weekend engagement at a place called Week's Tavern, where they ran into an assortment of problems. They were traveling with a mascot that happened to be a skunk. The manager of the hotel was rather upset, but a donation to his favorite charity resolved that matter. Then the group spent some time with fans during the weekend and by all accounts consumed a lot of alcohol. Somehow their performances remained unaffected. On stage they sang "Money Honey," "Warm Your Heart," "The Way I Feel," and "Someday," among others. All complete with Gerhart Thrasher's acrobatics with the mike. The others seemed able to cope with all the drink, but Baughan again found it all too much to handle.

In August 1955, Little David left the group and was replaced by the returning Johnny Moore. Baughan's failure to fit in was partly due to his drinking, but Jerry Wexler also felt that his vocals lacked projection and that this, combined with his other problems, meant he would never be a stable and long-term member of the group.

(When he left the Drifters, Baughan formed a group called the Harps, who recorded for Savoy as Little David and the Harps. They cut four tracks for the label, two of which—"I Won't Cry"/"You'll Pay"—were issued (Savoy 1178). In December 1956, he recorded four tracks for Atlantic—"All My Life," "Fire Fire," "Early in the Morning," and "It's a Sin"—but none was issued. He was with Mercury Records around 1958 as

56

Little Dave, but that was his last attempt at solo stardom.)

While playing in Los Angeles in September 1955, the Drifters, now fronted by Johnny Moore, were taken to the studios of Master Recorders by Ahmet Ertegun's older brother, Nesuhi. This session was a departure from the usual for not only were Ertegun and Wexler absent, but, ironically, the group recorded a cover version of the Colts' "Adorable," written by the Platters' manager, Buck Ram, who also managed the Colts. Wexler had asked Nesuhi to record the Drifters on the number, which had been doing well in regional markets. Previously, of course, Atlantic had usually been the one subjected to cover versions. Jerry Wexler chose well on this occasion, for the song was the perfect vehicle to introduce Johnny Moore and easily outsold the original when issued with the version of "Steamboat" cut at the same session. The latter was a re-recorded version, although the river boat effects came from the earlier track waxed by the ill-starred David Baughan lineup.

At the Los Angeles studios, the Drifters recorded "Ruby Baby," the first song written for them by the fast-rising rhythm and blues writers Jerry Leiber and Mike Stoller. In addition, Jimmy Oliver provided Gerhart Thrasher with the ballad Jerry Wexler thought their best, "Your Promise to Be Mine." Finally, the last song recorded was yet another attempt at the previous April's "Drifting Away from You."

When "Adorable" was issued in October 1955, it sold well enough to make the rhythm and blues Top 10 by January 1956, but "Ruby Baby," which followed in March 1956, failed to do as well as expected, despite the fact the group featured both it and the flip-side, "Promise to Be Mine," on Alan Freed's Rock and Roll Dance Party.

During 1954 and 1955, rock and roll was starting to make its presence felt on the American music scene; even the major labels were now getting into the act in a more determined manner. Bill Haley and His Comets had several original hits, although the tendency to cover black hits was still prevalent—among Haley's successes was a much watered-down version of Joe Turner's "Shake Rattle and Roll," which Turner originally had out on Atlantic. Mercury also joined in the race, signing the Platters from King/Federal, who proved an instant smash.

Although Chuck Berry's "Maybellene" on Chess was a massive seller, the more significant record was Little Richard's "Tutti Frutti," which reached number seventeen in the *Billboard* Top 100 in December 1955. This record struck a huge blow for both independent record companies and black music. Although it lost out to Pat Boone's inferior cover version in the charts, it did prove that black originals could compete with white covers despite all the advantages the latter had going for them.

In the wake of Little Richard's success, the Teenagers' original of "Why Do Fools Fall in Love" eclipsed the Diamonds' cover on Mercury.

If the door had not yet fully opened, it was certainly ajar. The stage was now set for the Drifters to break into the white mass market. Since their recordings, particularly "Ruby Baby," fit easily into the new genre and they were regulars on Alan Freed's radio and package shows—at a time when Freed was probably at the peak of his popularity—it was not unreasonable to suppose they would soon cross over to the pop charts in a big way. But they did not. Their failure to do so before had been somewhat understandable, for their early material had been too earthy for the mass market of the time; their failure to hit big now, during the initial rock explosion, was, and is, puzzling.

As a live act they were still much in demand, and in January 1956 they joined Irving Feld's most ambitious rock and roll package to date, lining up with the then king of rock and roll, Bill Haley and His Comets, the Five Keys (who, like the Drifters had flirted with "white" success), Bo Diddley, Roy Hamilton, the Turbans, LaVern Baker, Big Joe Turner, and the Platters, who were one of the hottest acts in the country. All were major rhythm and blues stars (with the obvious exception of Bill Haley, although he did score hits on the black charts), and they would all score significant "pop" hits, invariably before the Drifters did.

Atlantic, desperately keen to break the Drifters into the burgeoning rock and roll market, handed over production duties to Leiber and Stoller; Jerry Wexler assumed the role of executive producer with final say over the material, but in reality control rested with the new producers.

Lieber and Stoller had been active in the rhythm and blues field for several years, had teamed up when Leiber (born on April 25, 1933, in Baltimore) met Stoller (born March 13, 1933, in Belle Harbor, New York) in Los Angeles in the mid-forties. Leiber had been raised in a predominantly black community where he had grown to love the blues, while Stoller, although sharing his enthusiasm for blues, had a background in "serious" music.

When Leiber and Stoller started collaborating, they produced a distinctive brand of pop blues, strong in melody, which saw them score several rhythm and blues hits. Their successes included Little Willie Littlefield's "K.C. Lovin" in 1952 (as "Kansas City" by Wilbert Harrison, the song went on to sell a million in 1959), and Big Mama Thornton's original version of "Hound Dog" in 1953. Other notable compositions were "One Bad Stud" by the Honey Bears (revived in 1984 by the Blasters and the British doo-wop group the Mint Juleps), and "Smokey Joe's Cafe" by the Robins in 1955. Their association with the

60

Robins dated back to 1953 when they recorded the group on their own Spark label. (Their partner in Spark was Lester Sill, who would appear ten years later as Phil Spector's partner in the Philles label.) It was "Smokey Joe's Cafe" that brought them to the attention of Atlantic.

A split in the Robins led to the formation of the Coasters, with whom Leiber and Stoller went on to have a succession of smash hits ("Searchin," "Young Blood," "Yakety Yak," and "Along Came Jones," to name a few), which made the group the most successful in the U.S.A. between 1957 and 1960.

The first Drifters' session of 1956 took place in New York on February 16 and proved unproductive; a session held on June 21 was more successful, but the elusive big hit failed to materialize.

On that day in June the group recorded the great ballad "Soldier of Fortune," which was almost Platter-ish in sound and style, and possibly their best rocker "Honky Tonky," which had been sent to Atlantic by Otis Blackwell, who would later compose many rock and roll hits. Jesse Stone gave them "I Gotta Get Myself a Woman," and Jan Rudy supplied the final track, "Sadie My Lady."

The Drifters gave a particularly strong performance of "Soldier of Fortune"; Bill Pinckney's "Honky Tonky" might have been just the song to break them into the rock and roll market, but inexplicably it was shelved and released later on an album. "I Gotta Get Myself a Woman" featured a shared vocal by Pinckney and Moore, and made effective use of tempo changes behind Moore's intense vocals; Moore's up-tempo "Sadie My Lady" suffered the fate of "Honky Tonky," though it did manage somehow to appear as a British b-side as late as 1961.

Atlantic chose "Soldier of Fortune" and "I Gotta Get Myself a Woman" as the next release; the platter was the more successful in the rhythm and blues market and was also a milestone in the Drifters' career for it was their first record released in Britain (on London-American HLE8344 in September 1956).

Their fame seemed to be growing, but storm clouds were brewing.

61

In August 1956, Bill Pinckney, who was now both road manager and spokesman, approached George Treadwell and asked that the Drifters, who were all on salary, be given a raise. Treadwell, who owned the copyright to the Drifters name, refused, even though Pinckney threatened they would all quit. Treadwell called the other members together and told them Pinckney had been fired. (Pinckney later claimed he had been unaware of this and had been told he was no longer a Drifter only when he showed up a few days later in Washington for a concert. He also claimed that it had been the Drifters' valet, Lacy Hollingsworth, who had passed on the news.) When Andrew Thrasher protested, he, too, was fired.

This account is the one that has been quoted down through the years but, as with most stories, there are two sides. Apparently there were discrepancies in the Drifters' road accounts, and Pinckney, in his capacity as road manager, was the one responsible for the takings on tour. When George Treadwell became aware of the situation, he questioned Pinckney and, after a heated exchange, felt he had no option but to fire the bass singer. (This version of the story has been corroborated by Johnny Moore, who was there at the time.)

Since the group had been reduced almost over night from a quartet to a duo (Gerhart Thrasher and Johnny Moore), Jimmy Oliver called his friend Tommy Evans, who sang bass, and invited him to join the Drifters. Evans had been a member of the Ravens from 1954 to 1956 (he had replaced Jimmy Ricks) and had sung with the Carols on Savoy Records.

When Treadwell held auditions for Andrew Thrasher's replacement in New York at 1650 Broadway, he chanced upon (in the men's room) his friend Carnation Charlie Hughes. Hughes had been in the Du-Droppers on Groove Records and had replaced Ernest "Rocky" Ward in the Diamonds (not the same Diamonds who recorded "Little Darlin'"), though he had never recorded with them. Treadwell asked him to audition and immediately sent the other applicants home.

Thus, on November 8, 1956, Johnny Moore, Gerhart Thrasher, Charlie Hughes, and Tommy Evans presented themselves to Jerry Wexler as the Drifters. The combination was

Two shots of the Drifters, August 1956-Late 1957
▲ Rear (l. to r.): Tommy Evans, Charlie Hughes; Middle (l. to r): Gerhart Thrasher, Johnny Moore; Front: Jimmy Oliver.

► Rear (l. to r.): TommyEvans. Gerhart Thrasher, Johnny Moore, Charlie Hughes; Seated: Jimmy Oliver.

vastly different from that of three years before, but Leiber and Stoller were undeterred and recorded them on their own "Fools Fall in Love" (it took fifty-six takes to get it right, though). Jimmy Oliver's medium-paced "It Was a Tear" was released as the b-side.

Jerry Wexler was none too happy with the changes in the lineup, for having worked with artists such as Clyde McPhatter and Bill Pinckney, whom he rated very highly, he found Charlie Hughes a poor substitute, even though he liked him.

"Fools Fall in Love" nevertheless managed to reach number sixty-nine in the *Billboard* Hot 100, higher than any other Drifters' release—only "White Christmas" had made the pop charts back in 1954. In rhythm and blues terms it was not successful for it failed to dent the charts; it seemed to appeal more to the white rock and roll audience. Perhaps at last they had made the breakthrough.

Stepping Out!

"FOOLS FALL IN LOVE IN A HURRY"
"IT WAS A TEAR"
The Drifters
1123

ATLANTIC RECORDING CORP.
157 West 57 St., N.Y.C.

Bill Pinckney had in the meantime assembled the Flyers, who included Bobby Hendricks (born 1937 in Columbus, Ohio, on lead tenor), Dee Ernie Bailey (on baritone/tenor), and Billy Kennedy (on baritone). He took the group to Atlantic, who issued "On Bended Knee"/"My Heart's Desire" on their Atco subsidiary (Atco 6088). Hendricks bore more than a passing resemblance to Clyde McPhatter, especially on the up-tempo "On Bended Knee," which was very similar in feeling to the early recordings of the Drifters.

The Atco single failed to take off, however. But Pinckney tried again, this time on the Sun subsidiary Phillips International, which was based in Memphis. Danny and the Juniors had recorded "At the Hop," which had sold a million copies, and Pinckney countered with "After the Hop"—which was issued with a backing dubbed by the Turks—on Phillips International 3524. This, too, failed to take off, but Pinckney was by no means out of the music business and would continue to haunt the Drifters throughout the coming years.

The Drifters continued to tour, and they were often on the same bill as the one and only Screamin' Jay Hawkins (he reputedly had sold over a million copies of "I Put a Spell on You" on Okeh, without making any of the hit lists), who had the first horror act in rock and roll history. Hawkins shared the stage with bats, smoking skulls, and skeletons; but his stage entrance was the *piece de resistance*: he was carried on in a coffin. Because they so often toured together, the Drifters had become his unofficial pallbearers. One night they decided, as a joke, to seal Jay in the coffin before bringing him on stage. As the band played the introduction, Hawkins, locked in the coffin, was literally *screamin'*, but because the music was so loud no one heard him. He managed to free himself

SCREAMIN' JAY HAWKINS

by rocking the coffin back and forth; the lid fell off and he toppled onto the stage just before the air inside ran out. The Drifters made themselves scarce, which was rather wise since Jay had a bad temper. (He had blown his chance of recording for Atlantic several years before when he punched Ahmet Ertegun during a recording session. Apparently, Ertegun had wanted Hawkins to sound like Fats Domino, and Screamin' Jay had told Ertegun to go to hell.)

Flushed with the comparative success of "Fools Fall in Love," the Drifters, once more supervised by Jerry Wexler, recorded Terry Noland's rock-a-billy number "Hypnotized" on April 16, 1957. They also cut the straight rock and roll song "Yodee Yakee," and two ballads, "Souvenirs" and a revival of the 1953 Prisonaires song "I Know."

"Hypnotized" came out in May 1957, backed with the old "Drifting Away from You," and took the Drifters to number seventy-nine in the charts—not as successful as "Fools Fall in

65

Love," but it did outsell the Terry Noland original.

Though they were still selling records, the lack of real chart success started to affect their bookings. This and some personnel changes (from time to time, Treadwell had been forced to ask Bill Pinckney and Andrew Thrasher to come back and appear on live concert dates; neither, though, recorded with the Drifters after 1956) forced the Drifters to masquerade as the Coasters and the Ravens to get bookings.

To make matters worse, Johnny Moore was drafted in the autumn of 1957. He was quickly replaced by Bobby Hendricks of Bill Pinckney's Flyers. In fact, it was Pinckney himself, once again back with the Drifters, who recommended him. (In early 1958, Pinckney would once again be let go, this time replaced just in time for the April 1958 recording session by Tommy Evans.)

The Drifters were part of "The Biggest Show of Stars of 1957," which included Paul Williams, Chuck Berry, the Spaniels, Johnny and Joe, Tommy Brown, the Bobettes, the Teenagers, Paul Anka, LaVern Baker, the Everly Brothers, Jimmy Bowen, the Crickets, and old friend Clyde McPhatter. The show had both black and white acts, but because of the segregation laws in force at the time, none of the white acts performed on the Southern dates in Memphis, Columbus, and Birmingham (old habits seem to have died hard in the South). Such segregation was not practiced by the artists themselves, however. The tour ran from September 1 through November 24 and was an exceptionally long one, and since the acts usually travelled by bus, they had plenty of time to get to know one another. The Drifters became very friendly with Buddy Holly's Crickets. Nikki Sullivan of the Crickets, whom the Drifters had treated as the white sheep of the family, was particularly sad when the tour wound down at the Mosque in Richmond, Virginia.

On the record front, "Yodee Yakee" had been issued in October while the group was on tour. It failed to achieve the success of the earlier releases and missed out on the pop charts; it did have some success in the regional markets and registered on the rhythm and blues charts.

66

The "drifting" continued. Uncle Sam came knocking once again in January 1958, this time for Charlie Hughes. Jimmy Milner was brought in as his replacement and joined the Drifters in the Atlantic studios on April 28, 1958, for their first recording session since April 1957 (Atlantic had decided that "Souvenirs" was not strong enough for release).

The Drifters were placed once more in the hands of Leiber and Stoller, who had since become well known in the field of rock and roll, and now had several hits by the Coasters and Elvis Presley to their credit. On this occasion, they gave the Drifters "Drip Drop" and decided to record the then pop hit "Suddenly There's a Valley." For some strange reason, they selected the ancient and beloved-by-many-a-bar-singer "On Moonlight Bay" as the third number.

Leiber and Stoller gave "Suddenly There's a Valley" a radical reworking, featuring the bass vocals of Tommy Evans complemented by the wailing tenor of Bobby Hendricks. (For many years, fans believed Bill Pinckney supplied the bass, but it *was* in fact Tommy Evans.) The recording is outstanding and deserved more than its subsequent fate as a 1960 b-side—in Britain it failed even to make it that far and surfaced only on an album.

The idiosyncratic treatment given "Moonlight Bay" has also caused some confusion. The arrangement, which the Drifters found hard to follow, called for a chorale. They sang the number through once and then again on separate tracks which were later overdubbed. The effect was not the intended one, for instead of four voices echoed there were eight voices singing simultaneously. Because the recording sounds unlike anything else the Drifters ever did, some critics have concluded it was not made by the Drifters at all, but by the Ray Ellis Singers, a white, middle-of-the-road outfit. Bobby Hendricks's claim that the record featured Tommy Evans and himself, multi-tracked, has confused the issue even more. The Atlantic session files state that the recording was made by the Drifters—and we should add that they were most unhappy with it. Bobby Hendricks has been quoted as saying: "If Jimmy Oliver had been with us, we would never have done 'Moonlight Bay'."

When released in May 1958, both "Drip Drop" and "Moonlight Bay" entered the pop charts. But by the time the latter had risen to number seventy in June and "Drip Drop" had peaked at fifty-eight on August 24, 1958, changes had again taken place in the Drifters' lineup that would make all the previous upheavals seem trivial by comparison.

Just after the April session, Bobby Hendricks and Jimmy Oliver left and moved to Sue Records. Both agreed to return, however, for an engagement at the Apollo Theater at the end of May. During this week-long engagement, one of the Drifters, apparently "under the influence," physically abused Frank Schiffman, the owner of the theater. Treadwell was less than amused, for the Drifters' ten-year contract with the theater was now obviously in doubt. He was also troubled by the fact that once more alcohol abuse seemed to be a problem (Gerhart Thrasher in particular seemed to be putting away large quantities; he could still sing like a bird but unfortunately now drank like a fish). In short, the Drifters were a shambles. A frustrated George Treadwell fired them all.

What happened to the Drifters? Bobby Hendricks returned to Sue Records with Jimmy Oliver, who provided him with "Itchy Twitchy Feeling," which Oliver based on the Drifters' "Yodee Yakee" (it sold a million copies), and he had several smaller hits and appeared on Mercury in 1962, though never managing to achieve the success of his debut hit. Hendricks resumed his connection with the Drifters when he teamed up with Bill Pinckney in 1959. Jimmy Oliver had several instrumental releases, including "Stealin' Home" on Rainbow Records, "Slim Jim" on Port, and "The Sneak" on Juggy Murray's Sue label. He worked with Clyde McPhatter at Mercury, and together they formed the Olimac Publishing Company. Sue issued an album in the mid sixties (Sue 1041) on which Oliver covered Tamla-Motown tracks, and in 1970 he produced the Village Soul Choir's "Catwalk" (Abbott 2010). Tommy Evans went to California and joined Charlie Fuqua's Inkspots; he, too, later reappeared. Gerhart Thrasher initially went to Florida, but after receiving a call from Bill Pinckney was soon back on the road. Of Jimmy Milner, nothing is known; he seems to have dropped from sight after he left the Drifters.

George Treadwell was left with the name but no group. Far from being the end of the Drifters, though, June 1958 witnessed a rebirth that was to outdo almost all of what had gone before.

THE FIVE CROWNS (1952)
Rear (l. to r.): John Clark, Dock Green, James Clark;
Front (l. to r.): Wilbur "Yonkie" Paul, Nick Clark.
(Photo from the collection of Marv Goldberg)

CHAPTER 7

Crowning the Drifters

During that fateful week at the Apollo in June 1958, George Treadwell noticed a group from Harlem called the Crowns who were appearing further down the bill. Since he had a long-term contract for the Drifters at the Apollo, the idea occurred to him to replace the Drifters with the Crowns. He approached the Crowns' manager, Lover Patterson, and suggested his group become the Drifters. At the time, both Patterson and the Crowns thought Treadwell was joking or that he had had one drink too many. At the end of the week, though, when the Drifters did indeed disband, the Crowns found themselves in a downtown New York office discussing the details of Treadwell's plan. One of the members, James "Poppa" Clark, was none too happy with the arrangement and refused to continue with the group; the others were overjoyed to become the Drifters.

George Treadwell had staged quite a coup, for he had not only rid himself of the problems caused by his old group but had insured the continuity of the Drifters' name and was thus able to fulfill all the important bookings. (Jerry Wexler remembers the events differently, recalling that some time elapsed before *he* called Treadwell and suggested that Treadwell get a group together and revive the name.)

The Crowns, who had been promoting a recent release, "Kiss and Make Up," were not a new group; indeed, they had formed even before the Drifters had.

In 1952, long-time friends Dock Green and Wilbur "Yonkie" Paul decided to form a vocal group with three friends from their Harlem neighborhood, Richard Davis and twins Ralph and Joe Martin. The combination, called the Harmonaires, did not last very long, a fate common to many groups formed at the time. This was, after all, the age of street-corner vocal groups—

particularly so in New York City—where neighborhood youths singing *a cappella* could be found harmonizing under the street lamps.

Following the breakup of the Harmonaires, Green and Paul recruited the Clark brothers, Nick, John, and James, this time naming themselves the Five Crowns. Richard Davis and the Martin twins joined with John Thomas Steele and Tony Middleton to form the Five Willows, who would later score a major hit with "Church Bells May Ring" (on Melba in 1956; the record sold a million copies).

The Five Crowns were all basically tenors, although John Clark could sing baritone and Dock Green doubled on baritone and bass. The sound they produced was highly original for the time. They contacted Lover Patterson, supposedly the manager of the Orioles but in fact the group's valet, and impressed him enough that he left Sonny Til to look after their affairs.

Patterson got them a contract with Eddie Heller's Rainbow Records, for whom they recorded four tracks in July 1952. Rainbow issued "A Star"/"You're My Inspiration" (Rainbow 179) in September 1952, and followed it shortly with "$19.50 Bus"/"Who Can Be True" (Rainbow 184).

Following a disagreement with Heller, the group moved to Hy Weiss's Old Town Records, which released two singles, "Good Luck Darling"/"You Could Be My Love" (Old Town 790) and "Lullaby of the Bells"/"Later Baby" (Old Town 792). Two other singles emerged during 1953, "Why Don't You Believe Me"/"Keep It a Secret" (Old Town 202) and "Alone Again"/ "Don't Have to Hunt No More" (Old Town 206). These tracks were recorded during 1952 and 1953, along with four unissued tracks: "Again," "At the Fair," "Good Luck Darling" (an alternative take to the one issued), and "The Man in the Moon." These unreleased sides were found in the possession of Eddie Heller, but Dock Green and Wilbur Paul thought they were recorded for Old Town. The Five Crowns' version of "The Man in the Moon" was cut before the one issued by Joe Davis which featured the Crickets (not the Buddy Holly group). The song was a street song that had found its way from Harlem to the South

72

Bronx, the Crickets' home territory.

The first personnel change in the group came in 1953 when Nicky Clark (Nicky was a nickname—pardon the pun—he was actually called Claudie) left to join the Harptones, a group from the same neighborhood which was closely associated with the Five Crowns (Nicky led the Harptones on "I Depended on You"). Clark was not immediately replaced; his place in the publicity shots and on stage was taken by Lover Patterson, who simply pretended to sing in the live performances.

John "Sonny Boy" Clark was the next to leave; the group brought in new recruits Jesse Facing (tenor) and William "Bug Eye" Bailey (bass). Shortly after, James "Poppa" Clark left to join the Cadillacs.

With Richard Lewis in for James Clark, the Five Crowns recorded for Eddie Heller's new label Riviera in March 1955. Wilbur Paul lead the group on "Oo-Wee Baby"/"You Came to Me" (Riviera 990). These recordings resurfaced on Rainbow 335 a year later (by the Duvals, though, another group managed by Lover Patterson; the explanation may be that because the Crowns were at the time inactive, the record was re-released under the Duvals' name to promote them).

Following the release of their best record, "Popcorn Willie" (Transworld 717), the Five Crowns disbanded. Dock Green later said the group had worked up a song called "Castle in the Sky," with which the Bop Chords later had a hit. Unfortunately, the Five Crowns never recorded the number that might have broken them in a big way. Before their breakup William Bailey left, to be replaced by Leroy Brown.

Dock Green then formed a new Five Crowns, bringing in a tenor who is remembered only as J. D., Charlie Thomas on second tenor, Bernard Ward as yet another tenor, and Elsbeary Hobbs on bass (Wilbur Paul had joined the Harptones). This combination recorded one single—"Do You Remember"/"God Bless You" (Gee 1001)—before drifting into memory.

Never one to give up easily, Dock Green resurfaced in 1957 with yet another version of the Crowns. He dropped "Five" from the name since Nicky Clark occasionally joined Dock, tenors Charlie Thomas, Ben Nelson, Sy Palmer, and

THE CROWNS (1957)
(l. to r.): Charlie Thomas, Lover Patterson (standing in for Dock Green),
Ben Nelson (Ben E. King), Sy Palmer, Elsbeary Hobbs.
(Photo from the collection of Marv Goldberg)

Elsbeary Hobbs. Caravan Records reissued "Popcorn Willie" (Caravan 15609), and the lineup featured in the publicity shots continued on occasion to include the ever-silent Lover Patterson. Sy Palmer stayed only about six months and gave way to the returning James "Poppa" Clark.

In March 1958, the Crowns recorded two tracks for R&B Records, which was run by Doc Pomus and Mort Shuman. The resulting single featured Charlie Thomas singing "Kiss and Make Up" on the top-side and James Clark's dulcet tones on the flip-side's "I'll Forget About You." This was the record they were promoting when George Treadwell renamed them the Drifters.

With James Clark leaving the group, Treadwell placed guitarist Reggie Kimber (Kimber had toured occasionally with

74

the former Drifters and since the Crown/Drifters were unfamiliar with the terrain, he was considered right for the job) alongside Charlie Thomas, Dock Green, Ben Nelson, and Elsbeary Hobbs, sending them on the road as the Drifters. Lover Patterson accompanied them as road manager, although the full extent of his role was otherwise unclear (a circumstance that would later cause some problems). Charile Thomas was thought to have the voice closest to Clyde McPhatter's and was therefore the featured lead. The group, though, had a rough ride from audiences who felt they were being short-changed by a bogus line-up.

GREATEST COLORED SHOWS

APOLLO

125° ST. near 8° Ave · Tel. UNiversity 4-4490

One Week Only — Beg. Fri., May 30th

WWRL **DR. JIVE** And His RHYTHM 'n' BLUES Revue

"Yes, Indeed"

RAY CHARLES and Band

"DOWN ON MY KNEES"	"MOONLIGHT BAY"
HEARTBEATS	**DRIFTERS**
CADILLACS	**CROWNS**
TINY TOPSY	**ANN COLE**
SOLOMON BURKE	3 COOKIES
WED. NITE: AMATEURS	SAT.: MIDNITE SHOW

APOLLO THEATER SHOWBILL, EARLY JUNE 1958

After spending about eight months on the road, Atlantic called them back to the studios on March 6, 1959, to record with Leiber and Stoller. The musicians assembled seemed more suitable for a pop ballad session than a rhythm and blues one, as there was a large string section. Leiber and Stoller realized, however, that these Drifters were completely different from the group who had recorded "Drip Drop." (Atlantic had, in fact, distributed the Crowns' R&B-label single and thus were probably aware of who they were prior to their rebirth as the Drifters.) The session began with Lover Patterson's "Hey Senorita," a stylistic throwback to a primitive rock and roll number that had been cut two years before as "Dum Dum Dee Dum Dum" by the Cadillacs. It gave no hint of what would be recorded next.

Ben Nelson had written an up-tempo rhythm and blues song about Dock Green's girlfriend called "There Goes My Baby," which the Crowns had been rehearsing on the road. Leiber and Stoller saw the song in a completely different way. During the run-up, Charlie Thomas for some reason had difficulty singing it, and the producers asked Ben Nelson, who had

75

been trying to coach Thomas, to sing it himself. Leiber and Stoller slowed the song down and added a South American rhythm, which they both loved. Onto the basic rhythm and blues backing, they grafted a five-piece string section, creating the effect of two records played at once. At one point, Nelson came in too early. This mistake was left on the finished master and, combined with the general cacophony, resulted in a sound that was unlike anything that had ever been produced before. Strings had been used on rhythm and blues records as early as 1951 when the Orioles recorded "Everything Came True" and "You Are My First Love," but the way in which Leiber and Stoller used them was something else again.

Two other tracks rounded out the session: "Oh My Love," sung by Nelson, and "Baltimore," led by Charlie Thomas. After "There Goes My Baby," however, both were anticlimactic.

The recordings were taken to Ertegun and Wexler for their comments. To say they were less than impressed would be an understatement. Jerry Wexler nearly blew a fuse and almost choked on the tuna sandwich he was eating. He described "There Goes My Baby" as a "fucking mess"; Ahmet Ertegun put it slightly more charitably, saying that although they had an impressive track record, on this occasion they had, well, "bombed out."

Leiber and Stoller, however, thought "There Goes My Baby" would be a hit and persuaded Ertegun to let them work on it with Atlantic engineer Tom Dowd. Ertegun seems to have agreed only because he hoped to salvage something from the session; he finally allowed the record to be released on April 24, 1959. The Drifters played a major outdoor concert on May 29 at Herndon Stadium in Atlanta (with Ray Charles, B.B. King, and Jimmy Reed). By August 18, "There Goes My Baby" was number two on the *Billboard* Hot 100—on *Cashbox* and other charts it was number one.

This success did not go unnoticed by the members of the former Drifters. Bill Pinckney in particular was unhappy, for he resented the fact that after the years of hard work and struggle, a group of strangers had suddenly stepped in and reaped all the glory. Bill felt they were good singers and had a good sound, but that the sound was not the sound of the Drifters.

The distinctive voice leading the group was that of Ben Nelson, who was born Benjamin Earl Nelson on September 28, 1938, in Henderson, North Carolina; he changed his name to Ben E. King (the surname came from a favorite uncle, James King) at the suggestion of his agent, Frank Sands, shortly after the success of "There Goes My Baby."

As a child, King sang in church choirs before moving to Harlem with his family. While attending James Fenimore Cooper High School, he joined the Four B's (the first name of the members all began with the letter "b"); he auditioned for the Moonglows (unsuccessfully) in 1956 and joined the Crowns in 1957.

In the Crowns he was merely a backing tenor, and his parents thought he was going nowhere and would be better employed in his father's luncheonette. They changed their minds following the release of "There Goes My Baby," and could often be found seated in the front row at the Drifters' concerts.

Ben E. King may have become the Drifters' lead vocalist purely by chance, but his plaintive gospel wail quickly became their trademark and the recordings he made with the group over the next couple of years would forever link him to them.

THE CROWNS (1958)
Rear (l. to r.): Dock Green, Elsbeary Hobbs, Lover Patterson, James Clark;
Front (l. to r.): Benjamin Nelson (Ben E. King) and Charlie Thomas.

CHAPTER 8

Save the Last Dance for Me

The Drifters were aptly named, for since their formation in 1953 over a dozen members had drifted in and out, and the June 1958 upheaval failed to change the pattern.

In May 1959, George Treadwell and Lover Patterson, who had been the manager of the Crowns and had joined in the deal when they became the Drifters, had a disagreement which led to yet another change in personnel.

Apparently, Patterson was unhappy with his role in the new setup, which, as we have mentioned, was rather undefined. Obviously not the manager, he felt he was little more than a dog's body *cum* manager *cum* just about anything else. He *was* the manager of the Duvals, who, incidentally changed their name to the Crowns when the Crowns became the Drifters—confused?—and felt he was not getting the respect he thought he deserved from the Drifters' organization. Shrewdly, however, he had retained the contract of Ben E. King when he signed over the contracts of the other Crowns to George Treadwell. When he expressed his dissatisfaction to Treadwell and received no encouragement that things would change, he announced that he would no longer allow King to perform with the Drifters.

King himself was not happy with the setup, for though the Crowns were now members of a big name group, their financial situation had not improved. The members were salaried at seventy-five dollars a week, from which they had to pay their own expenses. King found himself in such dire straits that he offered to sell his interest in "There Goes My Baby" to Jerry Wexler for two hundred dollars.

King claimed to have written the song, but the credits also included Lover Patterson and George Treadwell. It was common practice at the time for label owners, disk jockeys, and producers (or even friends of such people) to append their names to songs to which they had no claim, the justification being that this would help the song to gain radio play or, at least, the interest of producers, who preferred to deal with people experienced in the business—in reality, though, it *all* came down to a share in the royalties. One classic case concerned Chuck Berry's "Maybellene," which though written solely by Berry was also credited to Alan Freed and Russ Fratto; Freed was there for giving the song radio play, but Fratto turned out to be the guy who supplied label owner Leonard Chess with stationery (seems only fair, doesn't it?).

Returning to the case of King versus Treadwell and Patterson, we must say that the situation was not quite that ludicrous, for both Treadwell and Patterson had backgrounds in music and both *had* contributed to the composition. To complicate matters even further, however, Dock Green later said he had also helped write the song. Doubtlessly, arguments could rage on indefinitely.

In any event, Jerry Wexler declined King's offer, only to receive a call from a lawyer he knew saying that King was in his office making him the same offer. Wexler told the lawyer (whom he has declined to name, in case you are wondering) to send King back to him; on his return, Wexler handed over two hundred dollars in exchange for a piece of "There Goes My Baby."

The squabble between Lover Patterson and George Treadwell brought matters to a head. When King's request for more money was refused because the new Drifters had yet to have a hit ("There Goes My Baby" would not hit the charts for several months; when it did, by the way, Wexler graciously tore up the agreement with King), King walked out of a group meeting, saying he would rather return to his old clerical job than continue singing. As he closed the door behind him, only Lover Patterson followed.

These problems could not, however, have surfaced at a more inopportune moment, for the stage had been set for a resurgence of innovative rhythm and blues and the Drifters, with a major hit now topping the charts, were obviously in a position to take advantage of the situation. Problems with their lead vocalists were the last thing they needed. Why was the stage set? Well, the music establishment, appalled by the hordes of screaming wild men and vocal groups of hoodlums who had since 1955 caused them problems, had begun to fight back, assimilating aspects of the original black sound and forming a pastiche of the music. Certain developments had aided their tasks. The real rock king, Little Richard, had given up the business for the Lord, Buddy Holly was dead, and Jerry Lee Lewis was an outcast following his bigamous marriage to his twelve-year-old cousin. Elvis Presley was now serving Uncle Sam, and many of his best days were behind him (a fact perhaps substantiated by most of his post-army output). To fill the places of these stars, the record industry had developed a succession of teen idols—Fabian, Frankie Avalon, and Bobby Rydell, to name but three. All had one thing in common: they were pretty boys whose pictures were certain to decorate the walls of most teenage girls. They may have sounded like rock and rollers on occasion, but they were nothing but pale copyists. And the industry was finding it harder and harder to con the record-buying public.

Though he would no longer tour with the Drifters, Ben E. King, fortunately (and surprisingly), agreed to continue fronting them. His place on stage was taken by Johnny Lee Williams, who came from Mobile, Alabama. Lead vocal duties reverted to Charlie Thomas.

Atlantic obviously wanted to keep the momentum created by "There Goes My Baby" going, but felt the two recordings they had in the can—"Baltimore" and "Hey Senorita"—were not strong enough for release as follow-ups.

Thus, the now five-strong recording Drifters assembled in the Atlantic studios on July 9, 1959. One of the songs selected by Leiber and Stoller came from the songwriting team of Doc Pomus and Mort Shuman, a seemingly unlikely duo who had met in 1955 when Shuman was dating Pomus' cousin. Pomus (thirty-four) had been crippled by polio in childhood but had not been prevented from becoming one of the few (if not the

81

only) white blues singers recording during the forties (his records rejoiced in titles such as "Fruity Woman Blues," "Send for the Doctor," and "Kiss My Wrist," but all fell on deaf ears). Shuman was a staunch doo-wop fan. After joining forces, they supplied Ray Charles and Big Joe Turner with hit songs ("Lonely Avenue" and "Boogie Woogie Country Girl," respectively) and co-wrote "Young Blood" with Leiber and Stoller, which brought the Coasters a hit in 1957. In early 1958, they started their own record company called R&B, which was distributed by Atlantic. The only new release on the label ("Kiss and Make Up") had been recorded, ironically, by the Crowns—more or less the same group now known as the Drifters.

The song they provided for the July 9 session was "True Love, True Love," and the task of singing it was given neither to King nor Thomas but to Johnny Lee Williams, whose high tenor voice recalled the days of the Drifters' past. The inventive arrangement gave the number an almost Eastern flavor, and it was destined to become a Drifters' classic.

Ben E. King took the lead on the second track, "Dance with Me," which though credited to Nahan, Treadwell, Lebish (an old accountant friend), and Elmo Glick (a pseudonym for Leiber and Stoller), King would later claim to have written by himself. Songwriting feuds aside, "Dance with Me" proved even more powerful than "True Love, True Love." The excellence of both was no doubt due to the meticulous approach of Leiber and Stoller, who thought nothing of doing sixty takes before editing the results to achieve what they wanted (Phil Spector, who worked as the assistant on many occasions, no doubt watched and took notes for future reference).

"Dance with Me" and "True Love, True Love" were released in October 1959. Both made it to the Top 100, the former reaching number fifteen, and latter (the b-side) number thirty-three. The record also saw the Drifters make their chart debut in Britain, where "Dance with Me" climbed to number seventeen on January 8, 1960, and re-entered the charts on March 10 at number thirty-five.

On December 23, 1959, Leiber and Stoller had the group back to record two other Pomus and Shuman songs: "Lonely

Winds" and "This Magic Moment." The latter in particular had a considerable Latin influence, which was not surprising for, like the Leiber-Stoller producing team, Pomus and Shuman were fascinated by the Latin American rhythms cultivated on Wednesday nights at the Palladium (53rd and Broadway), where the mambo rhythm of Tito Puente's orchestra could be found.

An attempt was made at the standard "Temptation," but it was shelved and appeared only in an altered form several years later.

Atlantic released "This Magic Moment" in February 1960, and it reached number sixteen on the national charts on March 29. One of their best recordings, the number has been revived (but never bettered) several times, most successfully by the Drifters' white copyists, Jay and the Americans, who took their version to number two in 1969.

When the follow-up, "Lonely Winds," stalled at number fifty-four, doubters came out of the woodwork, saying that the Drifters had peaked and could now only go down. Never were some more wrong.

Ben E. King would record only one more session with the Drifters; but, on May 19, 1960, they recorded the song that is possibly their greatest and certainly the one most closely associated with them—the Pomus and Shuman classic "Save the Last Dance for Me." Just about everybody and his uncle is familiar with this tune. In execution it is perfect—from King's soaring tenor lead to the wonderfully crafted backing vocals, from the string arrangement to the Latin rhythms, all is as it should be, with the bitter sweetness providing the icing on the cake.

But "Save the Last Dance for Me" almost never happened, for the powers that be at Atlantic did not like the song at all. Pomus himself had been rehearsing a teen idol named Jimmy Clanton and intended to have him record the number. Clanton had begun his career promisingly enough several years earlier with the New Orleans influenced ballad "Just a Dream" on Ace Records but had rapidly descended into the dross, endearing himself to adolescent females at the same time. He was annoyed when told he could no longer have the song

(Pomus told him it had been recorded without knowledge of the composers by someone else), and Pomus and Shuman placated him with "Go Jimmy Go," which they said they had written just for him but which had actually been penned for another teenager named Bobby Rydell as "Go Bobby Go." Happily, "Save the Last Dance for Me" was left to the more capable talents of the Drifters.

The other tracks cut that day were the Pomus and Shuman songs "Nobody but Me" and "I Count the Tears" (both nearly matched the greatness of "Dance"), and a Ben E. King rewrite of "There Goes My Baby" called "Sometimes I Wonder."

Wexler called Pomus to inform him that he and Shuman would have both sides of the next Drifters' release, but that the plug-side was to be "Nobody but Me." Following the record's release in 1960, the flip-side, "Save the Last Dance for Me," picked up quite a bit of regional chart action and radio plays, but Atlantic remained unconvinced until Dick Clark, the host of "American Bandstand," called to tell them they were going with the wrong side. Atlantic turned the record over. By October 18, 1960, "Save the Last Dance for Me" surveyed the rest of the records in the Top 100 from its number one position, nearly repeating the feat in Britain, where it reached number two on November 3, kept from the top spot only by Elvis Presley's neo-operatic "It's Now or Never." Its success resulted in answers by Damita Jo on Mercury with "I'll Save the Last Dance for You" and Billy Fury on U.K. Decca with "You're Saving the Last Dance for Me."

The Drifters' hit culminated a year of unprecedented success for Atlantic Records, for in August 1959 Ray Charles's "What'd I Say," which restored much of the primal spirit to rock and roll, reach number six, and by late 1959 Bobby Darin's "Mack the Knife" and the Coasters' "Poison Ivy" had each sold a million copies.

The Drifters seemed on a roll, but some internal problems had developed.

Shortly after the May 1960 recording session, they had an engagement in Mobile, Alabama, the hometown of Johnny Lee Williams. Overcome with a sudden bout of home sickness,

Williams refused to continue the tour and in effect left the group. (Williams went on to record as a solo act on Kent and Cub, and although at one time many believed him to be the vocalist on Drifter 101—"Rainbow Heart"/"Tear Drops and Memories"—this is untrue, as the vocalist on that recording was, in fact, white. He did front a Mobile, Alabama, group called the Embraceables in 1962, which recorded a track called "My Foolish Pride" on the Sigh (or Cy) label. The same group had an earlier single on Sandy called "From Someone Who Loves You," with lead vocals by Herman Bracey. (I have no information regarding Williams's fate after 1962.) Since they had a concert date in Nassau, replacing Williams was a matter of some urgency. Their prayers seemed to have been answered when James Poindexter appeared. He sang like a lark but, unfortunately, froze on stage, and his career with the Drifters was short-lived.

Charlie Thomas, Dock Green, and Elsbeary Hobbs completed the tour as a trio and returned to New York to find that the army apparently could not function without a Drifter—and so it was goodbye to Hobbs. Finding a suitable replacement proved difficult. William Van Dyke supplied the bass for about a month, to be ousted by George Grant, who managed to last a fortnight. George Treadwell finally solved the problem by calling Tommy Evans, who had been the bass in the Drifters' pre-Crown days. Evans, who had been doing Hoppy Jones impersonations with Charlie Fuqua's Inkspots, hastened back.

Guitarist Reggie Kimber had played his last note as a Drifter and had been replaced by Billy Davis. Davis was a composer, arranger, guitarist, and road manager (and probably made the tea, as well), and had been with Doc Bagsby's band before joining the Drifters (he later changed his name to Abdul Samad).

The problem of replacing Ben E. King was solved when Treadwell recruited Rudy Lewis, one of two men to sing with the Clara Ward Singers. He joined the Drifters in late 1960, in time to appear with them in Clay Cole's Brooklyn Paramount Christmas show, which also included Neil Sedaka, Bobby Vee, Bo Diddley, and Chubby Checker.

Ben E. King

Before closing this chapter, we should say a few words about the subsequent career of Ben E. King, who had in the meantime embarked full time on his solo career. Atlantic had issued two records (the Wexler produced "Show Me the Way" and the follow-up "Brace Yourself") when he was still officially a Drifter, but neither had caused much of a stir.

He made his breakthrough early in 1961 with the Spector-Leiber song "Spanish Harlem," which contained much of the Latin flavor beloved by Drifters fans. The b-side, "First Taste of Love," also fared well, but it was "Spanish Harlem" that took King to the Top 10 (some believed these were merely Drifters records issued under King's name, *a la* Buddy Holly and the Crickets, but the backing vocalists were the Duvals, Lover Patterson's old group).

"Spanish Harlem" was an important record for King, but the next release, the stark "Stand by Me," based on an old gospel song by the Soul Stirrers called "Lord, I'm Standing By," would cause tremors that would still be felt twenty-five years later. King has said he initially meant to cut the song with the Drifters, but his memory seems to have been dimmed by the passing years for in actuality he recorded the record nearly a year after leaving the Drifters. The version he did cut with the Duvals rose to number four and was followed by a succession of hits that included "Amor, Ecstasy," "Here Comes the Night," "Don't Play That Song," "I (Who Have Nothing)," "Too Bad," "Around the Corner," "Seven Letters" (which helped to get his marriage over a rough patch due to sentiments expressed in the song that struck a romantic chord in his wife), the seminal "What Is Soul," and "Tears, Tears, Tears."

Gradually, due in some degree to the Beatlization of the American record charts, his popularity began to decline. Unlike many others, though, he accepted it philosophically. He left Atlantic Records for Bob Crewe's Crewe Records, recording one album, *Rough Edges*, in 1970 before appearing the following year on Columbia with *The Beginning of It All*. Both albums attempted to update King's style but proved commercially unsuccessful.

In early 1975, Ahmet Ertegun saw him in concert in

Miami and invited him back to Atlantic for a one-off session. The result was "Supernatural Thing," which was a huge hit in America and led to the successful album *Benny and Us* with Scotland's Average White Band in 1977. Throughout the rest of the seventies, he continued to score on both the pop and rhythm and blues charts.

Faye Treadwell invited him to rejoin the Drifters in 1981. He accepted and toured with the then Drifters (Johnny Moore and company) until 1985. During this time he was featured on "You Better Move On" (Atlantic K11743), the last single to be issued by the group. When the 1986 film "Stand By Me" used his old hit as the theme song, King's recording reentered the American Top 10—as it did in Britain, although the source of its renewed strength there was its use in a jeans advertisement.

King is still in demand both on record and stage (in July 1987 his solo revival of "Save the Last Dance for Me" made the lower regions of the U.K. charts). Long established as one of the great vocalists in rhythm and blues and soul music, his name will always be linked with the Drifters, if for no other reason than that it is his voice one hears on the classic version of "Save the Last Dance for Me." With apologies to Clyde McPhatter fans, it remains *the* Drifters' record for most of their fans.

CHAPTER 9

Drifting Down Broadway

Atlantic Records, worried by the comings and goings within the Drifters and anxious to capitalize on the international success of "Save the Last Dance for Me," solved the immediate problem by issuing "I Count the Tears," which featured Ben E. King. This Pomus and Shuman song was nearly as strong as its predecessor but by January 31 had climbed only to number seventeen. Atlantic, for some strange reason, decided to use different b-sides on the American and British releases, neither of which had been recorded recently. For the American release, they resurrected "Suddenly There's a Valley," which had been recorded in April 1958 and featured Tommy Evans and Bobby Hendricks; for the British release, they went back even further and dug out "Sadie My Lady," which Johnny Moore had recorded way back in June 1956. Although "I Count the Tears" barely managed to creep into the U.K. Top Thirty (number twenty-nine), it did endear itself to an emerging group of British rockers when it became a stage favorite of the new rock groups—cover versions by the Searchers and the Aces appeared as late as 1963.

Over the years the Drifters had changed from a hard-edged rhythm and blues group to romantic balladeers, and Jerry Leiber and Mike Stoller thought their compositions no longer fitted the group (the songwriters perceived themselves as steeped in the former style) and decided to concentrate on their roles as the Drifters producers.

They had used Pomus and Shuman songs in the past, but the early sixties saw the emergence of a new breed of songwriter who worked mainly for Aldon Music, which was run by Don Kirshner (1650 Broadway), or were employed at the Brill Building (1619 Broadway), and Leiber and Stoller began to turn to these sources for material. Writers in such firms worked in cubby holes, usually in pairs, where they attempted to come up with *the* song that would capture the hearts of the nation's youth. They were, in effect, an updated version of the old publishing house writers since they were in the business of supplying tailor-made songs for different artists and were much in demand by rhythm and blues acts and the teen idols. The Brill Building was the more famous of the two, but Leiber and Stoller favored Don Kirshner's writers. (Kirshner, of course, had been phenominally successful over the course of just a few years, having started out co-writing jingles and pop tunes with old Bronx High School chum Bobby Darin; their first, "Bubblegum Pop," was copyrighted in January 1956.)

When the Drifters were called in to record on February 1, 1961, the revised line-up (Rudy Lewis, Charlie Thomas, Dock Green, and Tommy Evans) was presented with four songs. Two ("Sweets for My Sweet" and "Room Full of Tears") came from Pomus and Shuman, but the others were supplied by the new Broadway tunesmiths. "Some Kind of Wonderful" had been written by Carole King and Gerry Goffin; "Please Stay" had come from Burt Bacharach and Bob Hilliard. (Carole King—born Carole Klein, February 9, 1942, in Brooklyn—had in fact had several unsuccessful records released, among them "Short Mort," possibly a tribute to Mort Shuman, and "Oh Neil," an answer to the song Neil Sedaka had written for her, "Oh Carol.")

At this session was a quartet called the Gospelaires, which consisted of Dionne and Dee Dee Warwick, Cissy Houston, and Doris Troy. The recordings make clear how much the Drifters' sound had changed from the early days, inasmuch as the quartet tends to overshadow the group. Using a technique borrowed from gospel music, Leiber and Stoller highlighted the women's vocals behind the Drifters' lead vocal. Thus, on Rudy Lewis's "Some Kind of Wonderful" and Charlie Thomas's "Sweets for My Sweet" and "Room Full of Tears," the Drifters are almost inaudible and there is little trace of the group harmony. "Please Stay" did not suffer as badly because Rudy Lewis and the rest of the Drifters are well to the fore. But most of the

90

THE DRIFTERS (1962)
Rear (l. to r.): Charlie Thomas, Dock Green, Rudy Lewis;
Front: Tommy Evans.

hard-edged rhythm and blues roots were erased, along with Lewis's gospel background, which is barely noticeable since only on occasion was he allowed to show any of the emotionalism or intensity common to gospel-based vocalists.

Not that the records were bad. Far from it! All four tracks have stood the test of time. But Leiber and Stoller's producing did sometimes make the artists appear irrelevant.

"Some Kind of Wonderful" carried the Drifters into the Top 40 in May 1961, where it peaked at number thirty-two. At the same time it resurrected the ghost of David Baughan for his 1955 "Honey Bee" nestled uncomfortably on the flip of the smooth a-side.

Burt Bacharach attended the next session on July 13, 1961, ostensibly to watch the group record his "Mexican Divorce," a strange, quirky tune which though great was uncommercial. While there he was impressed by Dionne Warwick, so much so that shortly after he took her to Wand Records, where she was launched on a solo career. The rest, as they say, is history.

Nothing much really emerged from this session. Apart from Bacharach's song, the Drifters cut only "Loneliness or Happiness" and "Somebody New, Dancing with You," which bore more than a passing resemblance to "Save the Last Dance for Me." All three numbers wound up as future b-sides.

"Please Stay" had been released in May and climbed the charts to number fourteen on July 25. Bill Pinckney enjoyed a surprise reappearance on a Drifters' record when his "No Sweet Lovin'" from the David Baughan session of April 1955 was chosen to grace the back side.

They were back in the studio on October 26 just as "Sweets for My Sweet" peaked at number sixteen. On this occasion they recorded "When My Little Girl Is Smiling" (Charlie Thomas was featured, but Rudy Lewis did the slow introduction) and "She Never Talked to Me That Way" (led by Lewis). The former came from Goffin and King; the latter, from old faithfuls Pomus and Shuman. Both sounded like potential classics. They also recorded the wry Aaron Schroeder/Chuck Kaye "Jackpot."

The Goffin/King song was destined to become one of their most requested waxings. Released after the comparative flop of "Room Full of Tears" (number seventy-two, even though it featured one of Thomas's best vocals, so good in fact that many fans believed it to be Lewis's), "When My Little Girl Is Smiling" took them back into the Top 40 (number twenty-eight). It even managed to rise to the dizzy heights of number thirty-one in Britain, but its progress there was hampered by the inferior cover versions of Craig Douglas (a singing milkman, who sounded like one) and the Ben E. King copyist Jimmy Justice. Covers would continue to plague them in Britain for many years.

"She Never Talked to Me That Way" failed to see the light of day until it appeared on a British compilation in 1972, when it was erroneously attributed to the then Drifters' line-up, who were even credited with having written it (this may have been an Atlantic U.K. marketing ploy, though). Perhaps annoyed by Atlantic's decision not to release the song, Pomus and Shuman gave it to Del Shannon, who recorded it as "You Never Talked to Me That Way" on Big Top in 1962.

The Drifters were kept busy throughout this period with concert tours. The big package shows of the fifties had lost their popularity, but the Drifters still tended to tour in revue shows (often in the company of the teen idols, every second one of whom seemed to be named Bobby—Bobby Vee, Bobby Vinton, and so on and on) that restricted each act to four or five numbers.

On one such tour they encountered racism in North Carolina, where the audience was segregated into black and white sections. The Drifters featured a spot in which they talked to the audience, and on this occasion Charlie Thomas approached the rope which divided the whites from the blacks. The white section was full, the black section was not, and white fans had begun ducking under the rope into the black section. Disconcerted, the police weighed in heavy-handed to prevent any integration, a situation which prompted Charlie to say "Police, why don't you leave those people alone," only to see his plea provoke a near riot. Obviously, the inhabitants of the deep

South still had some way to go in achieving racial tolerance. The audiences in such areas still found it difficult to deal with racially integrated bills, and Thomas's words had an adverse effect on many of the whites present.

The South had always held dangers for black groups. Johnny Moore recalled in an interview that "It was always rough, hectic. Accomodations weren't easily found, especially in the South. But we were pioneers, and I'm proud of that. Sometimes we even had to sleep in cars." As late as 1962, things still weren't right; on one occasion members of the white vocal group the Dovells prevented Southern rednecks from attacking members of the Drifters.

Atlantic continued to record them whenever time could be found in their touring schedule. Their choice of one number on March 15, 1962, seemed, on the face of it, a strange one. Traditional jazz clarinetist Acker Bilk had had a massive international hit with the slow, sentimental "Stranger on the Shore," which had begun life as "Jenny" (in Britain it had been used as the theme on a television show—which no doubt helped it become successful over there). Despite a haunting melody, the tune was strictly middle-of-the-road. Rudy Lewis struggled manfully to give it some soul, but there was little doubt that it was better suited to balladeers such as Andy Williams, who also recorded it.

All was not lost, though. The flip-side, "What to Do," proved to be the record's salvation. Written by Abdul Samad (Billy Davis), Florence Davis, and Faye Treadwell, the song marked a return to the group's rhythm and blues roots, complete with bass interjections from Tommy Evans. Rudy Lewis, in particular, reveled in the freedom to come to grips with a rhythmic number after the ballads they had been given recently. Although the strings were still present, the instrumental break was taken by the old blues standby, the harmonica. It was a pity the record was consigned to the b-side of the Bilk opus. The Drifters' version of "Stranger on the Shore" managed to reach number seventy-three, but all in all it was not one of their best moments.

Atlantic had nothing in the can to follow up with, so

they released "Sometimes I Wonder" from the last Ben E. King session of May 1960. This was little more than "There Goes My Baby" revisited, but when issued in June 1962 along with "Jackpot," it became the first Drifters' release to fail to make any impression on either the rhythm and blues or pop charts since "Yodee Yakee" in 1957.

The next new material was cut on June 28, 1962, when they recorded another pair of Goffin/King songs—"Another Night with the Boys" and the immortal "Up on the Roof." The latter was a first for the Drifters because there were undertones of social commentary which hinted that perhaps all was not as happy as popular song would lead one to believe. For once, the female quartet seemed to be on leave, and the group indulged in some harmony both on "Up on the Roof" and the bluesy flip-side. They also laid down "I Feel Good All Over," which like "What to Do" seemed to belong to an earlier time—and probably surprised a lot of their detractors.

"Up on the Roof" took the Drifters high into the American Top 10 (it reached fifth position in 1963), although once again in Britain its chart status was affected by poor cover versions. It did appear on some hit listings, but Kenny Lynch scored the bigger hit with his truly abysmal attempt (Lynch later became some sort of television comedian, but the funniest thing he probably ever did was to try singing "Up on the Roof").

In case anyone had become complacent and thought the Drifters were now a stable unit, Dock Green left at the end of 1962. George Treadwell brought in a member of the Cleftones (one of his other groups), Gene Pearson. Pearson's resume went back to 1953, when as a member of the Embers he wrote "Paradise Hill," which they recorded on Herald. He next turned up in a 1955 line-up of the Rivileers, for whom he wrote the classic "A Thousand Stars" (the Rivileers had the song out on Baton, but Kathy Young and the Innocents were the ones to have a major success with it in 1961 on Instant). After the Rivileers, he joined the Cleftones around 1958 and was with the group when they recorded their 1961 hits "Heart and Soul," "For Sentimental Reasons," and "Glory of Love." He sang second tenor on these records and also wrote the b-sides. On joining the Drifters, Pearson, along with Charlie Thomas and Tommy Evans, dubbed the backing vocals to "Another Night with the Boys" (he is thus on the record but was not at the original session).

On January 22, 1963, while on their way to a Drifters' session, Leiber and Stoller met Phil Spector just off Broadway. Since Spector was carrying his guitar, they invited their former apprentice to come along. When the Drifters recorded "On Broadway" (written by Leiber and Stoller and another Aldon Music duo, Cynthia Weil and Barry Mann), Spector supplied the bluesy guitar solo—he would have been familiar with the song for he had recorded it the year before with the Crystals and had cut the number for his own Philles Records, which he had set up in Los Angeles with Lester Sill.

Following this session, Tommy Evans decided he had drifted long enough and bade the group farewell. He teamed up with Dock Green in a group called the Drapers—the other members were the familiar Carnation Charlie Hughes and Johnny Moore. The Drapers had one record out on the Gee label, "(I Know) Your Love has Gone Away"/"You Got to Look Up" (Gee 1081), and their resemblance to the Drifters was more than a coincidence. The Dock Green/Tommy Evans Drapers should not be confused with another group of the same name who were active about the same time—that group was, in fact, the Duvals (they recorded "Best Love"/"One More Time" on Vest 831). One other point of confusion should be cleared up: the Drapers' Gee record has been said to feature Jesse Facing, Richard Lewis, Wilbur Paul, Dock Green, and William Bailey—this is, of course, a Five Crowns' lineup from 1955, and how they came to be mentioned as the Drapers is rather a mystery. Dock Green also sang with Alexander Graves's Moonglows, but never recorded with them on Lana. Even though both Green and Evans were no longer in the Drifters, they continued overdubbing with them until "At the Club" in 1964, as a favor to George Treadwell (Johnny Moore disputes this).

Johnny Terry, formerly of the Famous Flames, the Knickerbockers (not the hit-making "Lies" group), and possibly

96

the Dominoes (there is some doubt about this), claimed membership in a group known as the Links. In any case, he joined the Drifters in early 1963, just in time to see "On Broadway" peak at number nine.

The next personnel change was something of a surprise —nobody left the group. Instead, Johnny Moore returned to bring the Drifters back to a quintet for the first time since the Ben E. King line-up.

After his discharge from the army in 1959, Moore had tried to launch a solo career. He recorded as Johnny Darrow to avoid being confused with other Johnny Moores (principally, the blues man who led the Three Blazes—Moore puts it this way: "Because the old Johnny Moore of the Blazes was still alive, I couldn't use my real name. One day I was reading an article about Clarence Darrow, the lawyer, in *Ebony*, and it just struck me that Johnny Darrow sounded good."). Johnny Moore "Darrow" had releases on both Sue and Melic. His best were the Sonny Boy Williamson "Don't Start Me to Talking" and "Spider Walk" on Sue, but neither set the world on fire. The Drapers had been only a one-off, however (all the members stayed in the business, though—Charlie Hughes was reported performing under the name "Sir Charles" as late as 1974), and when Treadwell offered Moore a chance to rejoin the Drifters, he was back. Treadwell may have been hedging his bets. Atlantic had issued a solo record by Rudy Lewis ("Hear What I Say"/"When the World Begins," which had cast him in the then popular mold of Jackie Wilson) that had failed to take off. Treadwell may have feared Lewis would follow in the footsteps of Ben E. King. His fear proved groundless, though, for Lewis and Moore got on so well that Lewis abandoned any plans he may have had for a solo career.

Moore's first session back with the Drifters took place on April 12, 1963. Moore and Lewis alternated leads; the latter led on "Only in America" and "Rat Race," Moore on "If You Don't Come Back" and "I'll Take You Home."

The Leiber and Stoller "Only in America," having been deemed too ironic for a black group because it extolled the virtues of America, was left unissued; the socially aware "Rat

THE DRIFTERS (1963)
(The night Johnny Moore returned.)
(L. to r.): Billy Davis (guitar), Gene Pearson, Johnny Terry,
Rudy Lewis, Charlie Thomas, Johnny Moore.
(Photo from the collection of Marv Goldberg)

JOHNNY MOORE AS A SOLO ACT "JOHNNY DARROW" (1959)
(Photo from the collection of Marv Goldberg)

Race" was chosen as the next release. It's chart placing of number seventy-three did neither the song nor the performance justice, but the jazz-like arrangement made it seem uncommercial. Johnny Moore's "If You Don't Come Back" on the b-side picked up enough action on its own to just miss the Top 100 (it reached 101). The Drifters' white copyist Jay and the Americans hit big with "Only in America" (rubbing salt into the wounds), but the Drifters' next release, the light "I'll Take You Home," restored them to the Top Thirty in October.

The Drifters reached their peak of popularity in America in 1963 (they received the accolade of recording commercials for Rheingold Beer and Coca Cola, an honor [?] reserved for only commercially "hot" artists), but were dealt a blow in the fall when Leiber and Stoller decided to leave Atlantic. The producers wanted another shot at running their own company and, along with veteran New York record man George Goldner, left to set up the Red Bird label. Their time with the Drifters is often looked upon with mixed emotions. Although their productions were highly creative, their concentration on lead vocalists to the exclusion of group harmony disturbed many vocal group fans, many of whom found the use of female vocalists (who on occasion included the classically trained Miriam Workman and Lil Clark) grating. But no one can dispute the fact that Leiber and Stoller produced many classic records, for their credits include some of the greatest recordings made at a time when American music was bland in the extreme: "There Goes My Baby," "Dance with Me," "Save the Last Dance for Me," "This Magic Moment," "Up on the Roof," "On Broadway," and "When My Little Girl Is Smiling." The main criticism leveled at them is that they reduced the Drifters to the playthings of writers and producers, and allowed the material to descend into formula. The Drifters' sound remained the same, and the public was probably unaware of the changes since what they heard was unaltered by the comings and goings.

Ertegun and Wexler already had a successor in mind, for they had been watching the progress of a thirty-four-year-old New Yorker named Bert Berns.

Berns had begun his career as a record salesman, and

had also worked as a music copyist and session pianist. In 1960, he started writing songs with Wes Farrell, Jerry Ragavoy, and Phil Medley; his credits included "Twist and Shout" (originally recorded on Atlantic by the Topnotes in 1960), "Cry to Me," and "Everybody Needs Somebody to Love" (both by Solomon Burke on Atlantic). He had run his own publishing company (Webb IV), operated a record label called Keetch, and freelanced in production work for Atlantic, United Artists, Cameo, and Jubilee. He had produced hits for the Jarmels ("A Little Bit of Soap"), Solomon Burke, and Barbara Lewis; but possibly his greatest was the seminal soul hit "Cry Baby" by Garnett Mimms and the Enchanters. Impressive credentials indeed! He had also recorded as Russell Byrd on Wand ("Little Bug"/"Nights of Mexico," Wand 121). His great talent was an ability to extract soulful performances from the artists he worked with, as the exemplary Mimms track suggests.

His first encounter with the Drifters came on August 22, 1963, when he produced the very emotional "In the Land of Make Believe" and "Didn't It." Three more tracks were recorded on December 11: "Beautiful Music," "One Way Love," and the standard "Vaya Con Dios." There was still a female quartet, but its role was diminished, especially on the first three songs where Berns seems to have allowed the group to assert itself.

Spearheaded by disk jockeys Murray the K and Dick Clark, the big package shows had made something of a comeback in 1963. Dick Clark presented his holiday revue at the Brooklyn Fox, where the Drifters joined Jay and the Americans, Gene Pitney, the Miracles, the Dovells, Ben E. King, the Shirelles, the Chiffons, Randy and the Rainbows, the Angels, Jan and Dean, the Tymes, and the Ronettes—when the package shows came back, they came back with a vengeance! The Drifters ran through four of their hits and finished with a frantic "There Goes My Baby," performed in a style more in keeping with its original format. This was featured on a subsequent live album on KFM Records (KFM 101).

January 1964 saw the release of "Vaya Con Dios," which had been given a gospel reading by Rudy Lewis, heavily sup-

100

ported by female vocalists. The record reached number forty-three. Little did the Drifters know that the significance of the sentiments would soon be brought home in the cruelest possible way.

In the spring of 1964, Jerry Wexler, who was still technically the executive producer (a title he rarely used), found a song at Ed Burton's publishers called "Under the Boardwalk." It had been written by Kenny Young and Artie Resnick, and Wexler felt it was perfect for the Drifters. But when he played a demo for Bert Berns and the group, no one thought much of it.

Flexing the muscle his status gave him, he insisted they record it; the date was set for May 20.

The day proved disastrous, for when members of the Drifters entourage called to collect Rudy Lewis, they found him dead. Although the rock press hinted that his death was connected with drug abuse, no evidence was found to substantiate this claim. The official cause of death was given as asphyxiation.

Johnny Moore was unaware of the tragedy, and only learned of what had happened when he bumped into Sylvia Robinson, of Mickey and Sylvia fame. She had heard on the radio that the Drifters' lead vocalist had died and initially thought it was Johnny Moore. Thus, on meeting Johnny she greeted him with "Thank God, it's not you" (or words to that effect), before telling him of Rudy's death. Johnny attributes Lewis's demise to his habit of eating large meals late at night, and believes Lewis choked after regurgitating one such meal in his sleep, cutting off his breathing.

Since union musicians were involved, Atlantic had to apply for approval to postpone the session. They were granted a twenty-four-hour extension.

The fact that Rudy Lewis had bowed out with "Vaya Con Dios" continued a rather macabre tradition in rhythm and blues, and rock and roll. Several artists had recorded prophetic titles as their swan songs: Chuck Willis died in 1958 shortly after recording "What Am I Living For"/"Hang Up My Rock and Roll Shoes"; when Buddy Holly died in February 1959, his

101

current release was "It Doesn't Matter Any More"; Eddie Cochran recorded "Three Steps to Heaven" at his last recording session in January 1960 before his death in April.

The Drifters regrouped the next day (May 21) and cut "Under the Boardwalk." What was basically a happy song celebrating summer was transformed into a wistful classic; Johnny Moore's vocal carried a sad and bitter edge to it which made nonsense of the song's sentiments. (The arranger, incidentally, was Englishman Mike Leander, who would surface in the U.K. in 1972 as the man behind the truly amazing Gary Glitter.)

With not a female quartet in sight, Charlie Thomas sang his heart out on "I Don't Want to Go on without You," which was recorded as a sorrowful tribute to Rudy Lewis. The recording was eerie because Thomas, whose vocals had always resembled Lewis's, sounded exactly like the departed Drifter. They finished the session with two versions of Berns's up-tempo "He's Just a Playboy," which somehow seemed out of place on such a traumatic occasion.

The up-tempo "One Way Love," which had come out in April, stalled at number fifty-six in June. But it was another Drifters' track that endeared itself to the new British rock bands—Cliff Bennett and the Rebel Rousers scored a U.K. hit with it, as they did with "I'll Take You Home"; but neither was really comparable to the original (Bennett's band was not really new; they had been treading the boards since 1959).

"Under the Boardwalk" catapulted the Drifters back into the American Top 10 in August (in Britain it managed only number thirty-five). Coupled with Berns and Wexler's poignant "I Don't Want to Go on without You," it remains one of their greatest releases to this day.

1964 was a year of turmoil on the American music scene. New York, which had been the center of the record industry, suddenly found its position challenged by London, Detroit, Memphis, and Los Angeles. The British invasion, spearheaded by the Beatles, who in April 1964 had the top five singles in the American Top 100, had turned the industry upside down; and much of the bland nonsense that had been passing for rock and

102

roll was cast aside. The Beatles and those who followed from Britain brought back much of the guts missing from American rock—and destroyed the careers of many teen idols in the process. On top of this, American labels based in Memphis (Stax) and Detroit (Motown) were beginning to flood the rhythm and blues market with a funkier sound.

The Drifters seemed to be weathering the storm well, for "Under the Boardwalk" had given them their biggest hit in years. But the new rhythm and blues which had been simmering for several years had finally boiled over and now threatened the older stars.

THE DRIFTERS (1963-1964)
(L. to r.): Gene Pearson, Johnny Terry,
Johnny Moore, Charlie Thomas, Rudy Lewis.

CHAPTER 10

The Times They Are A'Changing

During 1964 the popular music charts were dominated by the new white rock and roll groups, most of whom were imported from Britain, and the rhythm and blues of black America. Alongside the Beatles, the Rolling Stones, and Gerry and the Pacemakers nestled a seemingly endless stream of new black talent—from the Temptations to the Four Tops, Stevie Wonder to the Miracles, all of whom recorded for the Detroit-based Tamla-Motown operation. From the "new wave" rhythm and blues came the Impressions, Gene Chandler, and Major Lance; the Memphis-based Stax label scored via Otis Redding, Eddie Floyd, and Carla Thomas.

In one sense the market had returned to the pre-rock days of white and black music, but of course it was not the same. Black music was no longer restricted to a single audience, and rock and roll and rhythm and blues continued to interchange ideas because many of the white rockers, particularly the British ones, clearly showed black influences.

As has been said, this upheaval caused the collapse of many careers, but with "Under the Boardwalk" riding high, the Drifters seemed in no danger of falling out of favor. Moreover, the association with Bert Berns looked promising, for Berns was allowing them to perform in a style more natural to them than Leiber and Stoller had. Berns produced the follow-up to "Boardwalk" on August 4, 1964. This was another Young-Resnick song called "Sand in My Shoes" and very much in the same mold. Despite the similarity, Berns and the Drifters again created a classic of its kind; the sales, though, were disappointing and the record reached only number thirty-three. The flip-side, "He's Just a Playboy," recorded May 21, saw some action, placing 115 in the Top 150.

105

The Drifters appeared at the Up Town Theater in Philadelphia on July 24, alongside a few of the new rhythm and blues performers. Sharing the stage with them that night were Patty and the Emblems ("Mixed up Shook up Girl"), Barbara Lynn (who had hits with "You'll Lose a Good Thing" and "We Got a Good Thing Goin'"), Wilson Pickett, Patti La Belle and the Blue Bells, and the Vibrations (an older act who in a previous incarnation as the Jayhawks had had a 1956 hit with "Stranded in the Jungle").

Because of the number of acts, the Drifters were restricted to five songs: "Some Kind of Wonderful," "Ruby Baby," "Under the Boardwalk," "On Broadway," and "There Goes My Baby." A subsequent live album which featured part of their act would prove that their popularity had not diminished even when faced with the so-called hipper rising stars.

Taking advantage of this popularity, Lover Patterson put together a competing group in 1964 which featured Dock Green, Tommy Evans, and two of his Duvals (identified only as "Charly" on lead tenor and "Arnold" on baritone) and sent them on a tour of the Southern states. Nothing more was heard of them until 1966 when Green and Evans, along with Wilbur Paul and a tenor recalled only as "Snugs," recorded as the Floaters (no connection with the "Float On" group) on the B&B label. Green and Evans were both in Exciting Changes, alongside Hughie Beauregard and Leo Wright, in 1971. Tommy Evans turned up in the Masters (the other members were Freddie Sawyer, Rudy Stewart, Butch Ellis, Caesar Smith, and Joe Williams) and appeared with the Ravens at rock and roll revival shows in 1974. When last heard of, he intended to record with the members of that group.

The Atlantic Drifters, meanwhile, recorded the rather maudlin "Spanish Lace" with Bert Berns on October 20, and returned to the studios two days later to record a Christmas record which featured the old standard "The Christmas Song" and "I Remember Christmas." November saw the release of the Mann-Weil "Saturday Night at the Movies," which had been cut the previous August. By December 19, it had reached number eighteen but sadly proved to be the Drifters' last record to make an appearance in the American Top 20. The Christmas record failed to emulate "White Christmas" and was lost in the mass of seasonal releases.

The package tours started to bring them into contact with the new British groups—and at times there seems to have been some tensions. Many of these groups favored a hairstyle longer than what had been considered the norm, which made the Drifters doubt the virility of some of them. They ran into problems with the Nashville Teens, for example, who were in America to promote "Tobacco Road." Johnny Terry, who appeared to equate long hair with homosexuality, was especially unhappy, as the Teens' hairstyles were definitely longer than what he considered "normal." The situation was quickly resolved, however, as soon as Terry discovered that the British group were strictly heterosexual; to make amends for his attitude, he supplied them with a song he had co-written with Billy Davis, "Devil in Law."

George Treadwell, meanwhile, was making plans that would take the Drifters away from the package show circuit. He had taken a long look at the lounges and supper clubs of Las Vegas and had concluded that the real money lay there, and that the long-term future of the group would be more secure if they could break into that scene. Inasmuch as he knew the audiences who frequented such places would either be unfamiliar with the group or regard them merely as a teen attraction, he decided the Drifters would have to make an adult-oriented album.

The project got underway on October 23, 1964, when Atlantic laid down the backing tracks. But when the Drifters were brought in to add their vocals on November 10, unexpected problems arose. Unfamiliar with this so-called standard material, Charile Thomas, Gene Pearson, and Johnny Terry found it rather difficult to record their parts. Their attempts, in fact, were so poor that Atlantic engineers Tom Dowd and Arif Mardin had to dub backing vocals behind Johnny Moore's lead in order to salvage the tracks—one even proved beyond redemption. The story emanated from Atlantic Records; but when put to Johnny Moore, he vehemently denied it. According

107

to Johnny, the only personnel on the album are himself, Charlie Thomas, Gene Pearson, and Johnny Terry. Audio evidence fails to confirm or refute either version for only Moore is to the forefront, and the backing vocals are lost somewhere in the mix.

Two days later they were back on safer ground, recording Goffin and King's "At the Club." "In the Park," the other track laid down that day, was deemed unsuitable for release and was shelved.

Christmas once again found them at the Brooklyn Fox—this time joining Murray the K, old friends Dionne Warwick and Ben E. King, the Blue Bells, the Shangri-las, the Vibrations, Dick and Dee Dee, and Chuck Jackson. Treadwell no doubt hoped this would be one of the last times they would perform in this sort of package show.

"At the Club" had no suitable flip-side, so the Drifters took time off from the Fox to record "Answer the Phone" on New Year's Eve. The record features an interesting and, one must assume, unintended Ben E. King-Johnny Moore duet. Berns, perhaps to save time, used the backing track of the old King recording "He Will Break Your Heart"; the engineer apparently did not rub King completely off the track and at some points he can be heard in the background.

As "At the Club" climbed into the Top Fifty at the end of February 1965, the Drifters were getting ready for their first tour of Great Britain. Although they had only had two Top 20 hits in the U.K., they were highly regarded by rhythm and blues fans as well as members of the youth cult who called themselves Mods. They arrived in Britain in the middle of March and were a huge success. Some older fans found their performances mechanical, but most saw them for what they were—rhythm and blues legends who had sold over fifteen million records. They even managed two television appearances. On the Mod-dominated "Ready Steady Go," Charlie Thomas for some strange reason lipsynced to Ben E. King's "Lonely Winds," but they also sang "At the Club." They were featured on "Thank Your Lucky Stars" (a plug show for new releases) where they mimed "At the Club"—which no doubt helped it

THE DRIFTERS' FIRST TRIP TO ENGLAND (1965)
(L. to r.): George Treadwell, Charlie Thomas, Gene Pearson,
Johnny Moore, and Johnny Terry.

enter the U.K. Top 40. The press showed enough interest to publish several interviews, but all too soon they were gone.

Just before they left America, the Drifters cut the Mann-Weil "Looking through the Eyes of Love" and "Come over to My Place," and the Mort Shuman "Follow Me." The other songs recorded that day came from untried writers: Bishop-Gamble's "Chains of Love," Penn-Greene's "Far from the Maddening Crowd," and Kelly-Marcus's "The Outside World." Although some of these names would appear on later hit songs, they were new to the Drifters at the time. The Mann-Weil "Come on over to My Place" proved to be the most commercial of the recordings, though when released, it stalled at number sixty. Charlie Thomas's flip-side, "Chains of Love," split the sales, making it to the Top 100 (number ninety). Mann/Weil's "Looking through the Eyes Of Love," one of the strongest from the session, was left on the shelf.

Bert Berns had formed the Bang record label in 1964 with Ahmet and Nesuhi Ertegun and Gerald Wexler (the same Jerry Wexler of Atlantic Records, the first letter of whose forename, as in the case of the other partners, contributed to the makeup of the Bang label name), and saw it take off in 1965 with the McCoys' smash hit "Hang on Sloopy," an adaptation of "My Girl Sloopy," which had been recorded by the Vibrations for Atlantic. (The McCoys came from Indiana, and actually owed their big break to the Drifters. After graduating from the usual sock-hops and the college dance circuit, they managed to get bookings supporting the likes of Chuck Berry, the Four Seasons, and the Drifters. It was while supporting Johnny Moore and company that Bert Berns spotted them. As a tribute to the Drifters, the McCoys later cut "Sweets for My Sweet.") Berns had also been back and forth to London, where he had worked with Lulu and the Luvvers on his own "Here Comes the Night" (which he would later record with Them). Berns's trips to the U.K. led to an early involvement with Van Morrison when he went solo in 1967; in fact, Morrison's first recordings were cut for Bang, many featuring the Latin rhythms of the Drifters. All this combined with his other interests obviously put a strain on his ability to produce the Drifters, but he somehow managed to continue.

The so-called adult album finally appeared under the title *The Good Life with the Drifters*, but the response George Treadwell had hoped for failed to materialize. The album had such standards as the title track (made famous by Tony Bennett), "Tonight" (the love song from "West Side Story"), "I Wish You Love," and "More." "San Francisco" (the one track the engineers had not been able to salvage) was replaced with "Saturday Night at the Movies," even though this was completely out of place. The version of "Temptation" came from the 1959 master, with Johnny Moore dubbed on in the place of Ben E. King. Despite Moore's valiant efforts to inject some life, the whole project, in truth, seemed like a throwback to the days of Tin Pan Alley. The album crawled to number 123 in the album charts (it went as high as 103 in some listings) and failed to attract the adult cabaret audiences.

George Treadwell was not the only manager of a black rhythm and blues group who saw the lucrative supper clubs as the future. Berry Gordy, the founder and head of Tamla-Motown, also thought his acts would have to move into this market to sustain their careers, and so groomed the Four Tops, the Temptations, and the Supremes from early on to play places such as the Copa Cabana. All Gordy's groups made the transition; the Drifters did not. Why? The comings and goings within the group may have made it more difficult for audiences to identify with them. But the Drifters stayed truer to the close harmony of gospel and rhythm and blues, and this made it more difficult for them than for the Detroit-based groups to perform the required standards.

The failure of *The Good Life* was a blow, and the next release, "Follow Me," fell like a ton of bricks. The song was strong enough, but managed only a fleeting chart entry (number ninety-one) in July. Gene Pitney had in the meantime scored a huge hit with his version of the rejected "Looking through the Eyes of Love." The Drifters had also missed out on one of the biggest hits of early 1965 when Petula Clark recorded "Down Town," which the British writer Tony Hatch had written with the Drifters in mind.

"I'll Take You Where the Music's Playing," from the husband and wife team of Jeff Barry and Ellie Greenwich, which the Drifters recorded on June 30, took them somewhat higher in the charts; but even this stalled at number fifty-one. (Barry had recorded as a solo act on RCA and with his wife had formed the Raindrops, who had hits with "What a Guy" and "The Kind of Boy You Can't Forget." They had also worked as writers and performers with Leiber and Stoller's Red Bird label; Greenwich's "You Don't Know" was revered by collectors.)

The number fifty-one placing of "I'll Take You Where the Music's Playing" was a major success compared with the fate that befell the follow-up, "Nylon Stockings," which had been recorded at the same session. Coupled with another track from the session, "We Gotta Sing," it sank without a trace when issued in November—Atlantic U.K. flipped the record, to no avail.

At the end of 1965, the Drifters' career seemed to be floundering. The touring schedule remained full, but on occasion they were forced to accept dates they would have rejected in the past. This was probably inevitable after so many years as the leader of the pack. But Atlantic was not much help. As the turmoil in the record industry continued, with new trends such as folk-rock constantly appearing and disappearing, Atlantic, in common with other companies, had been seeking out and recording new teen messiahs wherever and whenever they could. Their roster included their answer to the Beatles, the Young Rascals, and Sonny and Cher, whom Atlantic had promoted heavily during the summer. This pair had massive hits with "I Got You Babe" and "But Your Mine," and caused a sensation with their far-out dress. (Sonny Bono was in fact a thirty-year-old teenager from Detroit, who had worked with the classic rock and roll label Specialty in the fifties.) The promotional department spent so much time on these new acts that some of Atlantic's established stars were neglected.

Possibly an omen, the Drifters recorded old crooner Dean Martin's "Memories Are Made of This" on January 27, 1966. Radically rearranged by Bert Berns, the record shot to number forty-eight in the charts when issued with the calypso-ish "My Islands in the Sun" (recorded on February 8). This was their best showing since "At the Club," fourteen months earlier.

Bert Berns's days as producer were numbered, however, for his other commitments finally caught up with him. A song he had written for the January 27 session, "Up in the Streets of Harlem," failed to make the Top 100 when issued in May, even though it had been one of their strongest records for some time. He produced the group only one more time, when he recorded the unissued "Takes a Good Woman" and his own composition "Aretha" on July 26.

And so Bert Berns was gone. During the two years he worked with the Drifters, he restored much of their credibility as a group by allowing them more free rein to display their talents. Only the ill-starred *Good Life* marred an otherwise excellent and productive association with the Drifters. The chance to work together again disappeared forever on New Years Eve 1967 when Berns died of a heart attack at age thirty-eight.

The departure of Bert Berns in July 1966 heralded a frantic round of changes within the Drifters.

The first to go was Johnny Terry, who left after a couple of months to get married. He was replaced initially by Dan Danbridge, who left within weeks, his place taken by William Brent (the same William Brent who had been in the 1954 Hornets with Johnny Moore; Moore, in fact, went to Cleveland to recruit him). Then, Gene Pearson left. He had been unhappy with his role as a dancer on stage and also with the places the group was playing—he felt many of the engagements were beneath them (he seems to have been so disillusioned that he left the music business altogether and took up manual labor for five years, returning only in the early seventies when he joined the Cleftones at oldies shows).

George Treadwell recruited Rick Sheppard, who had recorded as a solo artist on the Capitol and Shout (Bert Berns's) labels, in time for the recording session held on October 12, 1966. The Drifters were now Johnny Moore, Charlie Thomas,

William Brent, and Rick Sheppard. The producer was Bob Gallo, assisted by studio engineer Tom Dowd; the result was the Motown-ish "Baby What I Need"—the other track recorded, "My Baby Is Gone," was unissued. On its release the following March, "Baby What I Mean," coupled with the excellent "Aretha," did quite well in comparison to some of the recent efforts, making a showing at number sixty-two in *Billboard* and even managing a forty-ninth place in the U.K. charts. But this was the last good news for a while.

More changes. William Brent's career as a Drifter proved non-pensionable and he was quickly followed by Bill Fredericks (formerly of the Packards, who had some success with "Ding Dong"), who was in place when Ronny Savoy supplied them with "Ain't It the Truth" and "Up Jumped the Devil." Savoy produced these tracks in May 1967—seven months after the last session. Atlantic had issued nothing since "Baby What I Mean," and when they finally got around to putting out the Savoy tracks in July 1967, the record went unnoticed; it even failed to obtain a British release.

To complicate matters further, Dean Barlow (former lead of the Crickets—*not* the Buddy Holly group) has stated that, in 1967, Treadwell formed a group with Barlow and Joe Duncan (formerly of the Vocaleers) as primary members. Treadwell had them rehearse songs in the Drifters' vein, giving rise to the possibility that George intended to create an entirely "new" Drifters even as the lineups shifted and crumbled.

With the Drifters' fortunes sinking, the news of the death of long-time manager George Treadwell came as a doubly hard blow. Since his importance to the Drifters cannot be understated, we should pause for a moment to sum up the career of this remarkable man.

Born George McKinley Treadwell in New Rochelle, New York, on the December 21, 1919, he came to prominence as a jazz trumpeter in the early forties when he witnessed the birth of modern jazz at Monroe's Up Town in New York City. His playing took him into the bands of Benny Carter, Ace Harris, and Tiny Bradshaw; and between 1943 and 1946 he recorded with Cootie Williams's band. While a member of J.C. Heard's

DRIFTER'S LINE-UP FOLLOWING GEORGE TREADWELL'S DEATH (MID 1967)
(L. to r.): Bill Fredericks, Rick Sheppard, Johnny Moore,
Charlie Thomas and Abdul Samad (Billy Davis).

group in 1946, he met and recorded with Sarah Vaughan, and was featured on records by Dicky Wells and Ethel Waters and prominently featured on J.C. Heard's recording of the "Walk." He gave up playing to manage Sarah Vaughan (to whom he was briefly married—he continued to manage her after their subsequent divorce). Treadwell's talent agency had been set up in May 1953, and during the fifties he managed such notables as Sammy Davis, Jr., and Billie Holiday. Also, in the early fifties, he took on Atlantic's Ruth Brown and then the Drifters—the shrewdest move he would make.

His association with the Drifters has provoked both criticism and controversy through the years when he has been cast as a demon in his dealings with members such as Bill Pinckney and Ben E. King. Both, however, returned to work for him when he asked them, which would seem to suggest that he could not have been the ogre he has been portrayed as being. Indeed, Dock Green and Tommy Evans also maintained contact with the Drifters after leaving, strictly as a favor to Treadwell. There is no doubt, however, that it was Treadwell's foresight that kept the Drifters popular for as long as they were, for it was Treadwell who took them in the direction which saw them turn doo-wop into solid gold.

His funeral was attended by the Atlantic hierarchy and was given an especially poignant touch when the Drifters sang "Vaya Con Dios." On his death, the management of the group passed to his widow Faye (they had met in 1954 and married in 1957; they had one child, a daughter Tina, who was born in 1958).

During 1966 and 1967, Atlantic Records enjoyed an unprecedented success to which the Drifters contributed next to nothing. The new rock and roll bands Iron Butterfly, Buffalo Springfield, and the Rascals (no longer young) ruled the roost. In the rhythm and blues field, the label scored hits with Wilson Pickett and Otis Redding (licensed from Stax), while Jerry Wexler produced the new queen of soul, Aretha Franklin.

The Drifters seemed to have outlived their time, overtaken by the funkie rhythms coming from Memphis (the deep

AT A PARTY GIVEN BY THE TREADWELLS FOR SAMMY DAVIS, JR.
Top (l. to r.): Sammy Davis, Jr., his wife Mai Britt, and Faye Treadwell;
Inset (l. to r): Ben Wright, George Treadwell, Alan Lomax.

BILLIE HOLIDAY WITH FAYE TREADWELL
In the year before her death, George Treadwell managed Billie Holiday (left),
shown here enjoying a drink with Faye Treadwell just before leaving for London.

soul of Percy Sledge and O.V. Wright) and the mixture of uptown hipness and psychedelic soul coming from Motown. Where they had once led, they now followed. And Atlantic seemed blasé about their fate. To make matters even worse, Charlie Thomas, the sole survivor of the old Crowns and a Drifter for nine years, left in August 1967. (He set up a cab company in New York but returned to the music business in 1971.)

Charles Baskerville, who had been with Shep and the Limelites (of "Daddy's Home" fame), came in for a few months but was not present when Johnny Moore, Rick Sheppard, and Bill Fredericks recorded "I Dig Your Act," "Still Burning in My Heart," "I Need You Now," and "Country to the City," with Lou Courtney and Bob Bateman on November 8, 1967. Atlantic failed to issue "I Dig Your Act," and the O'Jays covered the song (this group from Canton, Ohio, was heavily influenced by the Drifters and had a small hit with the song before going on to score a series of international successes). "Country to the City" was also rejected, although it did appear on the same 1972 British compilation as "She Never Talked to Me That Way" (again, both the composition and performance were mistakenly credited to the lineup of the time). In fact, it was probably the best recording in many years for overdubbing made the Drifters' trio sound like a larger group. During 1968, Atlantic released only "Still Burning in My Heart"/"I Need You Now," which rose to what was then for the Drifters the dizzy heights of 112 on the *Billboard* charts.

The group again became a quartet in December 1967 when Milton Turner, who had been with the Packards alongside Bill Fredericks, joined. They lost Abdul Samad (Billy Davis) about the same time, his guitar stool passing to Butch Mann, who had played with the Chiffons ("Tonight's the Night" on Big Deal, which was number seventy-six in 1960) and Ruby and the Romantics (best remembered for "Our Day Will Come").

Atlantic did not bother to record them again until March 10, 1969, when Gary Sherman produced them on "You and Me Together Forever," "Your Best Friend," and a secular version of the old gospel song "Steal Away." Probably sensing that the first would hardly be appropriate given the Drifters turbulent history, Atlantic went with "Your Best Friend"/"Steal Away," but the record proved a non-event chartwise when released in April 1969.

In late 1969, Milton Turner stole away, making way for the introduction of yet another Charlie Thomas—he was known to the former Drifter of the same name since they both came from Virginia. To avoid confusion, the new Charlie became Don Thomas. (He had been with the Mystics—not the "Hushabye" group—on King Records; the Mystics later changed their name to the Dealers. Thomas may be the same Don Thomas who put out a couple of soul records around the end of the sixties.)

The Drifters were now at their lowest ebb since June 1958, but Atlantic decided to try one more time, on February 24, 1970. The session produced Bill Fredericks singing "You Got to Pay Your Dues" and Johnny Moore leading on "Black Silk." The record failed to register, but the top-side did become a club favorite both in America and Britain, where demand caused it to be belatedly released in 1976 (its popularity resulted in an American bootleg pressing in the late seventies).

Faced with such apathy, the Drifters more or less broke up in March 1970. At first, Johnny Moore, Rick Sheppard, and Don Thomas wanted to continue, but nothing came of this. Rick Sheppard traded in his rock and roll shoes for those of a New York cop, but Johnny Moore and Bill Fredericks eventually got together with Faye Treadwell and thus kept the name going in some form.

During 1970, Tony Orlando, a twenty-six-year-old New Yorker who had at one time recorded demos for the Drifters, was featured with Joyce Vincent Wilson and Telma Hopkins in a group called Dawn. This combination had two major hits in 1970—"Candida" and "Knock Three Times," which was number one in January 1971—and both owed much to the Drifters' style. (Tony Orlando and company went on to record "Vaya Con Dios" and "Sweets for My Sweet.") This prompted Atlantic to take Moore and Fredericks into a Chicago studio in January 1971, where with two session vocalists (one of whom was Ronald Quinn) they recorded four tracks: "A Rose by Any Other

Name," "Be My Lady," "Guess Who" (the old Jesse Belvin number), and "I Depend on You." The American public was unmoved, however, by the Dawn-like "A Rose by Any Other Name" (backed with "Be My Lady")—which was issued in March 1971; and the other tracks remained unissued.

The record marked the end of an association which had lasted nearly eighteen years, during which the group produced some of the greatest records in rhythm and blues history. Before concluding this section, we should say that the rumors the Drifters provided vocal background to records by Ruth Brown, Ivory Joe Hunter, and Billy Storm appear to be untrue, for there is no evidence of this in the Atlantic files.

In 1972, Faye Treadwell brought the Drifters—now Johnny Moore, Bill Fredericks, Butch Leake (a friend of Fredericks who had been singing in New York bars), and Grant Kitchings (formerly of the Ravens, Inkspots, and Kingtoppers)—to Great Britain. They arrived just as Atlantic U.K. began re-releasing some of the old sixties records, and so embarked on a whole new phase in the ongoing saga.

THE DRIFTERS, INC., v. THOMAS
—Plaintiffs, the Drifters, Inc., motion
preliminary injunction to re-
dants from using the name
in connection with
cal group is
use of
er
ng
his
ab-
an
nter-
dants
intiff's
ct, the
tly in-
nts who
ion and
be pred-
of certain
by two of
ein. There
writings allege...
the named defendant
are serious questions raised respecting
the validity of the purported contracts and whether or not plaintiff has
fully complied with the contract terms
and conditions. Furthermore, there is
some questions assuming these contracts are to be valid, if the restraints
imposed by paragraph seven thereof
are reasonable or should be enforced
considering the circumstances of this
action or the fact that this relief is
sought some twelve years after the
making of his alleged agreements.

Mars...
Drifters Suit

■ NEW YORK — A federal judge
refused last month to enjoin
Larry Marshak, manager of the
Drifters, from informing club and
theater owners that the group he
manages is the only group
licensed to use the name "Drifters," and from pursuing further
legal action against a group of
the same name led by original
Drifter Dock Green.

Decision

In a decision d...
19, 1979 ...

Dock Green
...homas Drifters and tried
own Drifters. (IF THINGS WE-
SSED UP ENOUGH ALREADY!)
...er, booking agent for the Charlie
...o, informed us that Dock Green
...d with a court order to discon-
...g as the "Drifters". The Char-
...p has a patented trademark
A copy of those papers filed

Clampdown on 'fake' Drifters

DERBY-based venue The Top Hat In Spennymore has agreed to
withdraw its booking this month for a group billed as The Great
Sound of the Original Drifters, following complaints from interna-
tional manager Faye Treadwell, who holds the rights to the hit group's name, threatened legal
action if the rival band appeared as scheduled on May 26.

Treadwell, who holds the rights to the hit group's name, threatened legal
action if the rival band appeared as scheduled on May 26.
The club has now agreed to book Treadwell's Drifters instead for a later
date in June.

Treadwell told The Stage her legal representatives would take immediate
action against any outfit which attempts to use the Drifters' name in future.

"If they continue then we will go to court over this if necessary," she
warned.

Her solicitor Omek Marks said that the manager had already established
her sole right to the Drifters' name in a number of court cases in the United
States and in 1988 in Britain.

"There are various groups around the UK who are being passed off as our
client's group, the most recent of which has come to our client's knowledge
was to appear at the Top Hat Club," said Marks.

"Following contact from our client and from this firm and pointing out our
client's sole right to use the name The Drifters in the entertainment field, that
venue has agreed to withdraw that group from appearing."

Nº 1081338

THE DRIFTERS

CHAPTER 11
Live on Stage—The Drifters?

Before we conclude the story of the Drifters, some background on the confusion that surrounds the use of the group's name—there are and have been a multitude of "Drifters" groups—would seem to be in order.

No doubt most people have seen advertisements for appearances by the Drifters in their local press, only to find that the group using the name has no connection with any known Drifters' line-up. This is not a situation unique to the Drifters, as there are several permutations of the Platters, the Supremes, the Marvelettes, the Crystals, the Shangri-las, and, on the rock and roll nostalgia circuit, the Byrds. In most cases, the groups concerned have absolutely no connection with the famous names they bear. The Drifters, however, have fallen victim to such exploitation far more than others. This has been partly due to the ongoing popularity of their hit records, and partly due to the ever-fluctuating nature of the group's membership roster.

For those who are unsure about exactly who owns the name "The Drifters," it's important to state here and now that, legally, the Drifters trademark is the property of Faye Treadwell.

Back in 1954, when Clyde McPhatter left the group, the name passed to Faye's late husband, George Treadwell, who set up a corporation called "Drifters, Inc.," and copyrighted the group name. Following the departure of Gerhart Thrasher and company in May 1958, Treadwell transferred the name Drifters to the group previously called the Crowns, which he was perfectly entitled to do.

When George died in 1967, all rights to the Drifters name passed to his widow Faye, who has fought to protect her property through the ensuing years, winning the right to exclusive use of the name in several court battles (more on this will be said below).

The first time that George Treadwell had real problems regarding another group's use of the name "Drifters" was back in 1959, when Capitol Records issued a "Drifters" single—minus Cliff Richard—called "Don't Be a Fool"/"Feelin' Fine" (Capitol 4220) by the Drifters. These recordings turned out to be by Cliff Richard's backing group, a U.K. act who, along with Richard, were massively popular in their homeland but virtually unknown in the U.S. George Treadwell immediately filed suit against Capitol, and the record was quickly withdrawn. The erstwhile "Drifters," at the suggestion of their bass guitarist Jet Harris, changed their name to the Shadows, although they were probably unaware that there was already an American group using that name as well. Luckily for them, that group did not enjoy the high profile of George Treadwell's Drifters.

Like Cliff Richard's backing group, there have been others who made no attempt to exploit the name or the material of their illustrious namesake (see Appendix 5), but merely made the mistake of picking the wrong name: a white Michigan-based group, Jimmy Williams and the Drifters, whose "Rainbow Heart"/"Teardrops and Memories" (Drifter 101) was released in 1954; Jimmy Orr and The Drifters, a fifties hillbilly act, and Steve Day and The Drifters, part of the early Liverpool rock group explosion.

Far more damaging to George and then to Faye Treadwell have been the numerous groups which have used the name to further their own careers. Some have been talented enough in their own right but have found it easier to trade on the Drifters name rather than attempt to establish a following of their own. Such groups fall into two categories: those which contain no former members of the Drifters and therefore have no claim whatsoever to use of the name, and those which do include former members—like the groups operated by Charlie Thomas and Bill Pinckney, former members of Treadwell's groups—who have asserted their own claims of legitimacy to use of the name over the years, based, apparently, on the fact that they were instrumental in the success of the Treadwell Drifters. Assertions like these have persisted despite the fact that, upon joining the Drifters, all members sign an undertaking that, should they leave, they will not use the name of the group thereafter in connection with their own careers—something which many seem to forget once they do leave.

Among the first category of such groups, one called the Invitations toured Great Britain in 1968 billed as the Original Drifters. At that time, U.K. promoters were bringing in various American acts, such as the Fabulous Ronettes (they featured P.P. Arnold and the Flirtations) and the Fantastic Temptations (in reality the old doo-wop group the Velours, who became the Fantastics). The Invitations, who were part of this trend, had a minor U.S. hit called "Hallelujah" in their own name about the same time, and subsequently changed their name to New York City, under which they had a major international success with "I'm Doing Fine Now."

More recently, there have been acts like the Sounds of the Drifters from Norfolk, Virginia (not to be confused with a group of the same name which appeared in the U.K. in 1990, on which more later); the Texas-based Billy Williams' Drifters, who contributed a version of "Under the Boardwalk" to a 1981 blues album by guitarist Sherman Robinson (their version is actually not too bad, as the lead does a passable Johnny Moore impersonation; from Australia, Billy Washington's Drifters, who regularly tour the Far East; a group featuring Michael Andrews, Arvis Andres (the only female to sing as a Drifter!), Kenny Knight, and King Moses, who, in the early eighties, toured the Southern states; and the World Famous Drifters from Los Angeles, featuring such well-known names as Bobby Tharren, Delbert Smith, and Benjamin Mitchell, whoever they are. On top of all these, many will no doubt be aware of the Drifters that perform in Spain throughout the holiday season (this group apparently emanates from Florida), which, like all the others, have no legitimate claim to use of the name.

Then there are the groups who do have ties to the Treadwell Drifters. These include the 1964 formations put together by Lover Patterson, one of which featured Little David Baughan, and another which included Dock Green and Tommy

Evans. Patterson rounded out these groups with members of the Duvals/Drapers.

When Rick Sheppard left the Drifters in 1970, he initially joined the New York City police force, only to hang up his nightstick in 1974 to form the Brand New Drifters, Ltd., a group which at one point included Don Thomas from the Treadwell Drifters. Not too much has been heard from Rick in the intervening years, but apparently he has been recently active in Canada, where he has again tried to lay claim to the Drifters name with a new group.

The longest lasting and biggest problem for the Treadwell Drifters have been the groups fronted by Bill Pinckney and Charlie Thomas. As Pinckney's connections go back the farthest—to 1953, when he first joined Clyde McPhatter and the Drifters—we will look at his career first.

Following his somewhat acrimonious departure in 1956, Bill first formed the Flyers, and then recorded solo on Phillips International. He did return to George Treadwell's Drifters on occasion—he claims to have introduced Bobby Hendricks to the group—but by May 1958 he was doing nothing of particular note when he heard that George Treadwell had dissolved the Drifters (the point at which the Crowns line-up took over the Drifters name).

Having toyed with the idea of forming a group, Pinckney saw his chance to capitalize on his Drifters heritage. He called the Thrasher brothers to see if they would join him in his new venture. Gerhart and Andrew Thrasher said yes and, along with David Baughan, the foursome became the "Original Drifters," which, in all honesty, they very nearly were (except for David Baldwin, James Johnson and company from the Mt. Lebanon singers period). This lineup did not last very long, however. Andrew Thrasher had been replaced by Bobby Hendricks by the time the group recorded two singles for End Records in 1959—"I Could Have Told You"/"Am I to Be the One" (End 1051) and "Gee"/"Santa Claus Is Coming to Town" (End 1053)—the latter of which featured a rare lead vocal by Gerhart Thrasher. The record company, perhaps fearful of litigation from George Treadwell, called the group the Harmony Grits for those recordings.

Bookings for the Original Drifters were good, but as usual the members came and went. Bobby Hendricks, who had scored a million-selling solo hit on the Sue label in 1958 with "Itchy Twitchy Feeling," left soon after the release of the End singles in an attempt to revive his solo career. By 1963, the Original Drifters were comprised of Gerhart Thrasher, Bill Pinckney, Jimmy Lewis, and Bobby Lee Hollis. Hollis, who had been a member of the Sunbeams (not the "Come Back Baby" group), had also recorded as a solo artist for the Sue label under the name "Johnny Pancake," a moniker apparently dreamed up by Sue label owner Juggy Murray to avoid confusion with Bobby Lee, the lead singer of the Fiestas of "So Fine" fame.

The Original Drifters toured the Far East during 1963, and can be heard performing "On Broadway" on an album called *Memories of Cow Palace*, the result of an appearance at San Francisco's famed Cow Palace auditorium. There, backed by an orchestra led by Phil Spector, they performed other Drifters' favorites like "Save the Last Dance for Me," and "Up on the Roof," although only "On Broadway" made the album. (The original album has long since been deleted, and I have no information regarding label and catalog number, having heard this recording only from a tape.)

Pinckney's Drifters enjoyed quite a high profile in the U.S. at this point, calling upon James Brown to produce "I Do the Jerk" (vocal by Hollis)/"Don't Call Me" in 1964 for Fontana Records (Fontana 1964). The record did fairly well in regional rhythm and blues markets, although it failed to break out nationally.

Bobby Hendricks rejoined Pinckney's group in 1964, ousting Jimmy Lewis, who went on as a solo act. (In 1968, Lewis scored a minor rhythm and blues hit with "Girls from Texas" on the Minit Records, and the record is much sought after by British and European fans.) With Hendricks, they toured the U.K. in 1966, and were received with much enthusiasm by British fans of the 1950s Drifters, whose tastes were rooted in blues and early rock and roll.

127

In 1967, Veep Records, a subsidiary of United Artists, issued the "Masquerade Is Over"/"I Found Some Lovin' " (Veep 1264) by Bill Pinckney and the Originals, but it failed to make an impact. During that year, David Baughan returned briefly, but once again the unfortunate Little David did not last too long. After his departure this time, nothing more was heard of him, except for a rumor which surfaced in 1969 that he was destitute. Sadly, he died in 1970 at the age of thirty-two.

By 1968, Bobby Lee Hollis, Gerhart Thrasher and Bobby Hendricks decided that they had been rockin' and driftin' too long, and they left the group. Hendricks attempted to revive his solo career without too much success—his "Go on Home Girl" (Williams 1) was released in 1969—and in the late seventies he was back touring with his own "Drifters" group; Gerhart Thrasher and Bobby Lee Hollis formed a vocal group in Miami, Florida, leaving Bill Pinckney to pick up the pieces.

The split could not have happened at a less opportune time, as Pinckney had a European tour lined up, although there was a distinct lack of "original" Drifters ready to embark on the venture anyway. Lacy Hollingsworth, the Drifters' valet from the early days, suggested that Pinckney consider a group from Atlanta called the Tears to replace his departed Originals. This group, which consisted of Albert Fortson, Wallace Ezzard, Benny Anderson, and Mark Williams, had recorded for King Records in 1965 (the titles for those who like to know such things are "Sugar Girl," "I've Got a Love to Hold," "Confused Man," and "I Need Your Love"). At some point, the Tears had included Charles Pitman and Willie Pitts, but it was Fortson, Ezzard, Anderson, and Williams who joined Pinckney on the European tour as the Original Drifters.

Following the tour, Pinckney and the group did some Southern dates for a Charleston, South Carolina, booking agent named Harold Thomas, but Pinckney and Thomas had a disagreement, causing Bill to leave the agency. The remaining members stayed with Thomas, however, and he quickly dubbed them the "Original Drifters" and sent them out on the road.

Undeterred, Pinckney recruited rival set of "Originals," this time teaming up with Clarence Walker, Bruce Caesar, and

Tony Richardson (who had apparently been in a group from Winston-Salem, North Carolina, called Sacardos). With this line-up, the Original Drifters cut one single in 1971 on Game Records—"Ol' Man River"/"Millionaire" (Game 394)—before they, too, split up.

Never one to throw in the towel, Bill Pinckney continued to use the Original Drifters name. Subsequent group members included Ollie Woodston, Nebraska Turner, Russell "Pretty Boy" Henry (who seemingly did great versions of Clyde McPhatter's material), and Harold "Sundown" Beverly. In 1979, with Tony Cook (formerly of the Bluenotes), Chuck Cockerhan, Andrew Lawyer, and Harold Jackson now performing as the Original Drifters alongside Pinckney, Southern Charisma Records issued "60 Minute Man"/"Broke Blues" (Southern Charisma 3289). For trivia Fans, Pinckney's son, Bill Jr., played percussion on this record.

In August 1980, with Ronald Washington replacing Harold Jackson, the group recorded their *Live At The Crocket Stadium* album in Charlotte, North Carolina. Consisting mostly of post-1960s material—only "Money Honey" came from Bill's time with the early Drifters—the album is recommended only to fanatics who must have everything bearing the group's name. It managed to achieve a U.K. release on Bulldog (BDL1041) in 1982, and re-appeared in 1990 on the Legends of Rock label, deceptively billed as a product by "The Drifters." Although the sleeve notes mentioned briefly that the performers were Pinckney's group, the packaging bears a 1964 photo of a Johnny Moore-led group—obviously out to confuse. The perpetrators of the live album also cut a version of the Johnny Moore group's "You're More Than a Number in My Little Red Book" for S&J Records in 1979 or 1980, no doubt to cash in on the popularity of the Moore original on the Carolina beach scene.

As late as 1989, Bill Pinckney and the Originals were appearing on record, issuing a Christmas album, *A White Christmas* (Ripete 392181), which included a throwback rendition of Clyde McPhatter's standard version of the title song, along with cuts like "Christmas Just Ain't Christmas," "Santa Claus Got the Blues," and the Beach Boys' "Little St. Nick." They also

had a 45, "W.P.L.J."/"Gonna Move Across River (Ripete 3002).
To this day, Bill Pinckney continues to perform with various formations of Original Drifters, mostly in the South Carolina area, where the demand for old-style rhythm and blues remains high, mainly because of the aforementioned beach scene and the legendary "Shag" dance parties. Latter-day members have included Russell Johnston, James Ivory, and Charles Fowler (who also performed together as Special Blend), while former members such as Russell Henry and Harold Jackson have drifted in and out. Ideally, Bill sees his perfect line-up as himself, Johnny Moore, Bobby Hendricks, and Charlie Thomas, but this appears unlikely to occur.

Despite what has often been written by the misinformed, Pinckney's Drifters are an illegitimate group—he has no legal right to use the name. It has been said that his and Faye Treadwell's Drifters co-exist, as he stays in America and Faye operates in Europe. More accurately, Treadwell has left Pinckney to his own devices over the years because she has never perceived him as a threat to her interests, which for some time have involved working the more active U.K. and European rhythm and blues markets. When a U.K. promoter did try to bring Pinckney's group over to Europe in 1990, the attempt was swiftly quashed by Treadwell.

To further complicate matters, Bill Pinckney has apparently been operating for several years under some sort of lease given him by Larry Marshak, who manages the Charlie Thomas version of the Drifters. This lease purportedly allows Bill to use the name in specified areas of the U.S., although the very legality of the issuance of such a lease is doubtful. Before becoming further bogged down in legalities, however, a look at the career of the Tears—the group Pinckney recruited as his Original Drifters in 1968—should be worthwhile. Although the Tears included no previous members of the Drifters, their connection with Pinckney justifies their inclusion in this section.

As noted above, when Pinckney left them with agent Harold Thomas, they continued to tour as the Original Drifters, fronted by Benny Anderson. They even managed a record release billed simply as the Drifters on Sounds South Records. This album, *Something Old, Something New* (Sounds South 16089), is absolutely dreadful, as it contains horribly disco-fied versions of Drifters hits like "On Broadway," "There Goes My Baby," and "Some Kind of Wonderful," padded out with standards and new songs. To be fair, the vocals are not too bad, but the arrangements do nothing at all for the songs, which are rooted in late-seventies disco. The album was issued in the U.K. in 1987 as *On Broadway* on the budget-priced Warwick label, but it should still be avoided at any cost. Wonder Records also saw fit to reissue it in America on Wonder JKA 0001—but one wonders why (no pun intended).

These non-Pinckney Original Drifters, whose formation has altered through the years to include George Wallace and Andrew Odem as replacements for Ezzard and Williams, also recorded for Abet Records as Five Degrees Fahrenheit. For some time, both Benny Anderson and Harold Thomas maintained that this is not so, although recently Anderson admitted it was their recording. When last heard of, these Drifters were comprised of Anderson, Wallace, Fortson, and Chuck Alexander, and they were still looking for a major deal and still using the name they acquired during their six-month stint with Bill Pinckney.

Next, we come to Charlie Thomas. After four years out of the business, Thomas was approached in 1971 by a New Yorker promoter named Larry Marshak to form a group for an up-coming rock and roll oldies show. At this time, America was in the grip of a nostalgic 1950's oldies revival, and such shows, featuring names from bygone eras—the Spaniels, the Capris, the Penguins, the Five Satins, etc.—were more popular than ever, and Thomas readily agreed to Marshak's request.

Thomas called upon his old cohorts Dock Green and Elsbeary Hobbs, and with the addition of Al Hirst they performed as the Drifters on the show. Hirst soon left, to be replaced by Al Banks, the former lead singer of the Turbans, who had had hits in the fifties with "When You Dance" and "Bingo." This lineup performed at New York's Academy of Music in 1972, where they also sang a couple of songs with Ben

131

E. King. Al Banks was briefly replaced by Richie Booker, but was back with the group when they recorded the old Spaniels hit "Peace of Mind," for which he supplied the lead vocals. Charlie Thomas sang lead on the flip side ("The Juggler"), and the record was issued in 1973 by the Gary, Indiana-based Steeltown Records (Steeltown 671), probably the same label that issued some early singles by the Motown-bound Jackson 5. This Drifters formation also recorded the *Live At Harvard University* album in 1972 (R&D 8001), although it was not released until 1975.

Al Banks died around 1973, and Bobby Ruffin, formerly of the Royal Jokers, replaced him. Musicor recorded the group in 1974 on the surprisingly good "A Mid-Summer Night in Harlem," a song tailor-made for the Drifters' classic style. In 1975, they appeared on the former Shirelles lead singer, Shirley Alston's solo album *With a Little Help of My Friends* (Prodigal 10008), where they supplied the backing vocals for her rendition of "Save the Last Dance for Me."

Bobby Ruffin left in 1977, and Don Thomas—the same Don Thomas from the 1970 Treadwell line-up and Rick Sheppard's group—came back in. Thomas was present when the group sang behind Southside Johnny on his album *This Time It's for Real*, where they performed the Bruce Springsteen-penned song "Little Girl So Fine" behind the album's star.

Don Thomas was quickly gone, to be replaced by former Crests man Gary Lewis, while Bernard Ward deputized for Elsbeary Hobbs during 1978. This was supposedly the same Bernard Ward from the mid-1955 Five Crowns line-up.

Dock Green then left and immediately started his own Drifters with Bernard Jones, Lloyd "Butch" Phillips, and Matthew "Bubba" Stevenson, but under pressure from Larry Marshak, they relocated to Canada. Unfortunately, Dock Green died early in 1989.

Members of Charlie Thomas Drifters have continued to come and go throughout the eighties, with only the nucleus of Thomas and Hobbs remaining constant. Other members have included, at various times, Terry King and Webster Harris (formerly of Jive Five). Charlie's group has made records throughout their existence, mostly poor re-recordings of Drifters classics, which should be avoided if you like the original versions. Their best effort is "A Mid-Summer Night in Harlem," but their live version of "White Christmas" from the Harvard University album is also passable. Their recordings appear on a multitude of labels, usually budget-priced with a misleading line-up on the cover featuring Johnny Moore. As a rule, if it's not on the Atlantic or Bell/Arista labels, forget it.

All of which brings us back to the legal question—who has the right to call themselves the Drifters? In 1971, when Charlie Thomas first put together his group, Faye Treadwell attempted to stop him. Although Faye's group were not too active at the time, she still held the rights to the name, and she also had copies of the undertakings signed by Thomas, Dock Green, and Elsbeary Hobbs which prevented them from using the Drifters' name. At the time, however, the case was set aside, and no conclusive judgement was rendered.

In 1976 Thomas, Green, and Hobbs took out a copyright on the Drifters' name, at which time they stated that they knew of no other group who had, or may have had, claim to the name—something that was obviously untrue. When Dock Green left in the late seventies, Larry Marshak took legal action against him, at the same time calling in Bill Pinckney's "lease." In early 1989, Faye Treadwell reactivated her suit against Thomas and company, and, after much delay, she won the initial stages of her case. Thereafter, Charlie Thomas had ninety days to contest the court's decision, which he failed to do, so that there can now be little argument that the Drifters' name belongs to Faye Treadwell.

In early January 1992, however, Dick Fox staged a "Royalty of Rock" concert at Madison Square Garden in New York City. Subtitled "The Ultimate Reunion," the artists featured included Dion and the Belmonts, Little Anthony and the Imperials, Ronnie Spector and the Ronettes, and Ben E. King and the Drifters—at least the Charlie Thomas version of the Drifters. A review of this concert by Wayne Robbins in the January 13, 1992, issue of *Newsday* gave passing marks to the Belmonts, rated Little Anthony as excellent, but compared the

133

Drifters set to a clash of rival street gangs. Apparently there were ego problems between King and Thomas. After the former had performed lackluster versions of "Spanish Harlem" and "I (Who Have Nothing)"—although "Stand By Me" was apparently better—Thomas led his Drifters through a dreadful rendition of "Up on the Roof." When King and the group did perform together, the bad feelings emanating from them both destroyed the collaboration. Whether the court decision favoring Faye Treadwell stops the activities of Thomas or other pirate Drifters groups remains to be seen. Despite legal moves to prevent him, Thomas, for one, seems determined to destroy the Drifters' reputation, although the latest news is that he has quit performing and is back in the cab business in New York.

The final group worthy—if that's the proper word—of a mention in this section is the one currently calling itself The Sounds of the Drifters, not to be confused with the group of the same name mentioned at the beginning of this chapter. This group was formed in early 1990, and at the time was comprised of Billy Lewis, who was, of course, a former Drifter, Tony Jackson, who sang briefly with them in late 1989, Chuck Thomas, and J.J. Marshall. Currently, the group features Billy Lewis, Gillie LeRoy Jones, Mike Henry, and Milton Brown. In any event, their attempts to perform in the U.K. have been met with a string of legal actions by Faye Treadwell which have deterred clubs and theaters from booking them, as in many cases the box office take has been impounded. There are now existing court orders preventing them from calling themselves the Drifters, although they still occasionally surface under that name.

To sum up, if you see an advertisement for the Drifters, and on enquiring you are told that Clyde McPhatter is the lead singer, your best bet is to simply stay away—unless you learn that it's Johnny Moore and company, Faye Treadwell's Drifters.

CHAPTER 12

Bringing Back the Good Times

Early in 1972, Faye Treadwell decided to lift the Drifters from their post-Atlantic Records doldrums and make a fresh start. To achieve this, she decided to bring them to Europe, with London as their base. Her decision followed a three-week tour in 1971, during which she had been sufficiently encouraged to see the potential for reviving the group's fortunes.

As it turned out, she could hardly have chosen a more opportune time. Atlantic U.K., noticing the continued popularity of the Drifters' recordings in clubs and on the emerging disco scene, had begun to reissue some of their classic material from the sixties. Even they must have been surprised, how-

THE DRIFTERS (1972)
(L. to r.): Bill Fredericks, Johnny Moore, Grant Kitchings, Butch Leake.

135

ever, when "At the Club"/"Saturday Night at the Movies"/
"Memories Are Made of This" (K10148) reached number three
in the British charts on April 9, 1972. So popular was the record
that it remained there for nineteen weeks.

More was to follow as the Drifters' *Golden Hits* album
entered the LP charts, and a further Atlantic reissue, "Come on
over to My Place"/"Up on the Roof"/"I Don't Want to Go on
without You" (the latter title, although sung by Charlie Thomas, had been intended for Johnny Moore, who let Charlie sing
it as a favor), almost repeated the success of "At the Club,"
peaking at number nine on August 26.

The Drifters, who were now Johnny Moore, Bill Fredericks,
Grant Kitchings and Butch Leake, were soon constantly on
tour and, to capitalize on their record success, Faye Treadwell
signed them to Bell Records, the recording arm of the giant
Columbia Pictures corporation. The major problem was finding
suitable material to complement their style, because, as Bill
Fredericks pointed out, many of the songwriters who had supplied the early sixties hits—Barry Mann, Carole King, etc.—
were now pursuing their own careers and keeping their compositions for themselves.

Bell Records placed them under the supervision of British songwriting team Roger Greenaway and Roger Cooke, who
were proven hitmakers with songs like "Blue Mink" and "Family Dog," and who, along with old-time Drifters sidekick Abdul
Samad (Billy Davis), produced their first recordings with the
Drifters in late 1972. They drew mainly on their own songs,
but added a few which are now regarded as standards—Neil
Diamond's "Sweet Caroline," Burt Bacharach and Hal David's
"(There's) Always Something There to Remind Me" (a U.S. hit
for Lou Johnston and a U.K. success for Sandy Shaw, who was
perhaps more famous for performing in her bare feet), and a
revival of "Save the Last Dance for Me," led by Bill Fredericks.

The choice for a single was Paul McCartney's "Every
Night," backed with Cooke and Greenaway's "Something Tells
Me" (Bell 1269). Though the performance was excellent, the
record failed to emulate the achievements of the Atlantic oldies
when issued in October 1972; it did not even have an American

release.

The album *The Drifters Now* appeared at the end of February 1973 and established the pattern the group was to follow during their association with Cooke and Greenaway. The sound was more mellow and the producers' compositions complemented the Drifters' great hits of the past. There were some outstanding moments on the album, especially on the rerecorded "Save the Last Dance for Me," "I'm Feeling Sad," "Sweet Caroline" (which they still used on their live performances), and "The Songs We Used to Sing," in which they revisited their doo-wop roots.

Record success on their new label finally arrived in the summer of 1973 when the Fredericks-led ballad "Like Sister and Brother" (Bell 1313) sent them to number seven on the charts on August 4. The record stayed on the charts for twelve weeks and remained popular into the early eighties, when it was voted the all-time favorite Drifters' track in a BBC Radio One listeners' poll. The record was released in the States on Bell 387 but failed to do anything—U.S. Bell had, in fact, already issued "You've Got Your Troubles"/"I'm Feeling Sad" on Bell 320, to no avail.

The lineup of Johnny Moore, Bill Fredericks, Butch Leake, and Grant Kitchings rapidly gained a reputation as *the* act to see, for, quite apart from the constant excellence of Moore's vocals, Fredericks had an uncanny knack for reproducing the vocal styles of both Rudy Lewis and Ben E. King, and displayed a more than capable bass when the Drifters performed early fifties material such as "Ruby Baby" and "Money Honey."

Cooke and Greenaway used not only their own compositions but also those of fellow U.K. songwriters Geoff Stephens (he had co-written "Like Sister and Brother"), Les Reed, and Tony Macauley. When the follow-up to "Like Sister and Brother" ("I'm Free for the Rest of Your Life") flopped, Cooke and Greenaway came up with "Kissing in the Back Row of the Movies." Johnny Moore was not happy with this number, as he felt that the lyrics were too adolescent for him. The producers prevailed, however, and they were proven right when the song reached number two on June 15, 1974. Again, though, when issued in the States (Bell 600), it proved a stiff.

Some of the Drifters' records made at the time do not seem to have featured the entire group. BMG, who now own the Bell recordings, have not been entirely forthcoming with full information, to say the least; but it would seem that present on "Kissing in the Back Row" are Johnny Moore, Bill Fredericks, long-time session singer Tony Burrows (of Edison Lighthouse, Brotherhood of Man, Infamy), and Roger Greenaway. BMG denies all knowledge of the Drifters, so as a "fact" this is no doubt open to dispute. According to a reissue on the Old Gold label, however, these *are* the facts, although apparently the full group does appear on many Bell and later Arista sides.

"Kissing in the Back Row of the Movies" was followed into the Top 10 in October 1974 by "Down on the Beach Tonight" (Bell 1381), which came from the pens of Tony Macauley and Roger Greenaway, and again echoed the sound of the Atlantic material recorded in the early sixties. Its climb to number seven in the charts underlined the fact that the Drifters were now one of the top record sellers in the U.K.

The old problem of personnel changes reared its head once more in November of 1974 when Bill Fredericks left. He went on to a largely unsuccessful solo career, his best shot at stardom coming in the late seventies when he was produced by Andy Gibb of the then very popular Gibb-brothers group, The Bee-Gees (this was the time of the film "Saturday Night Fever"). The effort failed to give his career the boost needed to make him a star.

Fredericks was replaced by Clyde Brown (the nephew of gospel singer Inez Andrews; he had recorded as a solo act without too much success), and the Drifters carried on, reaching number thirty-three with "Love Games" (Bell 1396) in February 1975. The album of the same name charted only briefly at number fifty-one in late 1975, but the very popular *Twenty-Four Original Hits*, a combination of classic Atlantic recordings and newer Bell material, reached number two at the same time and remained on the album charts for thirty-four weeks.

THE DRIFTERS (1974-75)
Rear (l. to r.): Grant Kitchings, Clyde Brown, Butch Leake;
Seated: Johnny Moore.

THE DRIFTERS (1976-78)
Rear (l. to r.): Billy Lewis, Joe Blunt, Clyde Brown;
Seated: Johnny Moore.

Further success came their way in the fall of 1975 when "There Goes My First Love" (Bell 1443) returned them to the Top 10 on September 6 (it reached number three). By this time, Grant Kitchings had also left and been replaced by Billy Lewis, who came from New York and who had worked as a solo artist on a number of labels.

The year finished on a high note when "Can I Take You Home Little Girl" (Bell 1462) charted at number nine on November 29. Shortly afterwards, however, the Drifters were hit with another personnel change when Butch Leake left. Joe Blunt, a veteran of rhythm and blues groups (among them, the mid-sixties era Chancellors) joined. Leake was still featured on the sleeve of the Bell album *There Goes My First Love* when it was issued late in 1975. The album contained, as well as the recent hits, the excellent "Harlem Child," "Don't Cry on a Weekend," and the ballad "And With No Regrets," to which Johnny Moore gave a superb reading. Clyde Brown made his debut on "The Juggler," which had been co-written by Kenny Young of "Under the Boardwalk" fame.

Though now well established on the club and theater circuit in England and Wales, they had yet to venture over the border into Scotland. They did so in March of 1976, playing the famed Apollo Theatre in Glasgow. The date (March 16, to be precise) was such a success that the theater was forced to add an extra show, and such was the demand for tickets that the queues stretched almost endlessly, with scenes reminiscent of Beatlemania. They did not disappoint their Scottish fans, as their performance surpassed that of any comparable soul group. Along with the classic hits, they added one or two surprises such as "Please Stay," which was known and beloved by U.K. audiences from an inferior cover made in the mid sixties by the Cryin' Shame on Decca. While they were in Scotland, the Les Reed/Roger Greenaway song "Hello Happiness" reached number twelve in the U.K. charts.

Though Bell Records had enjoyed success with the Drifters, the Bay City Rollers, Gary Glitter, and Showaddywaddy, its days as a record label were numbered. The Drifters would have only one more release on the label—the reggae-influenced

141

"Every Nite's a Saturday Night with You" (Bell 1491). It reached number twenty-nine in September 1976, just before Bell ceased to operate and transferred its roster to the new Arista label.

The end of 1976 saw them repeat the scenes of the March at the Glasgow Apollo, and they also scored heavily on the record front with the Clyde Brown/Johnny Moore duet "You're More Than a Number in My Little Red Book" (Arista 78), which peaked at number five on December 18. It proved to be their last major singles chart hit, inasmuch as subsequent releases—"I'll Know When True Love Really Passes By," "It Looks Like I'm the Clown Again," "Honey You're Heaven to Me," and "Closely Guarded Secret"—though popular in the clubs, all missed out in the charts.

The U.K. releases meant little in America, although they were much sought after by the "beach" fans in the Carolinas. The Drifters made their final appearance in the U.K. charts with an Old Gold reissue of "Save the Last Dance for Me"/"When My Little Girl Is Smiling," which reached number sixty-nine in April 1979.

DRIFTERS' TWENTY-FIFTH ANNIVERSARY PARTY (1978)
(L. to r.): Johnny Moore, Billy Lewis, Faye Treadwell, Clyde Brown, Joe Blunt.

But they were now such an institution and had had so many more hit records than any comparable group that the hit parade hardly mattered any more; moreover, the growing nostalgia for fifties and sixties rock groups in both Britain and Europe seemed to guarantee them a constant audience.

In July 1979, Johnny Moore, the most recognizable face in the Drifters, left for another try at solo stardom. He signed to Magnet Records, which released "Still Can't Shake Your Love"/"Lady Loves to Dance" on Magnet MAG162. The record was credited to Johnny Darrow Moore, which recalled his first solo stint in the late fifties when he recorded for Sue and Melic as Johnny Darrow. The record was commercial, but failed to established him in his own right.

Meanwhile, Faye Treadwell had recruited Ray Lewis. Lewis was from Los Angeles and had recorded as a solo act; he had also appeared in a few television series.

The Drifters, who were now Billy Lewis, Clyde Brown, Joe Blunt, and Ray Lewis, signed to Epic Records, where they were put into the hands of disco whiz kid Biddhu, who produced them on "Pour Your Little Heart Out" (Epic 7806). Though the record was plugged in a Joan Collins (yes, of "Dynasty" fame) sexploitation movie, it failed to chart. Once again, though, it was a big club favorite. They were still in demand for television and live shows, and this probably encouraged Epic to issue "I'm Not That Kind of Guy"/"What Am I Doing" (Epic 8559)—but they never promoted it and without marketing behind it the record died.

The changes in the lineup continued. Johnny Moore returned in 1980 to replace Joe Blunt, only to leave again in 1981 to form Slightly Adrift with Clyde Brown and Joe Blunt. They cut one single for Tower Bell Records ("Broken Heart"/ "The Soul of Love"), but their career was hampered by Tower Bell's desire to call them the Drifters, which Moore refused to agree to.

Faye Treadwell had in the meantime pulled off a major coup by persuading Ben E. King to rejoin the group. Another name from the past—Bill Fredericks—returned at the same time. The lineup was completed by Ray Lewis and Louis Price.

SNAPSHOTS OF THE
1985 DRIFTERS ON THE MOVE
Top (l. to r.): Clyde Brown,
Ben E. King, fan Les Quinn,
Joe Blunt, and (front) Mrs Blunt;
◀ Left: Johnny Moore.

Price, who had first joined in 1980, had been performing since he was five years old and had sung with the Temptations before joining the Drifters. They recorded several tracks for U.K. Atlantic, but only "You Better Move On"/"Save the Last Dance for Me" (Atlantic K17743) saw the light of day. Throughout 1982 they toured constantly and appeared on several television shows, among them a prime time Christmas special.

During 1983, Ben E. King teamed up with Johnny Moore, Clyde Brown, and Joe Blunt, and together they toured to packed houses as the Drifters. The exceptional quality of King and Moore's lead vocals prompted critic Spencer Leigh, when

144

writing about King in *Record Collector* magazine (May 1987), to compare the combination to the Beatles, as that was the last time he had seen a group feature two such strong vocalists.

This line-up stayed together until 1985, when Ben E. King decided to revive his solo career, and the other members, Johnny Moore included, decided to take some time off the road.

Not that this meant the end of the Drifters. In early 1986, Faye Treadwell brought back Billy Lewis, Ray Lewis (no relation), Louis Price (for a European tour) and, after an attempt to lure Bill Fredericks failed, Jonah Ellis, who was to also be music director in addition to fourth vocalist. Ellis had been the Drifters' guitarist from 1974 to 1978, when he left to work with the Temptations. He subsequently became a songwriter and producer with Total Experience Records, where he produced hit records for Yarbough and People and the Gap Band.

Despite the lack of big names from the past, this foursome proved to be quite outstanding, Louis Price in particular. In concert, they featured most of the Drifters' popular hits, but the highlight was the section where they returned to the doo-wop roots of the fifties, performing the Dells' "Oh What A Night," the Teenagers' "Why Do Fools Fall In Love," plus a knockout workout on the Five Satins' classic hit, "In the Still of the Night."

These Drifters were very successful on stage, even attracting the attention of RCA-Victor Records (nothing came of this, however). Fans still wanted to see Johnny Moore, who duly returned in early 1987. Johnny joined alongside Ray Lewis, Billy Lewis, and a new member, Gene Jenkins, whose background has unfortunately remained a mystery.

Jonah Ellis had returned to session work, while Louis Price departed to obscurity, a fate which befalls many ex-members of famous vocal groups.

By March, George Chandler had joined Johnny Moore, Billy Lewis, and Ray Lewis, replacing the short-lived Gene Jenkins, who, incidentally, despite the brevity of his stay, managed a television appearance on the U.K. quiz show "Three-Two-One" in September 1987, the Drifters' portion of which had been filmed the previous February.

THE DRIFTERS (EARLY 1987)
Rear (l. to r.): George Chandler, Johnny Moore, Billy Lewis;
Front: Ray Lewis.

George Chandler was a long-time session vocalist and doo-wop fan, but his tenure with the Drifters was to be short, as by mid May John L. "J.T." Thurston, a former member of Millie Jackson's entourage, had replaced him. Chandler went on to join London Beat, who scored a U.K. hit with "9 A.M." late in 1988, before going on to top U.S. charts with "I've Been Thinking About You" in 1990.

On June 7, 1987, the Drifters played the London Paladium, the most prestigious of British theaters. Despite the fact that singles record success seemed to have become a thing of the past, crowds flocked to see them—the drawing power of the Drifters' name had been demonstrated by the popularity of the television-advertised album *The Very Best of the Drifters*, which climbed to number twenty-four in the album charts in the winter of 1986.

RECEIVING A TELSTAR AWARD FOR SELLING OVER 50,000 ALBUMS (1987)
(L. to r.): Johnny Moore, Billy Lewis, Faye Treadwell, John Thurston, Ray Lewis.

The next personnel change came in the summer of 1988 when Ray Lewis, who had been with the group for nearly ten years, left. In came Joe Cofie (born on September 9, 1964), a multi-talented instrumentalist and vocalist who had played keyboards for Tamla-Motown veterans Jimmy Ruffin and Junior Walker.

In late February 1989, Moore, Lewis, Thurston, and Cofie set off on an exhausting ten-month world tour which opened in Hong Kong. They found themselves traveling the Far East in the shadow of Billy Washington's Australian-based Drifters, but quickly won the audiences over to the real sound of the Drifters.

Billy Lewis said goodbye in October after many years with the group, and initially attempted a solo career. However, in early 1990, he moved to the Drifters' copyist group Sounds of the Drifters (see Chapter 11), and finding a replacement for him proved to be a problem because of the hectic touring schedule.

George Chandler took time off from London Beat and filled in for a few other dates, but due to the pressure of other engagements could not stay for long. Tony Jackson, formerly of Picketty Witch, an early seventies hit duo, was the next replacement, but he, too, proved to be short-lived. (For British fans, Jackson was the voice on the Wimpy hamburger advertisement which featured "Come on over to My Place" and ran for awhile during 1989-90. Jackson, along with Billy Lewis, later turned up in Sounds of the Drifters. Finally, Keith John, the son of the legendary rhythm and blues singer Little Willie John, stepped into the breach.

The exhausting world tour wound up just outside Leicester, England, and here on December 19, 1989, where, during a two-hour performance, they proved themselves more than worthy of the name the Drifters. After singing all the hits, in which each member was given a showcase, they finished with a spine-tingling version of "White Christmas," dedicated to the memory of Clyde McPhatter. Even Johnny Moore must have felt a twinge of nostalgia. (And a special thank you is due here to Keith John for his *a cappella* renditions of "Fever," "All

Around the World," and "Sleep," all hits by his father. He sang these in Room 212 of the Sketchley Grange Hotel, and made one aging rocker—namely, this writer—absolutely delirious.)

Keith John's stay with the Drifters was to prove, like so many others, all too brief, as he works most of the time as a member of Stevie Wonder's entourage. Thus, by early 1990, Peter Lamar, a Brooklyn-ite who had been singing in Canada, was in the group. Still more changes occurred when John Thurston left in mid 1990, his place going to Patrick Alan, a native of Los Angeles who had sung in various Prince offshoots.

Peter Lamar could not tour in late 1990 due to problems at home, and Roy Hemmings, who had been in the "J.A.L.N. Band" in the seventies before becoming a session singer, was brought into the group. Lamar returned at the expense of Patrick Alan in early 1991, but by the end of the year the Drifters consisted of Johnny Moore, Joe Cofie, Roy Hemmings, and Rohan Turner, whom Faye Treadwell discovered singing in a nightclub.

All these personnel changes no doubt confuse the public, or they should if any other group but the Drifters was involved. However, for some reason they do not affect their continuing popularity, as the strength of their material carries the day. Also, Faye Treadwell never puts a sub-standard version of the Drifters on stage, as all who have seen them would doubtless testify, and they remain one of the world's best live acts to this day.

Thus, we have reached the end of the story that began back in May 1953, when Ahmet Ertegun asked Clyde McPhatter to form a vocal group at a time that was virtually the dawn of rock and roll. As they celebrate their fortieth anniversary, the Drifters legacy of popular music is immense.

In 1953 their combination of gospel and blues led directly to the soul music of the sixties, a revolution for which they were the catalysts. Some—Ray Charles and the Five Royales, for example—may dispute this claim, but Clyde McPhatter showed the way in 1951 when the Dominoes first tentatively mixed rhythm with blues, sanctifying it properly two years later.

THE DRIFTERS (EARLY-MID 1990)
(L. to r.): Peter Lamarr, Johnny Moore, Joe Cofie, John Thurston.

THE DRIFTERS (OCTOBER 1990)
(L. to r.): Roy Hemmings, Johnny Moore, Patrick Alan, Joe Cofie.

THE DRIFTERS (MAY 1991)
(L. to r.): Joe Cofie, Roy Hemmings, Peter Lamarr, Johnny Moore.

Their use of strings in the late fifties also heralded a new sound which was followed by a host of vocal groups, both black and white. Rhythm and blues groups like the Shirelles, the Jarmels, and the Flamingos broke through to national prominence with string-laden hits, and although strings had been used in rhythm and blues recordings before the Drifters—the Orioles did it in the early fifties—"There Goes My Baby" and subsequent releases showed how innovative they could sound.

The Drifters have provided the world with superb vocalists in the shape of Clyde McPhatter, Johnny Moore, Bobby Hendricks, Ben E. King, Rudy Lewis, and Bill Fredericks, and have released some of the greatest records in popular music history. Everyone knows the Drifters hits, which have included "White Christmas," "Money Honey," "What'cha Gonna Do," "Ruby Baby," "There Goes My Baby," "Drip Drop," "Dance with Me," "Save the Last Dance for Me," "Kissing In the Back Row of the Movies," and on and on and on—the list seems endless.

The group has had forty-seven rhythm and blues and pop hits in America, and over twenty in Great Britain alone, without taking into account their popularity around the world. Their songs have been recorded by scores of major artists, among them Elvis Presley, Little Richard, Ry Cooder, the Rolling Stones, the Four Seasons, Pat Boone, the Persuasions, Dion, Neil Young, without mentioning the countless cover versions by lesser lights which have appeared through the years. Versions of Drifters' songs appear on bootlegs by the Beatles and Bruce Springsteen, and even actor Bruce Willis appeared determined to build a singing career on revivals of Drifters' tunes, recording an album which included "Under the Boardwalk" and "Save the Last Dance for Me."

Johnny Moore has proven to be one of the few survivors of the golden age of rhythm and blues vocal groups, and to the public at large he *is* the Drifters. Some people sing of the rock and roll lifestyle, but Johnny has lived it for nearly forty years, from his early days with the Hornets. He has played countless one-nighters, and appeared both in the Alan Freed shows of the fifties and the legendary Murray The K extravaganzas of the sixties.

THE DRIFTERS (JUNE 1992)
(L. to r.): Joe Cofie, Johnny Moore, Roy Hemmings, Rohan Turner.

Through it all he has maintained that distinctive tenor voice which signals to any listener that he or she is hearing a Drifters song. In January 1988, he was inducted into the Rock and Roll Hall of Fame, along with fellow Drifters Clyde McPhatter, Ben E. King, and Rudy Lewis. The classic sound of the Drifters will remain alive and well as long as Johnny Moore is around to front the group. Along with George and then Faye Treadwell, who have guided the Drifters throughout the years, Moore has been the most constant factor in their success story.

The Drifters are timeless, embodying the pure spirit of all that is best in popular music. Even after forty years, their audience remains huge, and they are one of the few acts in rock and roll/pop that does not suffer from a generation gap. Their concerts are attended by fans aged from fifteen to seventy years.

If this book has helped make all who have contributed to their success into household names, then it has served its purpose; this story belongs to them all—the Drifters.

APPENDICES

Name Variations

Any researcher into the history of the Drifters cannot help but be struck by the number of variations in the spelling of the names of individuals connected with the group. Most of these occur in general reference works which, in turn, rely on earlier general works with no claim to definitiveness, thus perpetuating and compounding errors from one volume to the next. In an attempt to set the record straight, there follows what I believe, as a result of my research and contacts with the group, to be the correct information.

BAUGHAN, DAVID: Found as "Baughn," "Baugn," and even "Baugh," Little David's surname is spelled "Baughan."

GREEN, DOCK: Almost invariably listed as "Doc," the correct spelling is "Dock."

HOBBS, ELSBEARY: One of the trickiest of them all. Usually encountered as "Elsberry," "Elsburry," or even "Elsbearry" (close), the given name bestowed upon bass singer Hobbs was "Elsbeary."

HOPKINS, TELMA: Often listed as Thelma Hopkins, although Telma is correct. Hopkins was a member of the group Dawn, and more currently a cast member of the American TV sitcoms "Family Matters" and "Getting By."

KING, BEN E.: Some have identified him as "Benjamin Earl Solomon," but in a conversation with him a few years ago he assured me his real name is Ben Nelson.

KITCHINGS, GRANT: Has appeared under this name in most references to him, although the Bell album *Drifters Now* refers to him as Kitching. Most evidence points to Kitchings.

LEWIS, RUDY: Has occasionally been identified as "Ruby"

Lewis (wrong gender!). "Rudy."

MOORE, JOHNNY: Has been referred to as "Johnnie," but, as with Charlie Thomas, this is a slight variant of the more widely used "Johnny," which is how he signs his name.

PINCKNEY, BILL: Often seen as "Pinkney" or "Pickney," Bill spells his name "Pinckney."

PRICE, LOUIS: Sometimes spelled "Lewis," the correct spelling is "Louis."

THOMAS, CHARLIE: Sometimes referred to as "Charley" Thomas, a slight variation from the more common (and correct) "Charlie."

TREADWELL, FAYE: Sometimes found referred to as "Fay," her name is Fayrene, for which she uses the shortened "Faye."

TURNER, ROHAN: Sometimes referred to as "Roland," especially by manager Faye Treadwell.

WARWICK, DIONNE: Occasionally seen as "Warwicke," the more frequently occurring "Warwick" seems to be correct.

Other Matters

GEORGE TREADWELL: Despite claims that he was at one time married to Dinah Washington, there appears to be no substance in this. Although the voracious Miss Washington married seven times in her thirty-nine years on the earth, it would seem that George was not among her husbands. George did act as her manager at one point, which may have given rise to an inaccurate rumor that the two were married. He was, however, married to Sarah Vaughan prior to marrying Fayrene Treadwell.

APPENDIX 2

The Drifters:
A Group Family Tree, 1953-1993

Author's Note: Although every care has been taken to make this listing as accurate as possible, some of the dates cited are only approximate and there remain a few gaps when personnel could not be determined with absolute certainty. Also, no attempt has been made to document some of the more shortlived reappearances of people like Bill Pinckney and Andrew Thrasher (in 1956) and Keith John (in 1991).

Following William Brent's departure from the Drifters, the group has not really had a natural bass vocalist although, as the members came and went, many have doubled as baritone/basses. In fact, many group members have tended to be very flexible vocally, moving laterally with ease, so that while designated as a tenor, etc., this should not be taken as gospel.

Finally, from their inception in 1953 until the mid 1970s, the Drifters carried a guitarist with them on the road to act as musical director. They have included Walter Adams (1953), Jimmy Oliver (1953-58), Reggie Kimber (1958-61), Billy Davis (a.k.a. Abdul Samad, 1962-69), Butch Mann (1969-71), and Jonah Ellis (1974-78). These guitarists often appear in Drifters' publicity shots—in particular, Jimmy Oliver and Billy Davis—but they did not play on the Drifters' recordings.

Clyde McPhatter and The Drifters (May - June 1953)

Clyde McPhatter (lead tenor)	David Baughan (tenor)	William Anderson (tenor)	David Baldwin (baritone)	James Johnson (bass)

Clyde McPhatter and The Drifters (August 1953)

Clyde McPhatter (lead tenor)	Gerhart Thrasher (tenor)	Bill Pinckney (tenor)	Andrew Thrasher (baritone)	Willie Ferbee (bass)

159

Clyde McPhatter and The Drifters (1953 - 1954)

Clyde McPhatter (lead tenor)	Gerhart Thrasher (tenor)	Andrew Thrasher (baritone)	Bill Pinckney (bass)

The Drifters (Mid 1954)

David Baughan (lead tenor)	Gerhart Thrasher (tenor)	Andrew Thrasher (baritone)	Bill Pinckney (bass)

The Drifters (Late 1954 - March 1955)

David Baughan (lead tenor)	Johnny Moore (tenor)	Gerhart Thrasher (tenor)	Andrew Thrasher (baritone)	Bill Pinckney (bass)

The Drifters (Mid 1955 - August 1955)

David Baughan (lead tenor)	Gerhart Thrasher (tenor)	Andrew Thrasher (baritone)	Bill Pinckney (bass)

The Drifters (August 1955 - August 1956)

Johnny Moore (lead tenor)	Gerhart Thrasher (tenor)	Andrew Thrasher (baritone)	Bill Pinckney (bass)

The Drifters (August 1956 - Late 1957)

Johnny Moore (lead tenor)	Gerhart Thrasher (tenor)	Charlie Hughes (baritone)	Tommy Evans (bass)

The Drifters (Late 1957 - May 1958)

Bobby Hendricks (lead tenor)	Gerhart Thrasher (tenor)	Jimmy Millinder (baritone)	Tommy Evans (bass)

The Drifters (June 1958 - Mid 1959)

Charlie Thomas (tenor)	Ben E. King (tenor)	Dock Green (baritone)	Elsbeary Hobbs (bass)

The Drifters (Mid 1959 - May 1960)

| Ben E. King (lead tenor - on record only) | Johnny Lee Williams (tenor) | Charlie Thomas (tenor) | Dock Green (baritone) | Elsbeary Hobbs (bass) |

The Drifters (Mid 1960)

| Charlie Thomas (tenor) | James Poindexter (tenor) | | Dock Green (baritone) | Elsbeary Hobbs (bass) |

The Drifters (Mid 1960)

| Charlie Thomas (tenor) | Rudy Lewis (tenor) | | Dock Green (baritone) | William Van Dyke (bass) |

The Drifters (Mid 1960 - Late 1960)

| Rudy Lewis (lead tenor) | Charlie Thomas (tenor) | | Dock Green (baritone) | George Grant (bass) |

The Drifters (Late 1960 - Mid 1962)

| Rudy Lewis (lead tenor) | Charlie Thomas (tenor) | | Dock Green (baritone) | Tommy Evans (bass) |

The Drifters (Mid 1962 - Late 1962)

| Rudy Lewis (lead tenor) | Charlie Thomas (tenor) | | Gene Pearson (baritone) | Tommy Evans (bass) |

The Drifters (Early 1963)

| Rudy Lewis (lead tenor) | Charlie Thomas (tenor) | | Gene Pearson (baritone) | Johnny Terry (bass) |

The Drifters (April 1963 - May 1964)

| Rudy Lewis (lead tenor) | Johnny Moore (tenor) | Charlie Thomas (tenor) | Gene Pearson (baritone) | Johnny Terry (bass) |

161

The Drifters (May 1964 - Mid 1966)

| Johnny Moore (lead tenor) | Charlie Thomas (tenor) | Gene Pearson (baritone) | Johnny Terry (bass) |

The Drifters (July 1966)

| Johnny Moore (lead tenor) | Charlie Thomas (tenor) | Gene Pearson (baritone) | Dan Danbridge (bass) |

The Drifters (August - September 1966)

| Johnny Moore (lead tenor) | Charlie Thomas (tenor) | Gene Pearson (baritone) | William Brent (bass) |

The Drifters (October 1966 - Early 1967)

| Johnny Moore (lead tenor) | Charlie Thomas (tenor) | Rick Sheppard (baritone) | William Brent (bass) |

The Drifters (Early 1967 - Mid 1967)

| Johnny Moore (lead tenor) | Charlie Thomas (tenor) | Rick Sheppard (baritone) | Bill Fredericks (baritone/bass) |

The Drifters (Mid 1967 - Late 1967)

| Johnny Moore (lead tenor) | Charles Baskerville (tenor) | Rick Sheppard (baritone) | Bill Fredericks (baritone/bass) |

The Drifters (November 1967)

| Johnny Moore (lead tenor) | | Rick Sheppard (baritone) | Bill Fredericks (baritone/bass) |

The Drifters (December 1967 - Late 1969)

| Johnny Moore (lead tenor) | Rick Sheppard (baritone) | Milton Turner (baritone) | Bill Fredericks (baritone/bass) |

162

The Drifters (Late 1969 - March 1970)

| Johnny Moore (lead tenor) | Rick Sheppard (baritone) | Don Thomas (baritone) | Bill Fredericks (baritone/ bass) |

The Drifters (January 1971)

| Johnny Moore (lead tenor) | Bill Fredericks (baritone) | Ronald Quinn (baritone) | (unsure of name) (unknown) |

The Drifters (Early 1972 - Mid 1974)

| Johnny Moore (lead tenor) | Bill Fredericks (baritone/bass) | Butch Leake (baritone) | Grant Kitchings (tenor) |

The Drifters (Mid 1974 - Early 1975)

| Johnny Moore (lead tenor) | Clyde Brown (baritone) | Butch Leake (baritone) | Grant Kitchings (tenor) |

The Drifters (Mid 1975 - Early 1976)

| Johnny Moore (lead tenor) | Clyde Brown (baritone) | Butch Leake (baritone) | Billy Lewis (tenor) |

The Drifters (Early 1976 - Mid 1978)

| Johnny Moore (lead tenor) | Clyde Brown (baritone) | Joe Blunt (baritone) | Billy Lewis (tenor) |

The Drifters (Mid 1978 - 1979)

| Ray Lewis (tenor) | Clyde Brown (baritone) | Joe Blunt (baritone) | Billy Lewis (tenor) |

The Drifters (1980 - 1981)

| Johnny Moore (lead tenor) | Clyde Brown (baritone) | Ray Lewis (tenor) | Louis Price (baritone) |

163

The Drifters (Late 1981 - 1983)

Ben E. King (tenor)	Bill Fredericks (baritone)	Ray Lewis (tenor)	Louis Price (baritone)

The Drifters (1983 - 1985)

Johnny. Moore (tenor)	Ben E. King (tenor)	Clyde Brown (baritone)	Joe Blunt (baritone)

The Drifters (Early 1986 - Late 1986)

Ray Lewis (tenor)	Billy Lewis (tenor)	Louis Price (baritone)	Jonah Ellis (baritone/ bass)

The Drifters (Early 1987)

Johnny Moore (tenor)	Ray Lewis (tenor)	Billy Lewis (tenor)	Gene Jenkins (baritone)

The Drifters (March - May 1987)

Johnny Moore (tenor)	Ray Lewis (tenor)	Billy Lewis (tenor)	George Chandler (baritone)

The Drifters (May 1987 - July 1988)

Johnny Moore (tenor)	Ray Lewis (tenor)	Billy Lewis (tenor)	John Thurston (baritone)

The Drifters (August 1988 - October 1989)

Johnny Moore (tenor)	Billy Lewis (tenor)	John Thurston (baritone)	Joe Cofie (baritone)

The Drifters (October - November 1989)

Johnny Moore (tenor)	George Chandler (tenor)	John Thurston (baritone)	Joe Cofie (baritone)

The Drifters (November 1989)

| Johnny Moore (tenor) | Tony Jackson (tenor) | John Thurston (baritone) | Joe Cofie (baritone) |

The Drifters (November - December 1989)

| Johnny Moore (tenor) | Keith John (tenor) | John Thurston (baritone) | Joe Cofie (baritone) |

The Drifters (Early 1990 - Mid 1990)

| Johnny Moore (tenor) | Peter Lamar (tenor) | John Thurston (baritone) | Joe Cofie (baritone) |

The Drifters (Late 1990)

| Johnny Moore (tenor) | Patrick Alan (tenor) | Roy Hemmings (baritone) | Joe Cofie (baritone) |

The Drifters (Early - Mid 1991)

| Johnny Moore (tenor) | Peter Lamar (tenor) | Roy Hemmings (baritone) | Joe Cofie (baritone) |

The Drifters (Mid 1991 - The Present)

| Johnny Moore (tenor) | Rohan Turner (tenor) | Roy Hemmings (baritone) | Joe Cofie (baritone) |

165

Discography

The Atlantic Recordings, 1953-1971:
A Sessionography

Author's Note: The complete Altantic recordings from 1953 to 1971 follow; some tracks appear on a number of U.K. albums, but only the initial release is listed.

Clyde McPhatter and the Drifters: Clyde McPhatter (lead tenor), David Baughan, William Anderson (tenors), David Baldwin (baritone), and James Johnson (bass).

1085	Gone	unissued
1086	Let the Boogie Woogie Roll	unissued
1087	Lucille	Atlantic 1019
1088	What'cha Gonna Do	unissued

New York, June 29, 1953

Clyde McPhatter and the Drifters: Clyde McPhatter (lead tenor), Gerhart Thrasher, Bill Pinckney (tenors), Willie Ferbee (bass), and Walter Adams (guitar).

1104	The Way I Feel	Atlantic 1006
1105	Money Honey	Atlantic 1006
1006	Gone	Atlantic 1055
1107	What'cha Gonna Do	unissued
1108	Let the Boogie Woogie Roll	Atlantic 2060

New York, August 9, 1953

The Great Holiday Hit!

White Christmas

by

Clyde McPhatter

AND HIS DRIFTERS

b/w

THE BELLS OF ST. MARY'S

Atlantic #1048

ATLANTIC RECORDING CORP.
234 WEST 56th St. NEW YORK 19, N. Y.

Clyde McPhatter and the Drifters: Clyde McPhatter (lead tenor), Gerhart Thrasher (tenor), Andrew Thrasher (baritone), and Bill Pinckney (bass).

1151	Don't Dog Me	Atlantic 2049
1152	Such a Night	Atlantic 1019
1153	Warm Your Heart	Atlantic 1029
1154	Bip Bam	Atlantic 1043

New York, November 12, 1953

Clyde McPhatter and the Drifters: Clyde McPhatter (lead tenor), Gerhart Thrasher (tenor), Andrew Thrasher (baritone), and Bill Pinckney (bass, joint lead on "White Christmas").

1201	Bells of Saint Mary's	Atlantic 1048
		K10538 (U.K.)
1202	White Christmas	Atlantic 1048
		K10538 (U.K.)
1203	Honey Love	Atlantic 1029
1204	What'cha Gonna Do	Atlantic 1055

New York, February, 4, 1954

Clyde McPhatter and the Drifters: Clyde McPhatter (lead tenor), Gerhart Thrasher (tenor), Andrew Thrasher (baritone), and Bill Pinckney (bass).

1228	If I Didn't Love You Like I Do	Atlantic 2082
1229	Someday You'll Want Me	
	to Want You	Atlantic 1043
1230	There You Go	Atlantic 2038
1231	Try Try Baby	Atlantic 2028

New York, March 14, 1954

Clyde McPhatter and the Drifters: Clyde McPhatter (lead tenor), Gerhart Thrasher (tenor), Andrew Thrasher (baritone), and Bill Pinckney (bass).

1339	Everyone's Laughing	Atlantic 1070
1340	Sugar Coated Kisses	unissued
1341	Hot Ziggety	Atlantic 1070
1342	Three Thirty Three	Atco LP 375

New York, October 24, 1954

The Drifters: David Baughan (tenor), Gerhart Thrasher (tenor; lead tenor, "Drifting Away from You"), Andrew Thrasher (baritone), and Bill Pinckney (bass; baritone lead "Steamboat" and "No Sweet Lovin'").

1509	Drifting Away from You	unissued
1510	No Sweet Lovin'	Atlantic 2105
1511	Steamboat	unissued
1512	Honey Bee	Atlantic 2096

New York, April 21, 1955

The Drifters: Johnny Moore (lead tenor), Gerhart Thrasher (tenor; lead tenor, "Your Promise to Be Mine" and "Drifting Away from You"), Andrew Thrasher (baritone), and Bill Pinckney (bass; baritone lead on "Steamboat").

1664	Adorable	Atlantic 1078
1665	Your Promise to Be Mine	Atlantic 1089
1666	Ruby Baby	Atlantic 1089
1667	Steamboat	Atlantic 1078
1668	Drifting Away from You	Atlantic 1141

Los Angeles, September 19, 1955

4 NEW ATLANTICS=4 NEW HITS

RUTH BROWN
IT'S LOVE BABY
(24 Hours A Day)
WHAT'D I SAY
=1072

JOE TURNER
HIDE and SEEK
MIDNIGHT
CANNON BALL
#1069

CLYDE McPHATTER
HOT ZIGGETY
EVERYONE'S LAUGHING
#1070

AL HIBBLER
DANNY BOY
NOW I LAY ME DOWN TO DREAM
#1071

ATLANTIC RECORDING CORPORATION

The Drifters: Johnny Moore (tenor), Gerhart Thrasher (tenor; lead tenor, "Your Promise to Be Mine"), Andrew Thrasher (baritone), and Bill Pinckney (bass; lead, "I Should Have Done Right").

| 1182 | Your Promise to Be Mine | unissued |
| 1183 | I Should Have Done Right | Atco LP 375 |

New York, February 16,1956

The Drifters: Johnny Moore (lead tenor), Gerhart Thrasher (tenor), Andrew Thrasher (baritone), and Bill Pinckney (bass; lead, "Honky Tonky").

2046	Soldier of Fortune	Atlantic 2046 London-American HLE8344 (U.K.)
2047	Honky Tonky	Atlantic LP 8041 Atlantic LP 590010 (U.K.)
2048	I Gotta Get Myself a Woman	Atlantic 1101, London-American HLE8344(U.K.)
2049	Sadie My Lady	Atlantic LP 8041, London-American HLK9287 (U.K.)

New York, June 21, 1956

The Drifters: Johnny Moore (lead tenor), Gerhart Thrasher (tenor), Charlie Hughes (baritone), and Tommy Evans (bass).

| 2184 | It Was a Tear | Atlantic 1123, Atlantic LP 590010 (U.K.) |
| 2188 | Fools Fall in Love | Atlantic 1123, Atlantic LP 500010 (U.K.) |

New York, November 8, 1956

The Drifters: Johnny Moore (lead tenor), Gerhart Thrasher (tenor), Charlie Hughes (baritone), and Tommy Evans (bass).

2374	Yodee Yakee	Atlantic 1161, Atlantic LP 590010 (U.K.)
2375	Souvenirs	Atlantic 8041, Atlantic LP 590010 (U.K.)
2376	Hypnotized	Atlantic 1141, Atlantic LP 590010 (U.K.)
2377	I Know	Atlantic 1161, Atlantic LP 590010 (U.K.)

New York April 16, 1957

The Drifters: Bobby Hendricks (lead tenor), Gerhart Thrasher (tenor), Jimmy Milner (baritone), and Tommy Evans (bass; shared lead, "Suddenly There's a Valley"). All sing on "Moonlight Bay."

3051	Drip Drop	Atlantic 1187, London HLE8686 (U.K.)
3052	Suddenly There's a Valley	Atlantic 2087, Atlantic LP 590010 (U.K.)
3053	Moonlight Bay	Atlantic 1187, London HLE8686 (U.K.)

New York, April 28, 1958

The Drifters: Ben E. King (lead tenor), Charlie Thomas (tenor; lead, "Hey Senorita" and "Baltimore"), Dock Green (baritone), and Elsbeary Hobbs (bass).

3396	Hey Senorita	Atlantic 2062, London HLK9145
3397	There Goes My Baby	Atlantic 2025, London HLE8892
3398	Baltimore	Atlantic 2050, London HLE9081
3399	Oh My Love	Atlantic 2025, London HLE8892

New York, March 6, 1959

The Drifters: Ben E. King (lead tenor), Johnny Lee Williams (tenor; lead, "True Love, True Love"), Charlie Thomas (tenor), Dock Green (baritone), and Elsbeary Hobbs (bass).

3726	(If You Cry) True Love, True Love	Atlantic 2040, London HLE8988
3727	Dance with Me	Atlantic 2040, London HLE8988

New York July 9, 1959

The Drifters: Ben E. King (lead tenor), Johnny Lee Williams, Charlie Thomas (tenors), Dock Green (baritone), and Elsbeary Hobbs (bass).

3987	This Magic Moment	Atlantic 2050, London HLE9081
3988	Lonely Winds	Atlantic 2062, Atlantic HLK9154
3989	Temptation	unissued

New York, December 23, 1959

The Drifters: Ben E. King (lead tenor), Johnny Lee Williams, Charlie Thomas (tenors), Dock Green (baritone), and Elsbeary Hobbs (bass).

4565	Save the Last Dance for Me	Atlantic 2071, London HLK9201
4566	Nobody but Me	Atlantic 2071, London HLK9201
4567	I Count the Tears	Atlantic 2087, London HLK9787
4568	Sometimes I Wonder	Atlantic 2151, London REK1355 (E.P.)

New York, May 19, 1960

The Drifters: Rudy Lewis (lead tenor), Charlie Thomas (tenor; lead, "Room Full of Tears" and "Sweets for My Sweet"), Dock Green (baritone), and Tommy Evans (bass).

5323	Room Full of Tears	Atlantic 2127, London HLK9582
5324	Please Stay	Atlantic 2105, London HLK9582
5325	Sweets for My Sweet	Atlantic 2117, London HLK9427
5326	Some Kind of Wonderful	Atlantic 2096, London HLK9326

New York, February 1, 1961

The Drifters: Rudy Lewis (lead tenor), Charlie Thomas (tenor), Dock Green (baritone), and Tommy Evans (bass).

5630	Loneliness or Happiness	Atlantic 2117, London HLK9427
5631	Mexican Divorce	Atlantic 2134, London HLK9522

175

| 5632 | Somebody New, Dancing With You | Atlantic 2127,w i t h London HLK9500 |

New York, July, 13,1961

The Drifters: Rudy Lewis (lead tenor), Charlie Thomas (tenor; lead, "When My Little Girl Is Smiling"), Dock Green, (baritone), and Tommy Evans (bass).

5743	Jackpot	Atlantic 2151, London REK1355
5744	When My Little Girl Is Smiling	Atlantic 2134, London HLK9522
5745	She Never Talked to Me That Way	Atlantic LP K40412 (U.K.)

New York, October, 26, 1961

The Drifters: Rudy Lewis (lead tenor), Charlie Thomas (tenor), Dock Green (baritone), and Tommy Evans (bass).

| 6031 | Stranger on the Shore | Atlantic 2143, London HLK9554 |
| 6032 | What to Do | Atlantic 2143, London HLK9554 |

New York, March 15, 1962

The Drifters: Rudy Lewis (lead tenor), Charlie Thomas (tenor; lead, "I Feel Good All Over"), Dock Green (baritone), and Tommy Evans (bass).

| 6356 | Another Night with the Boys | Atlantic 2162, London HLK9626 |
| 6357 | Up on the Roof | Atlantic 2162, London HLK9626 |

6358	I Feel Good All Over	Atlantic 2201, London HLK9785

New York, June 28, 1962

The Drifters: Rudy Lewis (lead tenor), Charlie Thomas (tenor), Dock Green (baritone), and Tommy Evans (bass).

6743	Let the Music Play	Atlantic 2182, London HLK9699
6744	On Broadway	Atlantic 2182, London HLK9699

New York, January 22, 1963

The Drifters: Rudy Lewis (lead tenor), Johnny Moore (tenor; lead, "If You Don't Come Back" and "I'll Take You Home"), Charlie Thomas (tenor), Gene Pearson (baritone), and Johnny Terry (bass).

6819	Only in America	Atlantic LP K40412 (U.K.)
6820	Rat Race	Atlantic 2191, London HLK9750
6821	If You Don't Come Back	Atlantic 2191, London HLK9750
6822	I'll Take You Home	Atlantic 2201, London HLK9785

New York, April 12, 1963

The Drifters: Rudy Lewis (lead tenor), Johnny Moore (tenor; lead, "Didn't It"), Charlie Thomas (tenor), Gene Pearson (baritone), and Johnny Terry (bass).

7172	In the Land of Make Believe	Atlantic 2216, London HLK9848

7173   Didn't It   Atlantic 2225,
London HLK9886

New York, August 22, 1963

The Drifters: Rudy Lewis (lead tenor), Johnny Moore (tenor; lead, "One Way Love"), Charlie Thomas (tenor), Gene Pearson (baritone), Johnny Terry (bass).

7486   Beautiful Music   Atlantic LP
K 40412 (U.K.)

7487   One Way Love   Atlantic 2725,
London HLK9886

7488   Vaya con Dios   Atlantic 2216,
London HLK9848

New York, December 11, 1963

The Drifters: Johnny Moore (lead tenor), Charlie Thomas (tenor; lead, "I Don't Want to Go on without You"), Gene Pearson (baritone), and Johnny Terry (bass).

7922   Under the Boardwalk   Atlantic 2237,
Atlantic 4001 (U.K.)

7923   He's Just a Playboy (key of E)   unissued

7924   He's Just a Playboy (key of G)   Atlantic 2253,
Atlantic 4008 (U.K.)

7925   I Don't Want to Go On Without You   Atlantic 2237,
Atlantic 4001 (U.K.)

New York, May 21, 1964

The Drifters: Johnny Moore (lead tenor), Charlie Thomas (tenor), Gene Pearson (baritone), Johnny Terry (bass).

8057   I've Got Sand in My Shoes   Atlantic 2253,
Atlantic 4008 (U.K.)

| 8058 | Saturday Night at the Movies | Atlantic 2260, Atlantic 4012 (U.K.) |

New York, August 4, 1964

The Drifters: Johnny Moore (lead tenor), Charlie Thomas (tenor; lead, "There Goes My Baby"), Gene Pearson (baritone), and Johnny Terry (bass).

8110	Ruby Baby	unissued
8111	Some Kind of Wonderful	unissued
8112	Under the Boardwalk	Atlantic 8101, Atlantic 5018 (U.K.)
8113	On Broadway	Atlantic 8101, Atlantic 5018 (U.K.)
8114	There Goes My Baby	Atlantic 8101, Atlantic 5018 (U.K.)
8119	What D'i Say	The Drifters plus other revue acts

Uptown Theater, Philadelphia, July 24, 1964
(Issued as "Saturday Night at the Uptown," recording features the Drifters, the Vibrations, Patty and the Emblems, and Barbara Lynn, among others.)

The Drifters: Johnny Moore (lead tenor), Charlie Thomas (tenor), Gene Pearson (baritone), and Johnny Terry (bass).

| 8234 | Spanish Lace | Atlantic 2260, Atlantic 4012 (U.K.) |

New York, October 20, 1964

The Drifters: Johnny Moore (lead tenor), Charlie Thomas (tenor), Gene Pearson (baritone), Johnny Terry (bass).

| 8265 | The Christmas Song | Atlantic 2261 |
| 8266 | I Remember Christmas | Atlantic 2261 |

New York, October 22, 1964

The Drifters: Johnny Moore (lead tenor), Charlie Thomas (tenor), Gene Pearson (baritione), and Johnny Terry (bass).

8349/8276	Quando, Quando, Quando	Atlantic LP8103, Atlantic 5023 (U.K.)
8341/8268	I Wish You Love	Atlantic LP8103, Atlantic 5023 (U.K.)
8342/8267	Tonight	Atlantic LP8103, Atlantic 5023 (U.K.)
8343/8272	More	Atlantic LP8103, Atlantic 5023 (U.K.)
8344/8273	What Kind of Fool Am I	Atlantic LP8103, Atlantic 5023 (U.K.)
8345/8271	The Good Life	Atlantic LP8103, Atlantic 5023 (U.K.)
8346/8269	As Long As She Needs Me	Atlantic LP8103, Atlantic 5023 (U.K.)
8347/8277	Desafinado	Atlantic LP8103, Atlantic 5023 (U.K.)
8348/8275	Who Can I Turn To	Atlantic LP8103, Atlantic 5023 (U.K.)
8349/8270	San Francisco	unissued
8350	Temptation	Atlantic LP8103, Atlantic 5023 (U.K.)
8351/8274	On The Street Where You Live	Atlantic LP8103, Atlantic 5023 (U.K.)

Note: The backing tracks for this material were released on October 13, 1964; the "82" numbers pertain to these. The version of "Temptation" is the track from 1959 (3989) with Johnny Moore's vocals dubbed on.

New York, November 10, 1964

180

The Drifters: Johnny Moore (lead tenor), Charlie Thomas (tenor), Gene Pearson (baritone), and Johnny Terry (bass).

8323	In the Park	unissued
8324	At the Club	Atlantic 2268,
		Atlantic 4019 (U.K.)

New York, November 12, 1964

The Drifters: Johnny Moore (lead tenor), Charlie Thomas (tenor), Gene Pearson (baritone), and Johnny Terry (bass).

8447	Answer the Phone	Atlantic 2268,
		Atlantic 4019 (U.K.)

New York, December 31, 1964

The Drifters: Johnny Moore (lead tenor), Charlie Thomas (tenor; lead, "Up on the Roof" and "There Goes My Baby"), Gene Pearson (baritone), and Johnny Terry (bass).

8669	Up on the Roof	unissued
8670	Saturday Night at the Movies	Brook-Lyn 301,
		Atlantic 5026 (U.K.)
8671	Under the Boardwalk	Brook-Lyn 301,
		Atlantic 5026 (U.K.)
8672	There Goes My Baby	unissued

Recorded at the Brooklyn Fox on December 30, 1964, and issued on the album *Murray The K Live at the Brooklyn Fox.* Although recorded prior to "Answer the Phone," the matrix numbers assigned to these recordings follow on from that session, thus their placement in this discography.

The Drifters: Johnny Moore (lead tenor), Charlie Thomas (tenor; lead, "Chains of Love" and "The Outside World"), Gene Pearson (baritone), and Johnny Terry (bass).

8745	Looking Through the Eyes of Love	unissued
8746	Follow Me	Atlantic 2292, Atlantic 4034 (U.K.)
8747	Chains of Love	Atlantic 2285, Atlantic 4023 (U.K.)
8748	Far From the Maddening Crowd	Atlantic 2298, Atlantic 4040 (U.K.)
8749	Come on over to My Place	Atlantic 2285, Atlantic 4023 (U.K.)
8940*	The Outside World	Atlantic 2292, Atlantic 4034 (U.K.)

*Above track is listed in the Atlantic files as having been recorded at this session, despite a difference of 200 numbers in the matrix series.

New York, March 17, 1965

The Drifters: Johnny Moore (lead tenor), Charlie Thomas (tenor), Gene Pearson (baritone), and Johnny Terry (bass).

9078	I'll Take You Where the Music's Playing	Atlantic 2298, Atlantic 4040 (U.K.)
9079	Nylon Stockings	Atlantic 2310, Atlantic 4062 (U.K.)
9080	We Gotta Sing	Atlantic 2310, Atlantic 4062 (U.K.)

New York, June 30, 1965

The Drifters: Johnny Moore (lead tenor), Charlie Thomas (tenor; lead, "You Can't Love Them All"), Gene Pearson (baritone), and Johnny Terry (bass).

| 9880 | Up in the Streets of Harlem | Atlantic 2336, Atlantic 584020 (UK) |

9881	Memories Are Made of This	Atlantic 2325,
		Atlantic 4084 (UK)
9882	You Can't Love Them All	Atlantic 2336,
		Atlantic 584020 (UK)

New York, January 27, 1966

The Drifters: Johnny Moore (lead tenor), Charlie Thomas (tenor), Gene Pearson (baritone), Johnny Terry (bass).

| 9912 | My Islands in the Sun | Atlantic 2352, |
| | | Atlantic 4084 (U.K.) |

New York, February 8, 1966

The Drifters: Johnny Moore (tenor), Charlie Thomas (tenor), Gene Pearson (baritone), and Johnny Terry (bass).

10544	Takes a Good Woman	unissued
10545	Aretha	Atlantic 2366,
		Atlantic 584065 (UK)

New York, July 26, 1966

The Drifters: Johnny Moore (lead tenor), Charlie Thomas (tenor), Rick Sheppard (baritone), and William Brent (bass).

11080	My Baby Is Gone	unissued
11081	Baby What I Mean	Atlantic 2366,
		Atlantic 584065 (UK)

New York, October 12, 1966

The Drifters: Bill Fredericks (lead tenor), Johnny Moore, Charlie Thomas (tenors), and Rick Sheppard (baritone).

12371	Ain't It the Truth	Atlantic 2426
12372*	Dood Song	unissued
	(Up Jumped the Devil)	
12373*	Devil	Atlantic 2426, Atlantic LP40412 (UK)

*The Atlantic files list these as the titles; the record label records them as "Up Jumped the Devil."

New York, May 5, 1967

The Drifters: Johnny Moore (lead tenor), Bill Fredericks (tenor; lead, "I Need You Now"), Rick Sheppard (baritone).

13452	I Dig Your Act	unissued
13454	Still Burning in My Heart	Atlantic 2471
13455	I Need You Now	Atlantic 2471
13456	Country to the City	Atlantic LP40412 (UK)

New York, November 8, 1967

The Drifters: Johnny Moore (lead tenor), Bill Fredericks (tenor; lead, "Steal Away"), Rick Sheppard (baritone), and Milton Turner (bass).

16506	You and Me Together Forever	unissued
16507	Your Best Friend	Atlantic 2624
16508	Steal Away	Atlantic 2624

New York, March 10, 1969

The Drifters: Johnny Moore (lead tenor), Bill Fredericks (tenor; lead, "Black Silk" and "You Got to Pay Your Dues"), Rick Sheppard (baritone), and Don Thomas (bass).

19179	Black Silk	Atlantic 2726
19180*	You Got to Pay Your Dues	Atlantic 2746,
		Atlantic K10700 (UK)
19181	On My Block	unissued
19182	The World Doesn't Matter Anymore	unissued

*This track was bootlegged on the Andee Andee label.

New York, February 24, 1970

The Drifters: Johnny Moore (lead tenor), Bill Fredericks (tenor), Ronald Quinn (baritone)*, and unknown bass.

20936	A Rose by Any Other Name	Atlantic 2786, Atlantic 2091064 (UK)
20937	Be My Lady	Atlantic 2786, Atlantic 2091064 (UK)
20938	I Depend on You	unissued
20939	Guess Who	unissued

*Ronald Quinn was a session vocalist, as was the unidentified fourth vocalist.

Chicago, January 5, 1971

Atlantic U.K. recorded several tracks with the Drifters in 1982, but full session details were unavailable. At that time, the line-up was Ben E. King (tenor), Ray Lewis (tenor), Louis Price (baritone), and Bill Fredericks (baritone/bass). Due to legal problems (which were unspecified), only one single appeared—"You Better Move On"/"Save the Last Dance for Me" (U.K. Atlantic K17743)—and the version of "Save the Last Dance for Me" was a re-cut, featuring Ben E. King on lead (some say it is the original version, but my information is otherwise).

The Atlantic material has appeared on scores of re-issued albums throughout the years, and for those wishing to replace their old records or hear the recordings for the first time the compact disc collections *Let The Boogie Woogie Roll—Greatest Hits 1953-1958* (Atlantic 7 81927) and *All Time Greatest Hits and More—1959-1965* (Atlantic 7 81931) are highly recommended. The former contains all the Drifters' recordings from 1953-58 with the exception of "Moonlight Bay," while the latter has the hits from "There Goes My Baby" to "Come On Over to My Place." It also contains "She Never Talked to Me That Way," which was previously unavailable in America.

As regards the instrumentalists at the Atlantic sessions, the label unfortunately did not specify accompanists in its files. However, during the period 1953-58, the group's session musicians usually included Mickey "Guitar" Baker (Drifters' guitarist Jimmy Oliver did not play on their recordings), Harry Van Walls or Jesse Stone (piano), Howard Biggs (occasionally), Sam "The Man" Taylor, Big Al Sears, Budd Johnson, Ben Webster (sax), Heywood Henry (baritone sax), Panama Francis, Joe Marshall or Connie Kay from the Modern Jazz Quartet (drums), Lloyd Trautman (bass), and Taft Jordan (trumpet).

During the sixties, with the switch away from small combo backings to full orchestra, musicians were usually hired for the sessions without notation as to who played what. Billy Davis/Abdul Samad claims to have played at most of the sessions during his time with the group, but Roy Buchanan was brought in to play guitar on "On Broadway." Buchanan gained almost legendary status with rock guitarists during the sixties, principally due to his work with Dale Hawkins (of "Susie Q" fame) in the late fifties, although solo recordings such as "After Hours" were also held in high regard. He had ongoing drinking and drug problems, however, and frequently missed sessions—Phil Spector took his place at the "On Broadway" session—but he does have a tenuous link to the group, as he provided the guitar on Cody Brennan and the Temptations 1961 revival of "Ruby Baby" (no relation to the Tamla-Motown Temptations). After a period out of the music business, Roy

186

resurfaced in the early seventies with a string of gold albums. Old habits die hard, however, his involvement with drink and drugs continued, and he committed suicide in August 1988 while in police custody—such are the hazards of the rock 'n' roll lifestyle.

The Bell/Arista Recordings

Author's Note: Bell 45s were released between September 1972 and September 1975, when the label ceased. Bell's roster of artists transferred to the new Arista label, where the Drifters remained until late 1978.

All attempts to obtain full information proved hopeless, as BMG, which now owns the rights to these recordings, denied all knowledge of them. Roger Greenaway, who co-produced these tracks, attempted to help, but did so from memory, not from session notes, although his help was much appreciated. Therefore, these recordings are, unfortunately, listed by catalogue number only:

Bell/Arista 45's
(UK except when otherwise noted)

Bell 320 (US) You've Got Your Troubles/I'm Feeling Sad
Bell 1269　　 Every Night/Something Tells Me
Bell 387 (US) Like Sister and Brother/The Songs We Used to Sing (Bell 1313 in U.K.)
Bell 1339　　 I'm Free for the Rest of Your Life/Say Goodbye to Angelina
Bell 600　　 Kissing in the Back Row of the Movies/I'm Feeling Sad (Bell 1358 in U.K.)
Bell 1381　　 Down on the Beach Tonight/Say Goodbye to Angelina
Bell 1396　　 Love Games/The Cut Is Deep
Bell 1433　　 There Goes My First Love/Don't Cry On aWeekend
Bell 1462　　 Can I Take You Home Little Girl/Please Help Me Down

Bell 1469	Hello Happiness/I Can't Get Away from You
Bell 1491	Every Nite's a Saturday Night with You/I'll Get to Know Your Name along the Way
Arista 78	You're More Than a Number in My Little Red Book/Do You Have to Go Now
Arista 94	I'll Know When True Love Really Passes By/ A Good Song Never Dies
Arista 124	It Looks Like I'm the Clown Again/I Can't Believe It's Over
Arista 190	Honey You're Heaven to Me/When Ya Comin' Home
Arista 202	Closely Guarded Secret/I Can't Believe It's Over

Bell/Arista Albums

Author's Note: On these recordings, the Drifters were augmented by session singers, the names of whom were supplied by Roger Greenaway.

The Drifters personnel listed are those at the time of issue, and the initials refer to the lead vocalists.

The Drifters Now (Bell 219)

Side One
> You've Got Your Troubles (JM)
> Four and Twenty Hours (JM)
> Sweet Caroline (JM)
> Love Me, Love the Life I Lead (BF/JM)
> Save the Last Dance for Me (BF)
> (There's) Always Something There to Remind Me (BF)

Side Two
> Every Night (JM)
> Something Tells Me (JM)
> Deep Down Inside (JM)
> I'm Feeling Sad (JM)
> Say Goodbye to Angelina (JM)
> The Songs We Used to Sing (JM)

Note: The line-up for this LP included Johnny Moore, Bill Fredericks, Butch Leake, and Grant Kitchings.

Issued February 1973

Love Games (Bell 246)

Side One
    Love Games (JM)
    Like Sister and Brother (BF)
    I'm Ready (JM)
    If You're Gonna Love Me (BF/JM)
    The Cut Is Deep (JM)
    I Can't Get Away from You (BF)
Side Two
    Kissing in the Back Row of the Movies (JM)
    I'm Free for the Rest of Your Life (BF)
    I Can't Live Without You (JM)
    If It Feels Good, Do It (BF)
    A Blessing in Disguise (BF)
    Down on the Beach Tonight (JM)

Note: The album sleeve features Clyde Brown instead of Bill Fredericks, but obviously Fredericks was present on at least some of the recordings. Roger Greenaway listed the group as Moore, Kitchings, Leake, and Brown, but this cannot be totally accurate.

Issued May 1975

The Drifters 24 Original Hits (Atlantic K 460 106)

Side One
    Saturday Night At the Movies
    Dance With Me
    Some Kind of Wonderful
    When My Little Girl is Smiling

Come on over to My Place
Save the Last Dance for Me
At the Club
Up on the Roof
On Broadway
There Goes My Baby
I'll Take You Where the Music's Playing
Under the Boardwalk

Side Two

Sweet Caroline
I'm Free for the Rest of Your Life
Every Night
Like Sister and Brother
The Songs We Used to Sing
There Goes My First Love
Love Games
Love Me, Love the Life I Lead
If It Feels Good, Do It
Blessing In Disguise
Down on the Beach Tonight

Note: In 1975, Atlantic and Bell collaborated on the release of this album (Side One was comprised of Atlantic recordings, Side Two, Bell). It was an enormous success in the U.K. (number 1), and continued its popularity throughout the world in subsequent years. Initial pressings featured a gatefold sleeve picturing various Drifters' lineups.

There Goes My First Love (Bell 260)

Side One

Hello Happiness (JM)
Harlem Child (JM)
The Juggler (CB)
Lovin' You Is Easy (JM)
And with No Regrets (JM)
If Only I Could Start Again (CB)

Side Two
    I've Got You on My Mind (JM)
    You Chose a Fine Time (JM)
    Don't Cry on a Weekend (JM)
    Please Help Me Down (JM)
    Can I Take You Home Little Girl (JM)
    There Goes My First Love (JM)

Note: At the time of this album's release, the Drifters were Johnny Moore, Clyde Brown, Butch Leake, and Billy Lewis, although Roger Greenaway stated that Moore, Clyde Brown and Bill Fredericks were the principals, augmented by session vocalists Tony Burrows, Brian Bennett, and Greenaway himself. This recollection seems a bit dubious, as Fredericks left the group during 1974. Without the session notes, who's to know for sure?

Issued January 1976

Every Nite's a Saturday Night with You (Arista 140)

Side One
    You're More Than a Number in My Little Red Book (CB/JM)
    I'll Get to Know Your Name Along the Way (JM)
    Do You Have to Go Now (JM)
    Like a Movie I've Seen Before (JB)
    Twice a Week (JM/JB)
    Another Kind of Sorrow (JM)
Side Two
    Sweet Little Rock 'n' Roller (JM)
    Midnight Cowboy (CB)
    Another Lonely Weekend (JM)
    I'll Know When True Love Really Passes By (JB)
    Summer in the City (CB)
    Every Nite's a Saturday Night with You (JM)

Note: Again, there are doubts about who is actually on these recordings. Greenaway, for example, feels that the lead on "Midnight Cowboy" is Joe Blunt, although it sounds like Clyde Brown.

The sleeve features Johnny Moore, Clyde Brown, Joe Blunt, and Billy Lewis, who were augmented by Tony Burrows, Russell Stone, and Roger Greenaway (again, according to Greenaway).

Issued October 1976

The Best of the Drifters   (Arista 4114 (US))

Side One
   Under the Boardwalk (JM)
   Like Sister and Brother (BF)
   Kissing in the Back Row of the Movies (JM)
   Love Games (JM)
   On Broadway (JM)
Side Two
   Save the Last Dance for Me (BF)
   There Goes My First Love (JM)
   Can I Take You Home Little Girl (JM)
   Hello Happiness (JM)
   Every Night (JM)

Note: This U.S. release features a re-cut version of "On Broadway" with Johnny Moore listed as the lead, but the rest of the record—except for "Under the Boardwalk" (which may also be a re-recording)—features various tracks from 1972-1975.

Issued November 1976

The Epic Recordings

Author's Note: Once again, all efforts to obtain the exact session details for these recordings proved fruitless. They appear to have been recorded in mid 1979; produced by Biddhu. Epic, like BMG, seems unaware that it has any Drifters recordings in its catalog.

Drifters personnel for these records included Clyde Brown (tenor), Ray Lewis (tenor), Joe Blunt (baritone), and Billy Lewis (baritone).

Epic EPC 7806	Pour Your Little Heart Out/Instrumental
Epic EPC 8559	I'm Not That Kind of Guy/What Am I Doing

Issued August 1979 and April 1980, respectively.

Miscellaneous Notes

This section deals with some recordings which will probably be of interest to Drifters fans.

First, the Drifters were featured on the *Live at the Brooklyn Fox* album (KFM 101) recorded during the Murray The K shows at that theater in 1963. The Drifters number on this record was an uptempo version of "There Goes My Baby" featuring Charlie Thomas, but it does not appear in the Atlantic files, so possibly this was a bootleg album. Other acts featured include the Ronettes, Shangri-las, Ben E. King, Jay and the Americans, and Jan and Dean.

There are several albums available by Charlie Thomas's Drifters, but these should simply be avoided. They include *The Drifters' 16 Greatest Hits* (Trip-Top 16-6), *The Drifters Meet the Coasters* (TVP 1002), *Save the Last Dance for Me* (51 West Records 016041), *The Drifters' Greatest Hits* (Gusto GT-0063). All these are U.S. issues, but copies frequently creep into the U.K., usually as budget-priced offerings, complete with a jacket photograph featuring the Johnny Moore group!

Speaking of Johnny Moore, the recordings he made with the Hornets prior to his joining the Drifters were issued around 1980 on an album called *The Hornets and the 5C's* (Pea Vine PLP 9036). The Hornets tracks include "Lonesome Baby," "You Played the Game," "Ridin' & Rockin'," "I Can't Believe," and "Big City Bounce."

The U.S. album *Savoy Vocal Group Album* (Savoy 2241), which came out in the early eighties, has several tracks of interest. It features four cuts by Little David Baughan and the Harps ("I Won't Cry," "You'll Pay," "Baby Dee," and "Wah Diddy Wah"), plus four by the Carols featuring Tommy Evans on bass ("Call on Me," "I Got a Feeling," "Mighty Lak a Rose," and "Fifty Million Women."

For obsessive fans, Jimmy Lewis, who never sang with the "official" Drifters, although he was lead vocalist with Bill Pinckney's Original Drifters from 1963-65, recorded "Feelin' In Mah Bones" (4J 508), "I Have Love (for You)" (4J 512) in 1963, and also had some success with "Wait Until Spring" (number unknown) prior to joining Pinckney. Lewis did, of course, have an r & b hit in 1968 with "The Girls from Texas" (Minit 32017).

In 1959, De Besth Records issued the Five Crowns' "I Want You" (De Besth 123), and while nothing concrete is known of this group, we can assume this was the Duvals, unless anyone cares to inform us of the contrary.

Finally, to round out this section of trivia, Bill Pinckney's Flyers recorded two unissued sides for Atco in 1956—"Careless Love" (Atco 56C 104) and "Hey Susan" (Atco 56C 105).

The Drifters' Hit Singles:
American & British Charts

Author's Note: The Drifters initial success in America was, with the exception of "White Christmas" in December 1954, restricted to the black-oriented rhythm and blues charts. Many of the group's hits from this period outsold dozens of records which appeared on the white-dominated national charts. One major reason why the group failed to cross over into the mainstream American market during the fifties was the presence of puerile white cover versions of black tunes, covers which invariably garnered radio airplay to the detriment of the originals. Racial prejudice, as prevalent in the American music business as anywhere else, maintained the separation of musical styles along color lines almost to the end of the decade.

Unfortunately, the information available from the r & b charts of that period tends to be incomplete, as on occasion the list was restricted to the top ten positions only. Additionally, *Billboard* magazine, for example, abandoned r & b as a chart category completely for two years during the sixties.

Despite these complicating factors, the r & b charts reveal that the early Drifters scored major hits beginning in the early fifties with the following Ertegun/Wexler productions, all of them Clyde McPhatter-led singles: "Money Honey" (#1, 1953), "Lucille" (#7, 1954), "Such a Night" (#5, 1954), "Honey Love" (#1, 1954), "White Christmas" (#3, 1955), and "What'cha Gonna Do" (#8, 1955). They also had a hit with "Bip Bam," although its exact high point is uncertain. In early 1956, they had a #9 r & b hit with "Steamboat" (sung by Bill Pinckney), while the Johnny Moore tracks "Adorable," "Ruby Baby," "Soldier of Fortune," "I Gotta Get Myself a Woman," and "Yodee Yakee" were all strong rhythm and blues sellers.

A record of the group's *Billboard* national chartings, detailing their successes outside the r & b category, follows.

The Drifters' Hit Singles:

Song Title	Lead Vocalist	Session Date
White Christmas*	Bill Pinckney and Clyde McPhatter	Feb. 14, 1954
Fools Fall In Love	Johnny Moore	Nov. 8, 1956
Hypnotized	Johnny Moore	Apr. 16, 1957
Moonlight Bay	Group vocal	Apr. 28, 1958
Drip Drop	Bobby Hendricks	Apr. 28, 1958
There Goes My Baby	Ben E. King	Mar. 6, 1959
Dance with Me	Ben E. King	Jul. 9, 1959
True Love, True Love	Johnny Williams	Jul. 9, 1959
This Magic Moment	Ben E. King	Dec. 23, 1959
Lonely Winds	Ben E. King	Dec. 23, 1959
Save the Last Dance for Me	Ben E. King	May 19, 1960
I Count the Tears	Ben E. King	May 19, 1960
Some Kind of Wonderful	Rudy Lewis	Feb. 1, 1961
Please Stay	Rudy Lewis	Feb. 1, 1961
Sweets for My Sweet	Charlie Thomas	Feb. 1, 1961
Room Full of Tears	Charlie Thomas	Feb. 1, 1961
When My Little Girl Is Smiling	Charlie Thomas	Oct. 26, 1961
Stranger on the Shore	Rudy Lewis	Mar. 15, 1962
Up on the Roof	Rudy Lewis	Jun. 28, 1962
On Broadway	Rudy Lewis	Jan. 22, 1963
Rat Race	Rudy Lewis	Apr. 12, 1963
If You Don't Come Back	Johnny Moore	Apr. 12, 1963
I'll Take You Home	Johnny Moore	Apr. 12, 1963
Vaya Con Dios	Rudy Lewis	Dec. 11, 1963
One Way Love	Johnny Moore	Dec. 11, 1963
Under the Boardwalk	Johnny Moore	May 21, 1964
I've Got Sand In My Shoes	Johnny Moore	Aug. 4, 1964
Saturday Night at the Movies	Johnny Moore	Aug. 4, 1964
At the Club	Johnny Moore	Nov. 12, 1964
Come on over to My Place	Johnny Moore	Mar. 17, 1965
Chains of Love	Charlie Thomas	Mar. 17, 1965
Follow Me	Johnny Moore	Mar. 17, 1965
I'll Take You Where the Music's Playing	Johnny Moore	Jun. 30, 1965
Memories Are Made of This	Johnny Moore	Jan. 27, 1966
Baby What I Mean	Johnny Moore	Oct. 12, 1966
Still Burning In My Heart	Johnny Moore	Nov. 8, 1967

*Initially charting in 1954, the song re-entered at #96 in 1960, and again in 1962 at #88.

196

The American Charts

Producer	Label/Catalog #	Release Date	Peak Position
Ahmet Ertegun and Jerry Wexler	Atlantic 1048	Nov. 1954	80
Leiber & Stoller	Atlantic 1123	Jan. 1957	69
Jerry Wexler	Atlantic 1141	May 1957	79
Leiber & Stoller	Atlantic 1187	May 1958	72
Leiber & Stoller	Atlantic 1187	May 1958	58
Leiber & Stoller	Atlantic 2025	May 1959	2
Leiber & Stoller	Atlantic 2040	Oct. 1959	15
Leiber & Stoller	Atlantic 2040	Oct. 1959	33
Leiber & Stoller	Atlantic 2050	Feb. 1960	16
Leiber & Stoller	Atlantic 2062	May 1960	54
Leiber & Stoller	Atlantic 2071	Aug. 1960	2
Leiber & Stoller	Atlantic 2087	Dec. 1960	17
Leiber & Stoller	Atlantic 2096	Mar. 1961	32
Leiber & Stoller	Atlantic 2105	May 1961	14
Leiber & Stoller	Atlantic 2117	Sep. 1961	16
Leiber & Stoller	Atlantic 2127	Dec. 1961	72
Leiber & Stoller	Atlantic 2134	Feb. 1962	28
Leiber & Stoller	Atlantic 2143	Apr. 1962	73
Leiber & Stoller	Atlantic 2162	Oct. 1962	5
Leiber & Stoller	Atlantic 2182	Mar. 1963	9
Leiber & Stoller	Atlantic 2191	May 1963	71
Leiber & Stoller	Atlantic 2191	May 1963	101
Leiber & Stoller	Atlantic 2201	Aug. 1963	25
Bert Berns	Atlantic 2216	Jan. 1964	43
Bert Berns	Atlantic 2225	Apr. 1964	56
Bert Berns	Atlantic 2237	Jun. 1964	4
Bert Berns	Atlantic 2253	Sep. 1964	33
Bert Berns	Atlantic 2260	Nov. 1964	18
Bert Berns	Atlantic 2268	Jan. 1965	43
Bert Berns	Atlantic 2285	Apr. 1965	60
Bert Berns	Atlantic 2285	Apr. 1965	90
Bert Berns	Atlantic 2292	Jun. 1965	91
Bert Berns	Atlantic 2298	Jul. 1965	51
Bert Berns	Atlantic 2325	Mar. 1966	48
Bob Gallo	Atlantic 2366	Nov. 1966	62
Lou Courtney and Bob Bateman	Atlantic 2471	Jan. 1968	115

The Drifters' Hit Singles:

Song Title	Lead Vocalist	Session Date
Dance with Me	Ben E. King	Jul. 9, 1959
Save the Last Dance for Me	Ben E. King	May 19, 1960
I Count the Tears	Ben E. King	May 19, 1960
When My Little Girl Is Smiling	Charlie Thomas	Oct. 26, 1961
I'll Take You Home	Johnny Moore	Apr. 12, 1963
Under the Boardwalk	Johnny Moore	May 21, 1964
At the Club	Johnny Moore	Nov. 12, 1964
Come on over to My Place	Johnny Moore	Mar. 17, 1965
Baby What I Mean	Johnny Moore	Oct. 12, 1966
At the Club/Saturday Night At the Movies (reissue)	Johnny Moore	Nov. 12,1964/ Aug. 4, 1964
Come on over to My Place	Johnny Moore	Mar. 17, 1965
Like Sister and Brother	Bill Fredericks	Unknown
Kissing In the Back Row of the Movies	Johnny Moore	Unknown
Down on the Beach Tonight	Johnny Moore	Unknown
Love Games	Johnny Moore	Unknown
There Goes My First Love	Johnny Moore	Unknown
Can I Take You Home Little Girl	Johnny Moore	Unknown
Hello Happiness	Johnny Moore	Unknown
Every Nite's a Saturday Night With You	Johnny Moore	Unknown
You're More Than a Number In My Little Red Book	Johnny Moore/Clyde Brown	Unknown
Save the Last Dance for Me/ When My Little Girl Is Smiling (reissue)	Ben E. King/Charlie Thomas	May 19, 1960/ Oct. 26, 1961

Although many of the Drifters' records (e.g., "There Goes My Baby," "This Magic Moment," "Please Stay," etc.) failed to make the singles charts at the time of release, these have all become familiar to U.K. fans through a sucession of huge-selling "greatest hits" and "best of" compilation albums.

198

The British Charts

Producer	Label/Catalog #	Release Date	Peak Position
Leiber & Stoller	London HLK 8988	Dec. 1959	17
Leiber & Stoller	London HLK 9201	Sep. 1960	2
Leiber & Stoller	London HLK 9287	Feb. 1961	28
Leiber & Stoller	London HLK 9522	Mar. 1962	31
Leiber & Stoller	London HLK 9785	Sep. 1963	37
Bert Berns	Atlantic AT 4001	Aug. 1964	45
Bert Berns	Atlantic AT 4019	Feb. 1965	39
Bert Berns	Atlantic AT 4023	Apr. 1965	40
Bob Gallo	Atlantic 584 065	Jan. 1967	49
Bert Berns	Atlantic K 10148	Mar. 1972	3
Bert Berns	Atlantic K 10216	Jul. 1972	9
Roger Greenaway	Bell 1313	Jun. 1973	7
Roger Greenaway	Bell 1358	Apr. 1974	2
Roger Greenaway	Bell 1381	Sep. 1974	7
Roger Greenaway	Bell 1396	Jan. 1975	33
Roger Greenaway	Bell 1433	Aug. 1975	3
Roger Greenaway	Bell 1462	Oct. 1975	10
Roger Greenaway	Bell 1469	Feb. 1976	12
Roger Greenaway	Bell 1491	Sep. 1976	29
Roger Greenaway	Arista 78	Dec. 1976	5
Leiber & Stoller	Lightning LIG 9014	Mar. 1979	69

APPENDIX 5

Non-related
"Drifters" Recordings

Label/Cat.#	Group	Songs	Date
Coral 65037	The Drifters	I'm the Caring Kind/ Wine Headed Woman	Sep. 1950
Coral 65040	The Drifters	I Had to Find Out for Myself/ And I Shook	Nov. 1950
London 16011	Ernie Andrews & The Drifters	I Don't Want to See You Cry Anymore/ The Dog, the Cat and Me	1950
Excelsior (#?)	The Drifters	Mobile/Honey Chile	1951
Rama 22*	The Drifters	Besame Mucho/Summertime	1953
Class 500**	The Drifters	Three Lies/That Lazy Mood	ca. 1953
Crown 108	The Drifters	The World Is Changing/ Sacroiliac Swing	1954
Drifter 101	Jimmy Williams	Rainbow Heart/Teardrops and Memories	1954
Capitol 4220⁺	The Drifters	Don't Be a Fool/Feelin' Fine	1959
ABC 10042⁺	Cliff Richard & The Drifters	Living Doll/Apron Strings	1959
QualityChekd⁺⁺	The Drifters	Cherry Chocolate Twist/(non-Drifters flip)	1963

*Probably unreleased.
**An early series from the Class label, owned by Leon Rene, for which Bobby Day later recorded. In all liklihood, this is the same group as the one on the Excelsior label, which was owned by Leon's brother Otis.
⁺These are the two records by the English instrumental group which subsequently changed its name to the Shadows (one pressing of the ABC record did say "Cliff Richard & The Drifters").
⁺⁺This is *not* The Drifters, but a Surfaris-style surf ditty produced by Quality Chekd to promote its products. No details available as to the identity of the performers —probably one of the multitude of garage bands populating the era.

Doc Pomus
and Mort Shuman

Finally, we would like to pay tribute to the above mentioned songwriters who both, sadly, died during 1991—Doc Pomus in New York City on March 14, Mort Shuman in London on November 2.

Together they wrote many of the classic songs from the golden age of rock and roll and rhythm and blues, their compositions having been recorded by Elvis Presley, Big Joe Turner, Dion and the Belmonts, Gene Vincent, Bobby Darin, the Coasters, Jerry Lee Lewis, the Everly Brothers, and Del Shannon, to name but a few.

For the Drifters, they supplied "True Love, True Love," "Lonely Winds," "This Magic Moment," "Nobody But Me," "I Count the Tears," "Sweets for My Sweet," "Room Full of Tears," "She Never Talked to Me That Way," and, of course, the immortal "Save the Last Dance for Me," which, no matter who revives it, will always belong to the Drifters.

Pomus and Shuman captured the innocence of their time, racking up sales of over thirty million dollars with their songs, and their likes will never be seen again. And while they may be gone, for as long as people sing, they will never be forgotten.

General Index

A

ABC Records 201
Abbott Records 68
Abet Records 131
Abramson, Herb 3
Academy Of Music, New York City 131
Ace Records 83
The Aces 89
Adams, Faye 55
Adams, Walter 25, 32, 159, 167
Adorable (song) 58, 59, 170, 195
After Hours (song) 186
Again (song) 72
Ain't It The Truth (song) 114, 184
Alan, Patrick 149, 165
Aldon Music 89, 96
Alexander, Chuck 131
All Around The World (song) 148
All My Life (song) 56
All Time Greatest Hits And More—1959-1965 (CD) 186
Alone Again (song) 72
Along Came Jones (song) 61
Alston, Shirley 132
Am I To Be The One (song) 126
American Bandstand (TV program) 84
Amor, Ecstasy (song) 87
Amy Records 48
And I Shook (song) 21, 201
And With No Regrets (song) 141, 190
Andee Andee Records 185
Anderson, Benny 128, 130, 131
Anderson, William "Chick" 17, 22, 24, 159, 167
Andres, Arvis 125

Andrews, Ernie 21, 201
Andrews, Inez 138
Andrews, Michael 125
The Angels 100
Anka, Paul 66
Another Kind Of Sorrow (song) 191
Another Lonely Weekend (song) 191
Another Night With The Boys (song) 95, 96, 176
Answer The Phone (song) 108, 181
Apollo Theater 17, 27, 33, 68, 71
Apollo Theatre (Glasgow) 141, 142
Applebaun, Stan 47
Apron Strings (song) 201
Aretha (song) 113, 114, 183
Arista Records 133, 138, 142, 187, 188, 191, 192, 199
Aristocrat Records 3
"Arnold" 106
Arnold, P.P. 125
Around The Corner (song) 87
As Long As She Needs Me (song) 180
Asch, Moses 24
At The Club (song) 96, 108, 113, 136, 181, 190, 196, 198
At The Fair (song) 72
At The Hop (song) 64
Atco Records 64, 172, 194
Atlantic Records 2, 3, 10, 19, 20, 22, 23, 25, 27, 29, 32, 36, 39, 41, 42, 44, 45, 49, 56, 58, 59, 60, 61, 64, 65, 67, 75, 76, 81, 82, 83, 84, 87, 88, 89, 93, 94, 97, 99, 100, 101, 106, 107, 110, 112, 114, 116, 119, 120, 121, 133, 135, 136, 138, 144, 167, 169, 170, 172, 173, 174, 175, 176, 177, 178, 179, 180, 181, 182, 183, 184, 185, 186, 189, 190, 193, 197, 199
Autry, Gene 1
Avalon, Frankie 81
Average White Band 88

B

B & B Records 106
B & C Records 49
BBC Radio One 137
BMG 138, 187, 193
Baby Dee (song) 194
Baby What I Mean (song) 114, 183, 196, 198
Bacharach, Burt 90, 92, 136
Bagsby, Doc 85
Bailey, Dee Ernie 64
Bailey, William "Bug Eye" 73, 96
Baker, LaVern 41, 55, 60, 66
Baker, Mickey "Guitar" 27, 186
Baldwin, David 17, 19, 22, 23, 24, 126, 159, 167
Baldwin, James 17
Baldwin, William "Lover" 17, 22
Ballard, Hank 35, 52
Baltimore (song) 76, 81, 174
Bang Records 110
Banks, Al 131, 132
Barbara Lee (song) 6
Barlow, Dean 114
"Barrelhouse Tommy" 14
Barry, Jeff 112
Barton, Eileen 1
Bartram's And Ringwold's Circus 42
Baskerville, Charles 119, 162

Bass, Ralph 19
Bateman, Bob 119, 197
Baton Records 95
Baughan, David ("Little David") 22, 24, 51, 53, 55, 56, 58, 92, 125, 126, 128, 157, 159, 160, 167, 170, 194
The Bay City Rollers 141
Be My Lady (song) 121, 185
The Beatles 87, 102, 103, 105, 112, 145, 152
Beauregard, Hughie 106
Beautiful Music (song) 100, 178
The Bee-Gees 138
Begin The Beguine (song) 31
The Beginning Of It All (LP) 87
Bell Records 133, 136, 137, 138, 141, 142, 157, 187, 188, 189, 190, 199
The Bells (song) 19
The Bells Of Saint Mary's (song) 34, 35, 36, 41, 51, 169
The Belmonts 133, 203
Belvin, Jesse 121
Bennett, Brain 191
Bennett, Cliff 102
Bennett, Tony 10, 111
Benny And Us (LP) 88
Benton, Brook 25, 46, 47
Berns, Bert 99, 100, 101, 102, 105, 106, 108, 110, 112, 113, 197, 199
Berry, Chuck 8, 59, 66, 80, 110
Bertha 50
Besame Mucho (song) 22, 201
Best Love (song) 96
The Best Of The Drifters (LP) 192
Beverly, Harold "Sundown" 129
Biddhu 143, 193
Big City Bounce (song)

55, 194
Big Deal Records 119
Big Top Records 93
Biggest Rhythm And Blues Show 55
Biggest Rock And Roll Show 41
The Biggest Show Of Stars 66
Biggs, Howard 35, 186
The Bihari Brothers 3
Bilk, Acker 94
Bill Haley And His Comets 59, 60
Bill Pinckney And The Originals 128
Billboard (magazine) 2, 20, 21, 29, 36, 45, 59, 64, 76, 114, 119, 195
Billy Ward And The Dominoes 18
Bingo (song) 131
Bip Bam (song) 31, 32, 39, 169, 195
Bishop-Gamble (songwriting team) 110
Black, Bill 47
Black Silk (song) 120, 184, 185
Blackwell, Otis 61
Blaine, Jerry 6
The Blasters 60
The Blenders 5
A Blessing In Disguise (song) 189, 190
The Blue Bells 106, 108
Blue Mink (song) 136
The Bluenotes 129
The Blues Serenaders 27
Blunt, Joe 141, 143, 144, 163, 164, 192, 193
"Bob B. Soxx" 51
Bobby Day And The Satellites 48
The Bobettes 66
Bono, Sonny 112
Boogie Chillen (song) 4
Boogie Woogie Country Girl (song) 82
Book Of Memories (song) 50

Booker, Richie 132
Boone, Pat 29, 52, 59, 152
The Bop Chords 73
Bowen, Jimmy 66
Brace Yourself (song) 87
Bracey, Herman 85
Bradshaw, Tiny 114
The Brand New Drifters Ltd. 126
Brennan, Cody 186
Brenston, Jackie 9
Brent, William 113, 114, 159, 162, 183
Brewster, William Herbert 14
Brill Building 89, 90
Broke Blues (song) 129
Broken Heart (song) 143
Brooklyn Fox Theater 100, 108, 181
Brook-Lyn Records 181
Broonzy, Big Bill 3, 20
Brotherhood Of Man 138
Brown, Bill 18, 53
Brown, Clyde 138, 141, 142, 143, 144, 163, 164, 189, 191, 192, 193, 198
Brown, James 127
Brown, Leroy 73
Brown, Milton 134
Brown, Roy 2, 4
Brown, Ruth 41, 116, 121
Brown, Tommy 66
Bryant, James 25
Bryant, Rusty 55
Bubblegum Pop (song) 90
Buchanan, Roy 186, 187
Buddy Holly And The Crickets 87
Buffalo Springfield 116
Bulldog Records 129
Burke, Solomon 100
Burn The Candle (song) 5
Burnette, Johnny 8
Burrows, Tony 138, 191, 192
Burton, Ed 101
But Your Mine (song) 112

Byrd, Russell 100
The Byrds 123

C

The Cadillacs 73, 75
Caesar, Bruce 128
Calhoun, Charles 31
Call On Me (song) 194
Camelot Inn 50
Cameo Records 100
Can I Take You Home
  Little Girl (song) 141,
  187, 191, 192, 198
Candida (song) 120
Capitol Records 3, 46,
  113, 124, 201
The Capris 131
Caravan Records 74
Careless Love (song)
  194
Carmichael, Hoagy 6
The Carols 62, 194
Carter, Benny 114
Cashbox (magazine) 76
Castle In The Sky (song)
  73
Catwalk (song) 68
Chains Of Love (song)
  110, 181, 182, 196
The Chancellors 141
Chandler, Gene 105
Chandler, George 145,
  147, 148, 164
Charles, Ray 20, 76, 82,
  84, 149
"Charly" 106
Chase, Lincoln 31
Checker, Chubby 85
The Checkers 53, 55
Chelsea Vocational
  School 17
Cherry Chocolate Twist
  (song) 201
Chess, Leonard 3, 80
Chess, Phil 3
Chess Records 3, 55, 59
Chessler, Dorothy 6
The Chiffons 100, 119
Christmas Just Ain't
  Christmas (song) 129
The Christmas Song
  (song) 106, 180
Chudd, Lew 3

Church Bells May Ring
  (song) 72
Clanton, Jimmy 83
The Clara Ward Singers
  85
Clark, Claudie 73
Clark, Dee 51
Clark, Dick 84, 100
Clark, James "Poppa"
  71, 72, 73, 74
Clark, John "Sonny Boy"
  72, 73
Clark, Lil 99
Clark, Nicky 72, 73
Clark, Petula 111
Class Records 22, 201
The Cleftones 95, 113
The Cleveland Quartet 55
Cliff Bennett And The
  Rebel Rousers 102
Closely Guarded Secret
  (song) 142, 188
The Clovers 22
The Coasters 61, 66, 67,
  82, 84, 203
Cochran, Eddie 102
Cockerhan, Chuck 129
Cody Brennan And The
  Temptations 186
Cofie, Joe 148, 149, 164,
  165
Cole, Clay 85
Cole, Nat "King" 20
Collins, Dorothy 42
Collins, Joan 143
The Colts 41, 58
Columbia Pictures Corp.
  136
Columbia Records 3, 10,
  32, 87
Come Back Baby (song)
  127
Come On Over To My
  Place (song) 110, 136,
  148, 182, 186, 190, 196,
  198
Come What May (song)
  44
The Comets 59, 60
Como, Perry 3, 10, 44
Confused Man (song) 128
Cooder, Ry 152
Cook, Tony 129

Cooke, Roger 136, 137
Cooke, Sam 52
Cooper Junior High
  School 17
Copa Cabana (nightclub)
  111
Coral Records 21, 201
Country To The City
  (song) 119, 184
The Counts 55
Courtney, Lou 119, 197
Cow Palace (auditorium)
  127
Craig, Francis 31
Crazy Man Crazy (song)
  10
The Crests 132
The Crew-Cuts 10, 42
Crewe, Bob 87
Crewe Records 87
The Crickets 66, 72, 73,
  87, 114
Crown Records 22, 201
The Crowns 71, 73, 74,
  75, 77, 79, 82, 85, 119,
  123, 126
Crudup, Arthur 10
Cry Baby (song) 100
Cry To Me (song) 100
The Cryin' Shame 141
Crying In The Chapel
  (song) 8
The Crystals 96, 123
Cub Records 85
The Cues 5
Curtis, King 47
The Cut Is Deep (song)
  187, 189
Cy Records 85

D

Daddy's Home (song)
  119
Danbridge, Dan 113,
  162
Dance With Me (song)
  82, 99, 152, 174, 189,
  196, 198
Danny And The Juniors
  64
Darin, Bobby 45, 84, 90,
  203

Darrow, Clarence 97
Darrow, Johnny 97, 143
The Darts 35
David, Hal 136
Davis, Billy 85, 94, 107,
  119, 136, 159, 186
Davis, Florence 94
Davis, Joe 72
Davis, Richard 71, 72
Davis, Sammy, Jr. 116
Dawn 120, 121, 157
Day, Bobby 48, 201
Day, Doris 2
Day, Steve 124
The Dealers 120
De Besth Records 194
Decca Records 3, 21, 31,
  45, 49, 50, 84, 141
Deep Down Inside (song)
  188
Dejection (song) 17
The Dells 145
Deluxe Records 4
Denver (song) 49
Deram Records 49
Desafinado (song) 180
Devil (song) 184
Devil In Law (song) 107
The Diablos 51
Diamond, Neil 136
The Diamonds 59, 62
Dick And Dee Dee 108
Diddley, Bo 41, 60, 85
Didn't It (song) 100,
  177, 178
DiMucci, Dion 133, 152,
  203
Ding Dong (song) 114
Dion 133, 152, 203
Dion And The Belmonts
  133, 152, 203
Dixon, Julius 36
Do Something For Me
  (song) 18
Do You Have To Go Now
  (song) 188, 191
Do You Remember (song)
  73
The Dog, The Cat, And
  Me (song) 21, 201
Domino, Fats 3, 65
The Dominoes 6, 17, 18,
  19, 22, 24, 29, 36, 47,
  51, 52, 53, 97, 149
Don't Be A Fool (song)
  124, 201
Don't Call Me (song)
  127
Don't Cry On A Weekend
  (song) 141, 187, 191
Don't Dog Me (song) 31,
  32, 169
Don't Have To Hunt No
  More (song) 72
Don't Knock The Rock
  (film) 8
Don't Play That Song
  (song) 87
Don't Start Me Talking
  (song) 97
Dood Song (Up Jumped
  The Devil) (song) 184
Dootone Records 10
Dorsey, Thomas A. 14,
  15, 17
Douglas, Craig 93
The Dovells 94, 100
Dowd, Tom 29, 31, 76,
  107, 114
Down On The Beach
  Tonight (song) 138,
  187, 189, 190, 198
Down Town (song) 111
The Drapers 96, 97, 126
Drifter Records 201
The Drifters' Greatest
  Hits (LP) 193
Drifters, Inc. 123
The Drifters Meet The
  Coasters (LP) 193
The Drifters Now (LP)
  137, 157, 188
The Drifters' 16 Greatest
  Hits (LP) 193
The Drifters 24 Original
  Hits (LP) 189
Drifting Away From You
  (song) 53, 59, 65, 170
Drip Drop (song) 67, 68,
  75, 152, 173, 196
The Du-Droppers 62
Dum Dum Dee Dum Dum
  (song) 75
Duncan, Joe 114
The Duvals 73, 79, 87,
  96, 106, 126, 194
Dynasty (TV program)
  143

E

Early In The Morning
  (song) 56
Earth Angel (song) 10
Easter Parade (song) 41
Ebony (magazine) 97
Eddy, Duane 45
Edison Lighthouse 138
Ellington, Duke 27
Ellis, Butch 106
Ellis, Jonah 145, 159,
  164
Ellis, Ray 42, 44, 67
Ember Records 46
The Embers 95
The Emblems 106, 179
The Embraceables 85
The Enchanters 100
End Records 126, 127
Epic Records 143, 193
Ernie Andrews And The
  Drifters 21
Ertegun, Ahmet 3, 19,
  20, 22, 23, 28, 31, 35,
  36, 39, 42, 53, 58, 65,
  76, 87, 99, 110, 149, 195,
  197
Ertegun, Nesuhi 58, 110
Essex Records 10
Evans, Tommy 62, 66,
  67, 68, 85, 89, 90, 94,
  96, 106, 116, 125, 160,
  161, 172, 173, 175, 176,
  177, 194
The Everly Brothers 66,
  203
Every Night (song) 136,
  187, 188, 190, 192
Every Nite's A Saturday
  Night With You (LP)
  191
Every Nite's A Saturday
  Night With You (song)
  142, 188, 191, 198
Everybody Needs
  Somebody To Love
  (song) 100
Everyone's Laughing
  (song) 39, 41, 170
Everything Came True

(song) 76
Excelsior Records 21, 201
Exciting Changes 106
Ezzard, Wallace 128, 131

F

Fabian 81
The Fabulous Ronettes 125
Facing, Jesse 73, 96
Family Dog (song) 136
Family Matters (TV program) 157
The Famous Flames 96
The Fantastic Temptations 125
The Fantastics 125
Far From The Maddening Crowd (song) 110, 182
Farrell, Wes 100
Federal Records 18, 29, 53, 59
Feelin' Fine (song) 124, 201
Feelin' In Mah Bones (song) 194
Feld, Irving 41, 42, 44, 60
Ferbee, Willie 25, 32, 159, 167
Fever (song) 148
The Fiestas 127
Fifty Million Women (song) 194
51 West Records 193
Fire Fire (song) 56
First Taste Of Love (song) 87
Fisher, Eddie 29
The Fisk Jubilee Singers 13, 15
The Five Crowns 72, 73, 96, 132, 194
Five Degrees Fahrenheit 131
The Five Internationals 18
The Five Keys 6, 8, 60
The Five Royales 149
The Five Satins 131, 145

The Five Willows 72
The Flamingos 41, 152
The Flirtations 125
Float On (song) 106
The Floaters 106
Floyd, Eddie 105
The Flyers 64, 66, 126, 194
Follow Me (song) 110, 111, 182, 196
Fontana Records 127
Fools Fall In Love (song) 64, 65, 172, 196
For Sentimental Reasons (song) 95
Ford, Emile 45
Fortson, Albert 128, 131
Fortune Records 51
Four And Twenty Hours (song) 188
The Four B's 77
The Four Internes 17
4J Records 194
The Four Knights 4, 27
The Four Seasons 36, 110, 152
The Four Tops 105, 111
The Four Tunes 4
Fowler, Charles 130
Fox, Dick 133
Francis, Connie 44
Francis, Panama 27, 186
Franklin, Aretha 49, 116
Fratto, Russ 80
Fredericks, Bill 114, 119, 120, 121, 136, 137, 138, 143, 145, 152, 162, 163, 164, 183, 184, 185, 189, 191, 198
Freed, Alan 7, 8, 9, 10, 28, 39, 59, 80, 152
From Someone Who Loves You (song) 85
Frosty The Snowman (song) 1
Fruity Woman Blues (song) 82
Fuqua, Charlie 4, 68, 85
Fury, Billy 84

G

Gaither, Tommy 6
Gale Agency 55
Gallashald, Matthew 24
Gallo, Bob 114, 197
Game Records 129
The Gap Band 145
Garnett Mimms And The Enchanters 100
Gee (song) 126
Gee Records 73, 96
Gene And Eunice 10
George Washington Memorial Park 51
"Georgia Tom" 14
Gerry And The Pacemakers 105
Getting By (TV program) 157
Gibb, Andy 138
The Girls From Texas (song) 127, 194
Git On Board, Little Children (song) 13
Glen, Darrel 8
Glick, Elmo 82
Glitter, Gary 102, 141
The Glory Of Love (song) 45, 95
Glover, David 24
Glover, Herbert 24
Go Bobby Go (song) 84
Go Down Moses (song) 13
Go Jimmy Go (song) 84
Go Johnny Go (film) 8
Go On Home Girl (song) 128
God Bless You (song) 73
Godfrey, Arthur 6
Goffin, Gerry 90, 92, 93, 95, 108
Goldberg, Marv 23, 24
Golden Hits (LP) 136
Goldner, George 99
Gone (song) 23, 28, 39, 56, 167
Gonna Move Across The River (song) 130
The Good Life (song) 180
The Good Life With The Drifters (LP) 111, 113

Good Luck Darling (song) 72
Good Night Irene (song) 18
Good Rockin' Tonight (song) 4
A Good Song Never Dies (song) 188
Goodman, Benny 27
Gordy, Berry 111
The Gospelaires 90
Grant, George 85, 161
Graves, Alexander 96
Greatest Recordings—The Early Years (LP) 36
Green, Dock 71, 72, 73, 75, 80, 85, 90, 95, 96, 106, 116, 125, 131, 132, 133, 157, 160, 161, 174, 175, 176, 177
Green, James 25
Greenaway, Roger 136, 137, 138, 141, 187, 188, 189, 191, 192, 199
Greenwich, Ellie 112
Griffen, Jimmy 25
Grisson, Dan 52
Groove Records 62
Guess Who (song) 121, 185
Gusto Records 193

H

Haley, Bill 9, 10, 41, 59, 60
Hallelujah (song) 125
Hamilton, Roy 55, 60
Hamm, Arthur 25
Hancock, Hunter 9
Hang On Sloopy (song) 110
Hang Up My Rock And Roll Shoes (song) 101
Hank Ballard And The Midnighters 52
Harlem Child (song) 141, 190
The Harmonaires 71, 72
The Harmony Grits 126
The Harps 56, 194
The Harptones 73
Harris, Ace 114
Harris, Jet 124

Harris, Webster 132
Harris, Wynonie 2
Harrison, Wilbert 60
Hatch, Tony 111
Have Mercy Baby (song) 19
Hawkins, Dale 186
Hawkins, Erskine 55
Hawkins, Screamin' Jay 50, 65
He Will Break Your Heart (song) 108
Hear What I Say (song) 97
Heard, J.C. 114, 116
Heart And Soul (song) 95
Heller, Eddie 72, 73
Hello Happiness (song) 141, 188, 190, 192, 198
Hemmings, Roy 149, 165
Hendricks, Belford 46
Hendricks, Bobby 51, 64, 66, 67, 68, 89, 126, 127, 128, 130, 152, 160, 173, 196
Henry, Heywood 27, 186
Henry, Mike 134
Henry, Russell "Pretty Boy" 129, 130
Herald Records 95
Here Comes The Night (song) 87, 110
Herndon Stadium 76
He's Just A Playboy (song) 102, 105, 178
Hey Senorita (song) 75, 81, 174
Hey Susan (song) 194
Heywood, Eddie 31
The High Steppers 47
Hilliard, Bob 90
Hinds, E. 23
Hip-Hop 5
Hirst, Al 131
Hite, Les 14
Hobbs, Elsbeary 73, 74, 75, 85, 131, 132, 133, 157, 160, 161, 174, 175
Hodges, Jimmy 36
The Hokum Boys 14
Hokum Jug Band 8

Holiday, Billie 116
Hollingsworth, Lacy 62, 128
Hollis, Bobby Lee 127, 128
Holly, Buddy 66, 72, 81, 87, 101, 114
The Honey Bears 60
Honey Bee (song) 53, 92, 170
Honey Chile (song) 21, 201
Honey Love (song) 35, 169, 195
Honey You're Heaven To Me (song) 142, 188
Honky Tonky (song) 61, 172
Hooker, John Lee 2, 4
Hopkins, Telma 120, 157
The Hornets 55, 56, 113, 152, 194
The Hornets And The 5C's (LP) 194
Hot Ziggety (song) 39, 41, 170
Hound Dog (song) 60
Houston, Cissy 90
How Much Is That Doggie In The Window (song) 28
Hughes, Charlie ("Carnation" Charlie) 62, 64, 67, 96, 97, 160, 172, 173
Hunter, Ivory Joe 7, 121
Hushabye (song) 120
Hypnotized (song) 65, 173, 196

I

I Ain't Givin' Up Nothing (song) 47
I Can't Believe (song) 194
I Can't Believe It's Over (song) 188
I Can't Get Away From You (song) 188, 189
I Can't Live Without You (song) 189
I Could Have Told You

(song) 126

I Count The Tears (song) 84, 89, 175, 196, 198, 203

I Depend On You (song) 121, 185

I Depended On You (song) 73

I Dig Your Act (song) 119, 184

I Do The Jerk (song) 127

I Don't Want To Go On Without You (song) 102, 136, 178

I Don't Want To See You Cry Anymore (song) 21, 201

I Feel Good All Over (song) 95, 177

I Found Some Lovin' (song) 128

I Got A Feeling (song) 194

I Got You Babe (song) 112

I Gotta Get Myself A Woman (song) 61, 172, 195

I Gotta Have You (song) 41

I Had To Find Out For Myself (song) 21, 201

I Have Love (For You) (song) 194

I Know (song) 65, 173

(I Know) Your Love Has Gone Away (song) 96

I Need You Now (song) 119, 184

I Need You So (song) 45

I Need Your Love (song) 128

I Never Knew (song) 47

I Put A Spell On You (song) 65

I Remember Christmas (song) 106, 180

I Should Have Done Right (song) 172

I Told Myself A Lie (song) 45

I Want You (song) 194

I (Who Have Nothing) (song) 87, 134

I Wish You Love (song) 111, 180

I Won't Cry (song) 56, 194

Idaho (song) 27

If I Didn't Care (song) 4

If I Didn't Love You Like I Do (song) 36, 169

If I Don't Get There (song) 14

If I'd Known You Were Coming, I'd Have Baked A Cake (song) 1

If It Feels Good, Do It (song) 189, 190

If Only I Could Start Again (song) 190

(If You Cry) True Love, True Love (song) 174

If You Don't Come Back (song) 97, 99, 177, 196

If You're Gonna Love Me (song) 189

I'll Forget About You (song) 74

I'll Get To Know Your Name Along The Way (song) 188, 191

I'll Know When True Love Really Passes By (song) 142, 188, 191

I'll Save The Last Dance For You (song) 84

I'll Take You Home (song) 97, 99, 102, 177, 196, 198

I'll Take You Where The Music's Playing (song) 112, 182, 190, 196

I'm Doing Fine Now (song) 125

I'm Feeling Sad (song) 137, 187, 188

I'm Free For The Rest Of My Life (song) 137, 187, 189, 190

I'm Not That Kind Of Guy (song) 143, 193

I'm Not Worthy (song) 42

I'm Ready (song) 189

I'm The Caring Kind (song) 21, 201

Imperial Records 3

The Imperials 133

The Impressions 105

In That Green Gettin' Up Morning (song) 13

In The Land Of Make Believe (song) 100, 177

In The Park (song) 108, 181

In The Still Of The Night (song) 145

Infamy 138

The Inkspots 2, 4, 5, 18, 21, 36, 68, 85, 121

The Innocents 95

The Invitations 125

Iron Butterfly 116

It Doesn't Matter Any More (song) 102

It Looks Like I'm The Clown Again (song) 142, 188

It Was A Tear (song) 64, 172

Itchy Twitchy Feeling (song) 68, 127

It's A Sin (song) 56

It's Just A Matter Of Time (song) 47

It's Now Or Never (song) 84

It's Too Soon To Know (song) 6

I've Been Thinking About You (song) 147

I've Got A Love To Hold (song) 128

I've Got Sand In My Shoes (song) 178, 196

I've Got You On My Mind (song) 191

Iverson, Ben 55

Ivory, James 130

J

J.A.L.N. Band 149

J.D. 73

Jackpot (song) 92, 95, 176

Jackson, Bullmoose 2
Jackson, Chuck 108
The Jackson 5 132
Jackson, Harold 129, 130
Jackson, L'il Son 8
Jackson, Mahalia 15
Jackson, Tony 134, 148, 165
James Fenimore Cooper High School 77
Jan And Dean 100, 193
The Jarmels 100, 152
Jaxon, Frankie 8
Jay And The Americans 83, 99, 100, 193
The Jayhawks 106
Jenkins, Gene 145, 164
Jenny (song) 94
The Jerusalem Stars 25
Jesse Stone And The Blues Serenaders 27
Jimmie Lunceford Band 52
Jimmy Orr And The Drifters 124
Jimmy Williams And The Drifters 124
The Jive Five 132
Jo, Damita 84
John, Keith 148, 149, 159, 165
John, Little Willie 148
Johnny And Joe 66
Johnny And The Hurri- canes 29
"Johnny Pancake" 127
Johnson, Blind Willie 15
Johnson, Budd 186
Johnson, James "Wrinkle" 17, 22, 24, 126, 159, 167
Johnson, Robert 8
Johnston, Lou 136
Johnston, Russell 130
Jones, Bernard 132
Jones, Gillie LeRoy 134
Jones, Hoppy 36, 85
Jones, Ollie 5
Jones, Orvil "Hoppy" 4, 5
Jordan, Taft 186
Jubilee Records 100

The Juggler (song) 132, 141, 190
Juke Box Baby (song) 44
Julliard School Of Music 17
Just A Dream (song) 83
Justice, Jimmy 93

K

K.C. Lovin' (song) 60
KFM Records 100
Kansas City (song) 60
Kathy Young And The Innocents 95
Kaufman, Murray 100, 108, 152, 193
Kay, Connie 27, 186
Kaye, Chuck 92
Keep It A Secret (song) 72
Keetch Records 100
Kelly-Marcus (songwriting team) 110
Kennedy, Billy 64
Kenny, Bill 4, 5, 18
Kent Records 85
Kimber, Reggie 74, 85, 159
The Kind Of Boy You Can't Forget (song) 112
King, B.B. 76
King, Ben E. 77, 79, 80, 81, 82, 83, 84, 85, 87, 88, 89, 93, 95, 97, 100, 108, 111, 116, 131, 133, 134, 137, 143, 144, 145, 152, 154, 157, 160, 161, 164, 174, 175, 185, 193, 196, 198
King, Carole 90, 92, 93, 95, 108, 136
King, James 77
King, Pee Wee 3
King Records 18, 35, 53, 59, 120, 128
King, Terry 132
The Kingtoppers 121
Kirk, Andy 52
Kirshner, Don 89, 90
Kiss And Make Up (song) 71, 74, 82

Kiss My Wrist (song) 82
Kissing In The Back Row Of The Movies (song) 137, 138, 187, 152, 189, 192, 198
Kitchings, Grant 121, 136, 137, 141, 157, 163, 189
Klein, Carole 90
The Knickerbockers 96
Knight, Kenny 125
Knock Three Times (song) 120
Knopfler, Mark 7
Kokomo (song) 10
Kruger, Jeff 46

L

LaBelle, Patti 106
Lady Loves To Dance (song) 143
Lamar, Peter 149, 165
Lamont, Joe 18
Lana Records 96
Lance, Major 105
The Larks 6, 8
Later Baby (song) 72
Lawson, Sammy 42
Lawyer, Andrew 129
Leadbelly 18
Leake, Butch 121, 136, 137, 141, 163, 189, 191
Leander, Mike 102
Leave It Here (song) 14
Lebish, Lew 33, 82
Lee, Bobby 127
Legends Of Rock Records 129
Leiber & Stoller 58, 60, 61, 64, 67, 75, 76, 81, 82, 83, 87, 89, 90, 92, 96, 97, 99, 105, 112, 197, 199
Leiber, Jerry see Leiber & Stoller
Leigh, Spencer 144
Let The Boogie Woogie Roll (song) 23, 24, 28, 39, 167
Let The Boogie Woogie Roll—Greatest Hits 1953-1958 (CD) 186
Let The Music Play (song) 177

Let's Start All Over Again (song) 45
Let's Try Again (song) 45
Lewis, Barbara 100
Lewis, Billy 134, 141, 143, 145, 148, 163, 164, 191, 192, 193
Lewis, Gary 132
Lewis, Jerry Lee 44, 81, 203
Lewis, Jimmy 127, 194
Lewis, Ray 143, 145, 148, 163, 164, 185, 193
Lewis, Richard 73, 96
Lewis, Rudy 85, 90, 92, 93, 94, 97, 100, 101, 102, 137, 152, 154, 157, 161, 175, 176, 177, 178, 196
Lies (song) 96
Lightning Records 199
Like A Movie I've Seen Before (song) 191
Like Sister And Brother (song) 137, 187, 189, 190, 192, 198
The Limelites 119
The Links 97
Little Anthony And The Imperials 133
A Little Bit Of Soap (song) 100
Little Bitty Pretty One (song) 48
Little Bug (song) 100
Little Darlin' (song) 62
Little Dave 58
Little David And The Harps 56
Little Girl So Fine (song) 132
Little Richard 8, 29, 44, 49, 51, 59, 81, 152
Little St. Nick (song) 129
Littlefield, Little Willie 60
Live At Harvard University (LP) 132
Live At The Brooklyn Fox (LP) 193
Live At The Crocket Stadium (LP) 129

Living Doll (song) 201
Livingstone, Percy 56
London Beat 147, 148
London Paladium 147
London Records 21, 173, 174, 175, 176, 177, 178, 199, 201
London-American Records 172
Loneliness Or Happiness (song) 92, 175
Lonely Avenue (song) 82
Lonely Winds (song) 83, 108, 174, 196, 203
Lonesome Baby (song) 194
Long, James "Sonny" 55
Long Lonely Nights (song) 44
Looking Through The Eyes Of Love (song) 110, 111, 182
Lord, I'm Standing By (song) 87
Louis Records 47
Love Games (LP) 189
Love Games (song) 138, 187, 189, 190, 192, 198
Love Has Joined Us Together (song) 41
Love Me, Love The Life I Lead (song) 188, 190
Lover Please (song) 47, 52
A Lover's Question (song) 44, 46, 48, 51, 52
Lovey Dovey (song) 44
Lovin' You Is Easy (song) 190
Lubic, Joe 15
Lucas, Buddy 53
Lucille (song) 23, 32, 41, 167, 195
Lullaby Of The Bells (song) 72
Lulu 110
Lulu And The Luvvers 110
Lunceford, Jimmie 52
The Luvvers 110
Lynch, Kenny 95
Lynn, Barbara 106, 179

M
MGM Records 3, 44, 45, 46
Macauley, Tony 137, 138
Mack, James 24
Mack The Knife (song) 84
Mack, Wesley 24
Madison Square Garden 133
Magnet Records 143
The Man In The Moon (song) 72
Mann, Barry 96, 106, 110, 136
Mann, Butch 119, 159
Mantovani 2
Mardin, Arif 107
Marsden, Gerry 105
Marshak, Larry 130, 131, 132, 133
Marshall, J.J. 134
Marshall, Joe 186
Marterie, Ralph 10
Martin, Dean 112
Martin, Joe 71, 72
Martin, Ralph 71, 72
Martin, Roberta 14
Martin, Sally 15
Martino, Al 3
The Marvelettes 123
The Masquerade Is Over (song) 45, 128
Massey, Bill 25
Master Recorders 58
The Masters 106
Maybelle, Big 55
Maybellene (song) 59, 80
McCartney, Paul 136
The McCoys 110
McPhatter, Beulah (Eva) 17
McPhatter, Bertha 17
McPhatter, Billy 48
McPhatter, Clyde 15, 17, 18, 19, 20, 22, 23, 24, 25, 28, 29, 31, 32, 33, 35, 36, 37, 39, 41, 42, 44, 45, 46, 47, 48, 49, 50, 51, 52, 53, 56, 64, 66, 68, 75, 88, 123, 126,

129, 134, 148, 149, 152, 154, 159, 160, 167, 169, 170, 195, 196
McPhatter, Esther   17
McPhatter, George   17
McPhatter, Gladys   17
McPhatter, James   17
McPhatter, Lena   48
McPhatter, Leroy   17
McPhatter, Nora   48
McPhatter, Patrick   48
Medley, Phil   100
Melba Records   72
Melic Records   97, 143
Memories Are Made Of This (song)   112, 136, 183, 196
Memories Of Cow Palace (LP)   127
Memphis Recording Service   3
Mercury Records   3, 10, 46, 47, 48, 56, 59, 68, 84
Mexican Divorce (song)   92, 175
Mickey And Sylvia   101
Middleton, Tony   72
Midnight Cowboy (song)   191
The Midnighters   52
A Mid-Summer Night In Harlem (song)   132, 133
Mighty Lak A Rose (song)   194
Miller, Gus   55
Millinder, Jimmy   160
Millionaire (song)   129
The Mills Brothers   2, 4, 5
Milner, Jimmy   68, 173
Milner, John   67
Milt Mirley And The High Steppers   47
Mimms, Garnett   100
Minit Records   127, 194
The Mint Juleps   60
Mintz, Leo   7
The Miracles   100, 105
Mirley, Milt   47
Mitchell, Benjamin   125
The Mixed Up Cup (song)   50

Mixed Up Shook Up Girl (song)   106
Mobile (song)   21, 201
The Modern Jazz Quartet   186
Modern Records   3, 4
Money (song)   51
Money Honey (song)   25, 27, 28, 29, 31, 32, 33, 52, 55, 56, 129, 137, 152, 167, 195
Monroe's Up Town (jazz club)   32, 114
Moondog's Rock And Roll Party (radio program)   7
The Moonglows   48, 77, 96
Moonlight Bay (song)   67, 68, 173, 186, 196
Moore, Johnny   51, 55, 56, 58, 61, 62, 66, 88, 89, 94, 96, 97, 99, 101, 102, 107, 108, 110, 111, 113, 119, 120, 121, 125, 129, 130, 133, 134, 136, 137, 138, 141, 142, 143, 144, 145, 148, 149, 152, 154, 158, 160, 161, 162, 163, 164, 165, 170, 172, 173, 177, 178, 179, 180, 181, 182, 183, 184, 185, 189, 191, 192, 193, 194, 195, 196, 198
Moore, Merrill   46
More (song)   111, 180
Morrison, Van   110
Moses, King   125
Moses Smote The Waters (song)   24
Motown Records   68, 103, 105, 111, 119, 132, 148, 186
The Mount Lebanon Singers   17, 24
Mr. Rock And Roll (film)   8
Mumford, Gene   6, 17
Murray, Juggy   68, 127
Murray The K   100, 108, 152, 193
Murray The K Live At The Brooklyn Fox (LP)   181

Musicor Records   132
My Baby Is Gone (song)   114, 183
My Baby Rocks Me (With A Steady Roll) (song)   8
My Definition Of The Blues (song)   42
My Foolish Pride (song)   85
My Girl Sloopy (song)   110
My Heart's Desire (song)   64
My Islands In The Sun (song)   113, 183
The Mystics   120

N
Nahan   82
The Nashville Teens   107
Nathan, Syd   18, 35
National Convention of Gospel Choirs And Choruses   15
National Records   5
Natural Records   6
Near You (song)   31
Needham, "Waxie Maxie"   46
Nelson, Ben   73, 75, 76, 77, 157
Nelson, George   6
New York Blue Sox   25
Newsday (magazine)   133
Nights Of Mexico (song)   100
9 A.M. (song)   147
$19.50 Bus (song)   72
No Sweet Lovin' (song)   53, 92, 170
Nobody But Me (song)   84, 175, 203
Noland, Terry   65, 66
Nylon Stockings (song)   112, 182

O
Odem, Andrew   131
Oh, Carol (song)   90
Oh My Love (song)   76, 174

Oh My Papa (song) 29
Oh, Neil (song) 90
Oh What A Night (song) 145
The O'Jays 119
Okeh Records 27, 65
Ol' Man River (song) 5, 129
Old Gold Records 138, 142
Old Town Records 27, 72
Olimac Publishing Company 68
Oliver, Jimmy 25, 32, 47, 58, 62, 64, 67, 68, 159, 186
Oliver, King 14
On Bended Knee (song) 64
On BrOAdway (LP) 131
On Broadway (song) 48, 96, 97, 99, 106, 127, 131, 177, 179, 186, 190, 192, 196
On Moonlight Bay (song) 67
On My Block (song) 185
On The Street Where You Live (song) 180
One Bad Stud (song) 60
One More Time (song) 96
One Right After Another (song) 45
One Way Love (song) 100, 102, 178, 196
Only A Fool (song) 49
Only In America (song) 97, 99, 177
Oo-Wee-Baby (song) 73
The Original Drifters 125, 126, 127, 128, 129, 130, 131, 194
The Originals 128
The Orioles 2, 5, 6, 8, 18, 28, 51, 72, 76, 152
Orlando, Tony 120
Orr, Jimmy 124
Otis, Clyde 46, 47, 49
Otis, Johnny 9, 36
Our Day Will Come (song) 119
The Outside World (song) 110, 181, 182

P

P. P. Arnold And The Flirtations 125
The Packards 114, 119
Page, Patti 28
Palladium Theatre 83
Palmer, Sy 73, 74
Paradise Hill (song) 95
Paramount Records 14
Paramount Theater 85
Parker, Johnny 27
Patterson, Lover 71, 72, 73, 74, 75, 79, 80, 87, 106, 125, 126
Patti LaBelle And The Blue Bells 106
Patty And The Emblems 106, 179
Paul, Wilbur "Yonkie" 71, 72, 73, 96, 106
Pea Vine Records 194
Peace Of Mind (song) 132
Pearson, Gene 95, 96, 107, 108, 113, 161, 162, 177, 178, 179, 180, 181, 182, 183
The Penguins 10, 131
Penn-Greene (songwriting team) 110
Penny, Hank 3
The Percolating Puppies 4
The Persuasions 152
Philles Records 61, 96
Phillips International Records 64, 126
Phillips, Lloyd "Butch" 132
Phillips, Sam 3, 9
Pickett, Wilson 52, 106, 116
Picketty Witch 148
Pinckney, Bill 18, 24, 25, 32, 35, 36, 41, 46, 53, 55, 56, 61, 62, 64, 66, 67, 68, 76, 92, 116, 124, 126, 127, 128, 129, 130, 131, 133, 158, 159, 160, 167, 169, 170, 172, 194, 195, 196
Pinckney, Bill, Jr. 129

Pitman, Charles 128
Pitney, Gene 100, 111
Pitts, Willie 128
The Platters 10, 41, 58, 59, 60, 123
Please Help Me Down (song) 187, 191
Please Stay (song) 90, 92, 141, 175, 196
Poindexter, James 85, 161
Poison Ivy (song) 84
Pomus, Doc 74, 81, 82, 83, 84, 89, 90, 92, 93, 203
Popcorn Willie (song) 73, 74
Port Records 68
Pour Your Little Heart Out (song) 143, 193
Powell, Jimmy 25
Presley, Elvis 5, 10, 29, 35, 44, 47, 52, 67, 81, 84, 152, 203
Preston, Jimmy 9
Price, Louis 143, 144, 145, 158, 163, 164, 185
Prince 149
The Prisonaires 65
Prodigal Records 132
Prysock, Red 7
Public Enemy 5
Puente, Tito 83
Puzey, Leonard 5

Q

Quality Chekd 201
Quando, Quando, Quando (song) 180
The Ques 18
Quinn, Ronald 120, 163, 185

R

R & B Records 74, 82
R & D Records 132
RCA-Victor Records 2, 3, 10, 112, 145
RFM Records 193
RPM Records 3
Rackley, Lena 48
Rae, David 27
Ragavoy, Jerry 100

Rainbow Heart (song) 85, 124, 201

Rainbow Records 68, 72, 73

The Raindrops 112

Rainey, Gertrude "Ma" 14

Ram, Buck 58

Rama Records 22, 201

Randy And The Rainbows 100

The Rascals 116

Rat Race (song) 97, 177, 196

The Ravens 5, 23, 35, 62, 66, 106, 121

The Ray Ellis Singers 67

Ray, Johnny 10, 32, 52

Ready Steady Go (TV program) 108

The Rebel Rousers 102

Record Collector (magazine) 145

Red Bird Records 99, 112

Red, Tampa 8

Redding, Otis 51, 52, 105, 116

Reed, Jimmy 76

Reed, Johnny 6

Reed, Les 137, 141

Rene, Leon 201

Rene, Otis 201

Resnick, Artie 101, 105

Richard, Cliff 124, 201

Richardson, Tony 129

Ricks, Jimmy 5, 62

Ridin' & Rockin' (song) 194

Ripete Records 129, 130

Riverside Blues (song) 14

Riviera Records 73

The Rivileers 95

Robbins, Wayne 133

Robeson, Paul 5

The Robins 60, 61

Robinson, Bob 14

Robinson, Sherman 125

Robinson, Smokey 51

Robinson, Sylvia 101

Rock And Cry (song) 42

Rock And Roll Dance Party 59

Rock And Roll Hall Of Fame 154

Rock Around The Clock (film) 8

Rock 'N' Roll (song) 8

Rock This Joint (song) 9

Rocket 88 (song) 9

Rockin' And Ridin' (song) 55

The Rolling Stones 105, 152

The Romantics 119

The Ronettes 100, 133, 193

Room Full Of Tears (song) 90, 93, 175, 196, 203

A Rose By Any Other Name (song) 121, 185

Rough Edges (LP) 87

The Royal Jokers 132

Royalty Of Rock (concert) 133

Ruby And The Romantics 119

Ruby Baby (song) 58, 59, 106, 137, 152, 170, 179, 186, 195

Rudy, Jan 61

Ruffin, Bobby 132

Ruffin, Jimmy 148

Rupe, Art 3

Rydell, Bobby 81, 84

S

S & J Records 129

The Sacardos 129

Sacroiliac Swing (song) 201

Sadie My Lady (song) 61, 89, 172

Samad, Abdul 85, 94, 119, 136, 159, 186

San Francisco (song) 111, 180

Sand In My Shoes 105

Sands, Frank 77

Sandy Records 85

Santa Claus Got The Blues (song) 129

Santa Claus Is Coming To Town (song) 126

The Satellites 48

Saturday Night At The Movies (song) 106, 111, 136, 179, 181, 189, 196, 198

Saturday Night At The Uptown (LP) 179

Saturday Night Fever (film) 138

Save The Last Dance For Me (LP) 193

Save The Last Dance For Me (song) 83, 84, 88, 89, 92, 99, 127, 132, 136, 137, 142, 144, 152, 175, 185, 188, 190, 192, 196, 198, 203

Savoy Records 56, 62, 194

Savoy, Ronny 114

Savoy Vocal Group Album (LP) 194

Sawyer, Freddie 106

Say Goodbye To Angelina (song) 187, 188

Schiffman, Frank 33, 68

Schroeder, Aaron 92

The Searchers 89

Searchin' (song) 61

Sears, Big Al 7, 186

Sedaka, Neil 85, 90

Send For The Doctor (song) 82

Seven Days (song) 42

Seven Letters (song) 87

The Shadows 124, 201

Shake, Rattle And Roll (song) 31, 59

The Shangri-las 108, 123, 193

Shannon, Del 93, 203

Sharp, Alexander 6

Shaw, Sandy 136

She Never Talked To Me That Way (song) 92, 93, 119, 176, 186, 203

Sheen, Bobby 51

Shep And The Limelites 119

Sheppard, Rick 113, 114, 119, 120, 126, 132, 162, 163, 183, 184

Sherman, Gary 119
The Shirelles 100, 132, 152
Short Mort (song) 90
Shout Records 113
Show Boat (musical) 5
Show Me The Way (song) 87
Showaddywaddy 141
Shuman, Mort 74, 81, 82, 83, 84, 89, 90, 92, 93, 110, 203
Sigh Records 85
Sill, Lester 61, 96
The Silvertone Singers 24
Sinatra, Frank 1, 45
The Singing Cousins 24
Singleton, Shelby 47, 48
"Sir Charles" 97
60 Minute Man (song) 18, 129
Sketchley Grange Hotel 149
Sledge, Percy 119
Sleep (song) 149
Slightly Adrift 143
Slim Jim (song) 68
Smith, Caesar 106
Smith, Delbert 125
Smokey Joe's Cafe (song) 60, 61
Snakey Feeling (song) 27
The Sneak (song) 68
"Snugs" 106
So Fine (song) 127
Soldier Of Fortune (song) 61, 172, 195
Solomon, Benjamin Earl 157
Some Kind Of Wonderful (song) 90, 92, 106, 131, 175, 179, 189, 196
Somebody New, Dancing You (song) 92, 176
Someday (song) 41, 51, 56
Someday, Somewhere (song) 14
Someday You'll Want Me To Want You (song) 36, 169

Something Old, Something New (LP) 131
Something Tells Me (song) 136, 187, 188
Sometimes I Wonder (song) 84, 95, 175
Songs From The Big City (LP) 48
The Songs We Used To Sing (song) 137, 187, 188, 190
Sonny And Cher 112
The Soul Of Love (song) 143
The Soul Stirrers 15, 87
The Sounds Of The Drifters 125, 134, 148
Sounds South Records 131
Southern Charisma Records 129
The Southern Knights 25
Southside Johnny 132
Souvenirs (song) 65, 67, 173
The Spaniels 55, 66, 131, 132
Spanish Harlem (song) 48, 87, 134
Spanish Lace (song) 106, 179
Spark Records 61
Special Blend 130
Specialty Records 3, 112
Spector, Phil 51, 61, 87, 96, 127, 186
Spector, Ronnie 133
Spider Walk (song) 97
Springsteen, Bruce 132, 152
St. Nicholas Arena 41
Stand By Me (film) 88
Stand By Me (song) 14, 87, 134
A Star (song) 72
Stardust (song) 6
Starvation Blues (song) 27
Stax Records 103, 105, 116
Steal Away (song) 13, 119, 120, 184

Stealin' Home (song) 68
Steamboat (song) 53, 58, 170, 195
Steele, John Thomas 72
Steeltown Records 132
Stephens, Geoff 137
Steve Day And The Drifters 124
Stevenson, Matthew "Bubba" 132
Stewart, Rudy 106
Still Burning In My Heart (song) 119, 184, 196
Still Can't Shake Your Love (song) 143
Stoller, Mike see Leiber & Stoller
Stone, Fred 25
Stone, Jesse 25, 27, 28, 31, 61, 186
Stone, Julia 25
Stone, Russell 192
Storm, Billy 121
Stranded In The Jungle (song) 106
Stranger On The Shore (song) 94, 176, 196
Strong, Barrett 51
Strong, Nolan 51
Such A Night (song) 10, 31, 32, 35, 169, 195
Suddenly There's A Valley (song) 67, 89, 173
Sue Records 68, 97, 127, 143
Sugar Coated Kisses (song) 39, 170
Sugar Girl (song) 128
Sullivan, Nikki 66
The Sultans Of Swing 7
Summer In The City (song) 191
Summertime (song) 22, 201
Sun Records 3, 64
The Sunbeams 127
Superdisc Records 41
Supernatural Thing (song) 88
The Supremes 111, 123
Susie Q (song) 186
Suttles, Warren 5

Swan, Billy 47
The Swan Silvertones
15
Sweet Caroline (song)
136, 137, 188, 190
Sweet Little Rock 'n'
Roller (song) 191
Sweets For My Sweet
(song) 90, 92, 110,
120, 175, 196, 203
Swing Low Sweet Chariot
(song) 13
Symphony (song) 49

T
TVP Records 193
Ta Ta (song) 47
Take A Step (song) 45
Takes A Good Woman
(song) 113, 183
Talent Scouts (TV show)
6
Tamla Records 68, 105,
111, 148, 186
Tampa Red 14
Taylor, Sam "The Man"
27, 186
Tear Drops And Memories
(song) 85, 124, 201
The Tears 128, 130
Tears, Tears, Tears (song)
87
The Teen Queens 41
The Teenagers 8, 41, 59,
66, 145
Tell Me (song) 49
Temptation (song) 83,
111, 174, 180
The Temptations 105,
111, 144, 145, 186
Terrell, Pha 52
Terry, Dossie 53
Terry, Johnny 96, 107,
108, 113, 161, 162, 177,
178, 179, 180, 181, 182,
183
Thank You Love (song)
49
Thank Your Lucky Stars
(TV show) 108
Tharpe, Sister Rosetta
15
Tharren, Bobby 125

That Lazy Mood (song)
201
That's All Right, Mama
(song) 10
Them 110
There Goes My Baby
(song) 75, 77, 79, 80,
81, 84, 95, 99, 100, 106,
131, 152, 174, 179, 181,
186, 190, 193, 196
There Goes My First Love
(LP) 141, 190
There Goes My First Love
(song) 141, 187, 190,
191, 192, 198
There You Go (song) 36,
169
There's Always Some-
thing There To Remind
Me (song) 136
(There's) Always Some-
thing There To Remind
Me (song) 136, 188
Think Me A Kiss (song)
45
Thirty Days (song) 42
This Is Not Goodby (song)
45
This Magic Moment
(song) 83, 99, 174,
196, 203
This Time It's For Real
(LP) 132
Thomas A. Dorsey Gospel
Songs Publishing Co.
14
Thomas, Carla 105
Thomas, Charlie 73, 74,
75, 76, 81, 82, 85, 90,
92, 93, 96, 102, 107, 108,
110, 113, 119, 120, 124,
126, 130, 131, 132, 133,
134, 136, 158, 160, 161,
162, 174, 175, 176, 177,
178, 179, 180, 181, 182,
193, 196, 198
Thomas, Chuck 134
Thomas, Don 120, 126,
132, 163, 184
Thomas, Harold 128,
130, 131
Thornton, Big Mama 60
A Thousand Stars (song)
95

Thrasher, Andrew 24,
41, 62, 66, 126, 159,
160, 169, 170, 172
Thrasher, Bernice 24
Thrasher, Gerhart 24,
25, 33, 41, 53, 56, 58,
62, 68, 123, 126, 127,
128, 159, 160, 167, 169,
170, 172, 173
The Thrasher Wonders
24
The Three Blazes 97
Three Lies (song) 22,
201
Three Steps To Heaven
(song) 102
Three Thirty Three (song)
39, 170
Three-Two-One (TV
program) 145
Thurston, John L. "J.T."
147, 148, 149, 164, 165
Tight Like That (song)
14
Til, Sonny 6, 19, 51, 72
Tilghman, Earlington 6
Tindley, Charles 13, 15
Tobacco Road (song) 107
Tonight (song) 111, 180
Tonight's The Night
(song) 119
Too Bad (song) 87
The Topnotes 100
Total Experience Records
145
Tower Bell Records 143
Transworld Records 73
Trautman, Lloyd 186
Treadwell, Faye 88, 94,
116, 120, 121, 123, 130,
133, 134, 135, 136, 143,
145, 149, 154, 158
Treadwell, George 23, 32,
41, 62, 66, 68, 69, 71,
74, 79, 80, 82, 85, 95,
96, 97, 107, 108, 111,
113, 114, 116, 123, 124,
125, 126, 132, 154, 158
Treadwell, Tina 116
Treasure Of Love (song)
42, 45, 46
Trip-Top Records 193
Troy, Doris 90

218

True Love, True Love (song) 82, 174, 196, 203
Try Try Baby (song) 36, 169
The Turbans 60, 131
The Turks 64
Turner, Big Joe 27, 41, 59, 60, 82, 203
Turner, Denis 47
Turner, Ike 9
Turner, Milton 119, 120, 162, 184
Turner, Nebraska 129
Turner, Rohan 149, 165
Tutti Frutti (song) 59
Twenty-Four Original Hits (LP) 138
Twice A Week (song) 191
Twice As Nice (song) 45
The Twist (song) 35
Twist And Shout (song) 100
Twitty, Conway 44
The Tymes 100

U

Under The Boardwalk (song) 101, 102, 103, 105, 106, 125, 141, 152, 178, 179, 181, 190, 192, 196, 198
United Artists Records 100, 128
Universal Dancing 49
Up In The Streets Of Harlem (song) 113, 182
Up Jumped The Devil (song) 114, 184
Up On The Roof (song) 48, 95, 99, 127, 134, 136, 176, 181, 190, 196
Uptown Theater (Philadelphia) 106, 179

V

Van Dyke, William 85, 161
Van Walls, Harry 186
Vance, Narcia 50
Variety Records 27

Vaughan, Sarah 116, 158
Vaya Con Dios (song) 100, 101, 116, 120, 178, 196
Vee, Bobby 85, 93
Vee Jay Records 52
Veep Records 128
The Velours 125
The Very Best Of The Drifters (LP) 147
Vest Records 96
The Vibranaires 5
The Vibrations 106, 108, 110, 179
Village Soul Choir 68
Vincent, Gene 49, 203
Vinton, Bobby 93
The Vocaleers 114

W

WABC (radio station) 9
WINS (radio station) 8
WJW (radio station) 7
WKEL (radio station) 7
W.P.L.J. (song) 130
Wah Diddy Wah (song) 194
Wait Until Spring (song) 194
Walk (song) 116
Walker, Clarence 128
Walker, Junior 148
Wallace, George 131
Wand Records 92, 100
Ward, Bernard 73, 132
Ward, Billy 6, 17, 18, 19, 29, 36, 53
Ward, Clara 15
Ward, Ernest "Rocky" 62
Warm Your Heart (song) 31, 32, 56, 169
Warwick, Dee Dee 90
Warwick, Dionne 90, 92, 108, 158
Warwick Records 131
Washington, Billy 125, 148
Washington, Dinah 10, 32, 46, 55, 158
Washington, Ronald 129
Waters, Ethel 116

Waters, Muddy 2
Watson, Deek 4
The Way I Feel (song) 27, 28, 55, 56, 167
We Got A Good Thing Goin' (song) 106
We Gotta Sing (song) 112, 182
Webb IV (publishing company) 100
Webster, Ben 186
Week's Tavern 56
Weil, Cynthia 96, 106, 110
Weiss, Hy 27, 72
Welcome Home (LP) 50
We'll Understand It Better By And By (song) 14
Wells, Dicky 116
West Side Story (musical) 111
Westbrook, Chauncy 25
Wexler, Jerry 2, 20, 22, 23, 24, 27, 28, 31, 34, 35, 36, 39, 42, 44, 49, 53, 56, 58, 60, 62, 64, 65, 71, 76, 79, 80, 84, 87, 99, 101, 102, 110, 116, 195, 197
What A Guy (song) 112
What Am I Doing (song) 143, 193
What Am I Living For (song) 101
What D'i Say (song) 179
What Is Soul (song) 87
What Kind Of Fool Am I (song) 180
What To Do (song) 94, 95, 176
What'cha Gonna Do (song) 23, 24, 28, 35, 39, 56, 152, 167, 169, 195
What'd I Say (song) 84
When My Little Girl Is Smiling (song) 92, 93, 99, 142, 176, 189, 196, 198
When The Real Thing Comes Along (song) 45
When The World Begins (song) 97

When Ya Comin' Home
(song) 1881
When You Dance (song)
131
Where Did I Make My
Mistake (song) 45
The Whispering Seren-
aders 14
White, Charlie 17, 18,
22, 24
A White Christmas (LP)
129
White Christmas (song)
34, 35, 36, 41, 52, 56,
64, 107, 133, 148, 152,
169, 195, 196
The White Cliffs Of Dover
(song) 53
Who Can Be True (song)
72
Who Can I Turn To (song)
180
Why Do Fools Fall In
Love (song) 59, 145
Why Don't You Believe
Me (song) 72
Wildcats Jazz Band 14
Williams, Andy 94
Williams, Big Joe 3
Williams, Billy 125
Williams, Cootie 114
Williams, Jimmy 124,
201
Williams, Joe 106
Williams, Johnny Lee
51, 81, 82, 84, 85, 161,
174, 175, 196
Williams, Mark 128,
131
Williams, Paul 66
Williams Records 128
Williams, Reverend 50

Williamson, Sonny Boy
3, 97
Willis, Bruce 152
Willis, Chuck 8, 101
Wilson, Jackie 19, 51, 97
Wilson, Joyce Vincent
120
Wine Headed Woman
(song) 21, 201
With A Little Help From
My Friends (LP) 132
Without Love (song) 42,
51
Wonder Records 131
Wonder, Stevie 105, 149
Woodston, Ollie 129
Workman, Miriam 99
The World Doesn't Matter
Anymore (song) 185
The World Famous
Drifters 125
The World Is Changing
(song) 22, 201
Wright, Leo 106
Wright, O.V. 119

Y
Yakety Yak (song) 61
Yarbrough And People
145
Yodee Yakee (song) 65,
66, 68, 95, 173, 195
You And Me Together
Forever (song) 119,
184
You Are My First Love
(song) 76
You Better Move On
(song) 88, 144, 185
You Came To Me (song)
73
You Can't Love Them All

(song) 182, 183
You Chose A Fine Time
(song) 191
You Could Be My Love
(song) 72
You Don't Know (song)
112
You Got To Look Up
(song) 96
You Got To Pay Your
Dues (song) 120, 184,
185
You Never Talked To Me
That Way (song) 93
You Played The Game
(song) 194
You'll Lose A Good Thing
(song) 106
You'll Pay (song) 56,
194
Young Blood (song) 61,
82
Young, Kathy 95
Young, Kenny 101, 105,
141
Young, Neil 152
The Young Rascals 112
Your Best Friend (song)
119, 120, 184
Your Promise To Be Mine
(song) 58, 59, 170,
172
You're More Than A
Number In My Little
Red Book (song) 129,
142, 188, 191, 198
You're My Inspiration
(song) 72
You're Saving The Last
Dance For Me (song) 84
You've Got Your Troubles
(song) 137, 187, 188